AF615219

The Optic

Black Dog Publishing Limited

of Walter

The Optic of Walter Benjamin

Edited by Alex Coles

Benjamin

Volume 3

de-, dis-, ex-.

Historiography, Collecting, Ethnography and the Archive
Part One

Image project by Mark Dion
Cabinet of Curiosities for the Wexner Center for the Arts

Architectures, Arcades and Glass Surfaces

Part Two

Image project by Clifton Steinberg
Inside – Outside: Arcade – Department Store

Introduction

Alex Coles

More books on Benjamin, and still the pile grows .... Benjamin's prose breeds commentary like vaccine in a lab.
— Peter Osborne, *Radical Philosophy 88*, 1998.

Anyone paying the least attention to the reception of Walter Benjamin will know exactly what Peter Osborne means, while those with a keen interest can just glance across their study towards the guilty, sagging Benjamin shelf for confirmation. For some time now the Benjamin industry has been in full swing, but many of the books have become sloppy, often with the editor attempting to string together a series of contributions that cover a wide variety of themes – some of them excellent – through a pseudo-thematic. In part, underpinning such instances is the fact that the reception obeys the law of the supplement, namely, that as the reception grows, the more inadequate it becomes. While recent collections of essays have focused on deconstruction, history, modernity and philosophy (the latter co-bred by Peter Osborne in Routledge's laboratories) there has been little addressing art and architecture specifically. It is this specificity – or at least its continual displacing – that this volume insists upon.

Instead of lining up all the usual suspects for a show-down of hermetic Benjaminian debate, *The Optic of Walter Benjamin* brings together a number of specially commissioned contributions from practitioners in diverse fields. Furthermore, instead of using Benjamin as a motif – either of exile, modernity, or the messianic – as is often the current practice in cultural studies and visual culture, each contribution undertakes a (re)focusing of the optic of Walter Benjamin. Thus, the notion of optic put forward in the title does not so much suggest a theme that the contributions share but more an operational procedure – characterised by Benjamin in the *Arcades* project as the "telescoping of the past through the present." But as Benjamin brings into focus particular areas of debate previously overlooked, or only haphazardly worked through in discussions converging around art and architecture – such as the archive, ethnography and historiography – so the contemporary condition of these areas reveals fresh nuances in Benjamin's text. Thus the focusing apparatus is reflected upon in nearly all of the contributions at the same time as it is put into practise. The two visual projects only work to enhance this.

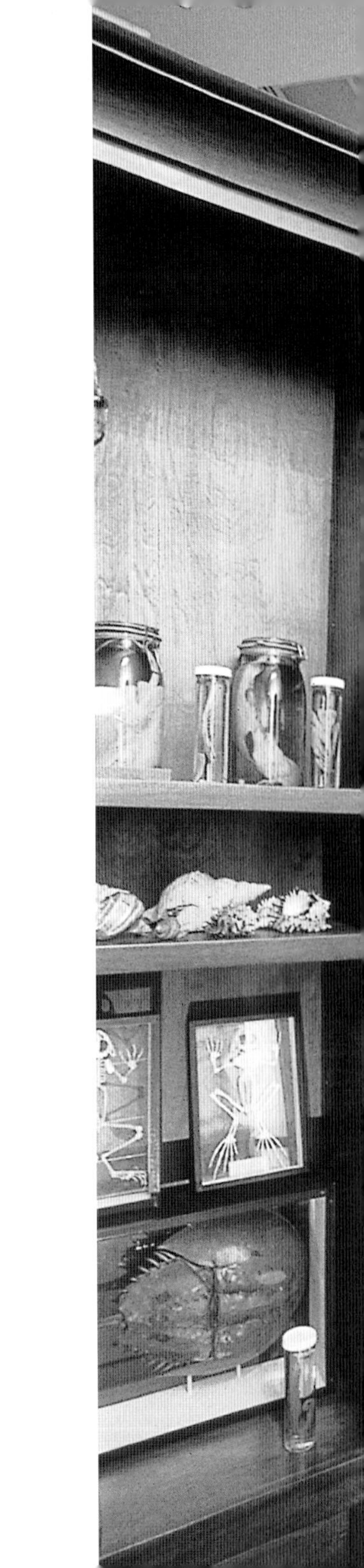

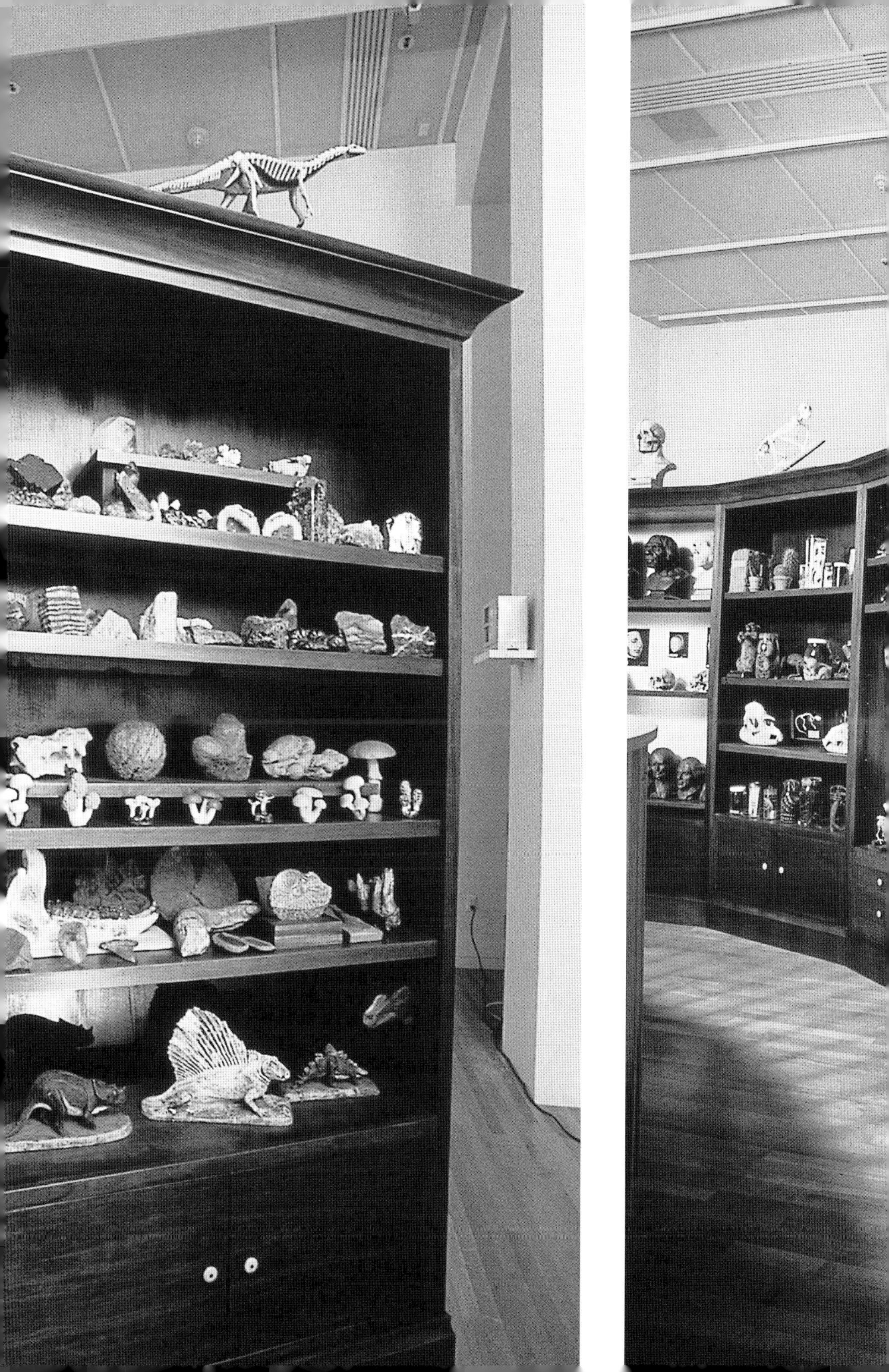

Atlas/Archive

Benjamin H.D. Buchloh

Gerhard Richter's Atlas: The Anomic Archive

Gerhard Richter's *Atlas* is one of several structurally similar, yet rather different projects by a number of European artists from the early to mid-1960s (one could also think of the forty-year-old collection of typologies of industrial architecture by Bernhard and Hilla Becher begun in 1958, or the work of Christian Boltanski begun in the late 1960s) whose formal procedures of accumulating found or intentionally produced photographs in more or less regular grid formations have remained enigmatic. They are either notable for their astonishing typological *homogeneity* and *continuity* (as is the case with the work of the Bechers) or for the equally remarkable *heterogeneity* and *discontinuity* that defines Richter's *Atlas*. Having made photography's innate structural order of the archive, its seemingly infinite multiplicity, serialisation and aim for comprehensive totality the principles of the work's formal organisation, these projects share first of all a condition of not being classifiable within the typology and terminology of avant-garde art history: neither the term 'collage' nor the term 'photomontage' would adequately describe the apparent formal and iconographic monotony of these photographic panels, nor the vast archival accumulations of their materials. Yet at the same time, the descriptive terms and genres from the more specialised segments of the history of photography, all of them operative in one way or the other in Richter's *Atlas*, appear equally inadequate to describe and classify these image accumulations.

Despite the first impression the *Atlas* might provide, neither the private album of the amateur, nor the cumulative projects of documentary photography could identify the discursive order of this photographic collection. And we could not argue either that the exactitude of topographical or architectural photography, or the massive image apparatus of surveillance and spectacularisation operative in photo-journalism, govern the peculiar "photographic condition" of Richter's *Atlas*. Lastly, in spite of their dominance among the genres presented, not even advertisement and fashion photography and its principles of fetishisation determine the reading of these panels.

By contrast, what could come to mind first of all are the terms with which one would describe instructional charts, teaching devices, technical or scientific illustrations found in textbooks or catalogues, the archival organisation of materials according to the principles of a still unidentifiable discipline. Avant-garde history, however, seems to have few, if any precedents for artistic procedures that organise knowledge systematically within didactic models of display. If such precedents do appear – as, for example, in the teaching panels produced by Kazimir Malevich between 1924 and 1927 to illustrate the theoretical efforts of the Institute of Artistic Culture in Leningrad – they are generally considered as mere supplements to the actual aesthetic objects.

This would also be the case with another crucial example that has equally remained outside the historian's terminological purview, Hannah Höch's *Media Scrap Book*, which the artist produced around 1933.[1] Höch's project points equally towards the earlier existence of various artistic strategies to organise and accommodate large quantities of found photographs in an archival manner. Rather than deploying fragmentation and fissure as the dynamic principles of photomontage, the archival order seems to be probing the subject's mnemonic competence in the face of rising media culture.

The tracing of historical processes, the establishment of typologies, chronologies and temporal continuities – even if only fictitious, as in Boltanski's case – seem to have conflicted for the longest time with the avant-garde's self-perception as providing instantaneous presence, shock and perceptual rupture.

The Beginnings of Richter's *Atlas*

After his transition from East to West Germany in 1961, Richter started a collection of photographic images whose ultimate purpose – at least initially – seems to have been unclear even to him: organised according to the most traditional display system of a rectangular grid, the images – at first glance at least – appear to have been chosen solely for their sentimental value of recording instances and subjects from family history. Only one of the images would later serve as a matrix for one of Richter's photo-paintings, begun at the time when the initial panels for the *Atlas* were assembled (*Christa and Wolfi,* 1964), whereas the others – including the third panel consisting almost entirely of amateur landscape photographs taken during holiday travels – would remain seemingly mute documents in the first four panels of the *Atlas*. Thus, these photographic images appear as though they had been torn out of the family album shortly before Richter's flight from East Germany, to serve as souvenirs of a past being left behind forever, or as though they might have been mailed to him from his relatives in the East, to console the young artist about his departure from his loved ones.[2] The desire to avert the traumatising loss of memory would have been activated all the more so since Richter exited the new Communist state of East Germany at the moment of a first solidification of identity, when he had finished his education as an artist, had gained his first professional experiences in a photographic laboratory and had just received his first commissions as a mural painter on behalf of the Communist Party.

But a second condition of a historically determined "memory crisis" could be recognised in the fact that the massive mobilisation of an apparatus of remembrance, such as Richter's *Atlas,* could have resulted not just from the loss of a geo-political order but also from a more general destruction of social identity, as was clearly the case for Richter (and for the Bechers) when they first confronted the shambles of German culture in the post-war period.

The photographic imagery of family members serve Richter – as it had all photographic theoreticians from Siegfried Kracauer in 1927 to Walter Benjamin in 1931 and again for Roland Barthes in 1979 (when the confrontation with the death of his mother made him write a contemporary phenomenology of photography) – as the point from which the reflection on the relationship between photography and historical memory would originate. As though photography's oscillating ambiguity, as a dubious agent simultaneously enacting and destroying mnemonic experience, could at least be fixed for one moment by situating the image in an analogue to the mnemonic imprint of the family relation itself. After all, this is the imprint where physical contiguity and the referent of psychic inscription could not be doubted, where the materiality of mnemonic experience appeared to be guaranteed. Whether this imprint and inscription would be defined as that of genetic and hereditary encoding (the foundation of a proto-racist theory, as suggested in the theory of memory developed by Aby Warburg's teacher, Richard Semon); or whether it would trace the more or less successful psycho-sexual organisation according to the Oedipal law that determines the formation of subjectivity (for example, Freud's inherent definition of psychic memory); or, indeed, whether memory would be conceived of as being determined by class and social institution (as proposed in Durkheim's theorisation of memory structure), it is in the reflection upon the family image that the power of mnemonic ties to the past and their impact on the present could be most credibly verified as material processes, alternatingly – like photography – assuring and assaulting the formation of identity.[3]

The assumption that the initial impulse to form the *Atlas* originated from Richter's recent experience of the loss of a familial and social context, and the encounter with the self-inflicted destruction of the German bourgeois culture of the nation state, would be confirmed by Richard Terdiman's analysis of the historical circumstances which engender a "memory crisis," and concomitant with it the desire to theorise the conditions and enact new possibilities of memory construction. This desire is activated in moments of extreme duress and destruction, in which the traditional material bonds among subjects, between subjects and objects, and between objects and their representation appear to be on the verge of displacement, if not outright disappearance.[4]

"Memory crisis" however, had also clearly originated in a less private type of menace, in a crisis of object experience and representational doubt that had afflicted Siegfried Kracauer and Walter Benjamin in the late 1920s. This was the moment when the rise of a new photographic media culture allowed a first vista into the newly emerging collective conditions of anomie and amnesia and when it became possible to imagine the destruction of mnemonic experience and the annihilation of historical thought altogether by newly emerging means of mass cultural representation. One of the puzzling arguments made by Benjamin suggests that the date 1860 should be considered as photography's historical climax, since at that moment the social promise of radically different forms of collective interaction and subjecthood could still be captured by photography as an emerging technology as much as the photograph itself embodied the transition from the auratic object to the increasingly emptied structure of mere technological reproduction.

Excursus on the *Atlas*: Aby Warburg and Walter Benjamin

The term "atlas" rings perhaps more familiar in the German language than it does in English, having been defined since the end of the sixteenth century as a book format that compiles and organises geographical and astronomical knowledge. We are told that this format received its name from one of Mercator's map collections in 1585 which carried a frontispiece showing an image of Atlas, the Titan of Greek mythology who held up the pillars of the universe at the threshold where day meets night. But later, in the nineteenth century, the term had been increasingly deployed to identify *any* tabular display of systematised knowledge and one could have encountered an atlas in almost all fields of the empirical sciences: an atlas of astronomy, of anatomy, geography and ethnography, and later even schoolbooks charted plants and animals and carried that name like the god had carried the pillars. When the confidence in empiricism and the aspiration towards comprehensive positivist systems of knowledge withered in the twentieth century, the term "atlas" seemed to fall into a more metaphorical usage.

Thus we encounter the most important example of this tendency around 1927 in a monumental project which sets out to gather identifiable forms of collective memory: the *Mnemosyne Atlas* was first conceived by the art historian Aby Warburg in 1925 after his release from Ludwig Binswanger's psychiatric clinic in 1924, and it was actively developed in 1928 and continued until his death in 1929. Warburg attempted to chart the continuity of primal or traumatic historical experiences through the various layers of cultural transmission (his primary focus being the reception and transformation of 'dynamograms' or 'Pathosformeln' from classical antiquity in Renaissance painting). When he argued in the unpublished introduction to his *Mnemosyne Atlas* that

> ... it is in the area of orgiastic mass seizure that one should look for the mint that stamps the expression of extreme emotional seizure on the memory with such intensity that the engrams of that experience of suffering live on, an inheritance preserved in the memory.[5]

Warburg signals in the introduction to his project not only an uncanny prognostic of the imminent future of social behaviour under the rise of German Fascism, but moreover that he would attempt to trace processes of collective historical memory to the extent that they were inextricably linked to traumatic experiences.

Soon thereafter, in a crucial text from 1931, Walter Benjamin's "A Short History of Photography", the scope of the term *Atlas* is once again strangely modified for the purposes of contemporary needs (and again, in an almost ominous prognosis of the needs of the future), when Benjamin discusses August Sander's *Antlitz der Zeit*, the key work of the German Neue Sachlichkeit photographer, as an "Übungsatlas". Eerily anticipating that only a few years later physiognomic observation would not only serve as the pretext for political persecution, but more brutally as the pseudo-scientific legitimation of racist persecution, this exercise-manual, as Benjamin claims, will educate its viewers in the physiognomic study of the relationships between the class identity of the depicted sitters and their political and ideological affiliations of the imminent future. Benjamin states that:

> ... overnight Sander's work could gain an unexpected actuality. Shifts within the power structure as they have become necessary in our society, tend to make the development and the sharpening of a physiognomic perception into a vital necessity. Whether one is on the left or on the right, one will have to get used to being looked at from where one comes. And one will have to see it for oneself in the others. Thus, Sander's work is more than simply a picture book: it is an atlas of exercise.[6]

Let me, however, return to Warburg's *Mnemosyne Atlas* for the moment. Even though the scholar had to leave the project behind in an unfinished state, more than sixty panels with over a thousand photographs had been assembled by Warburg at the time of his death. According to his aspirations as recorded in the diaries, the *Mnemosyne Atlas* would not only trace forms of social and collective memory by

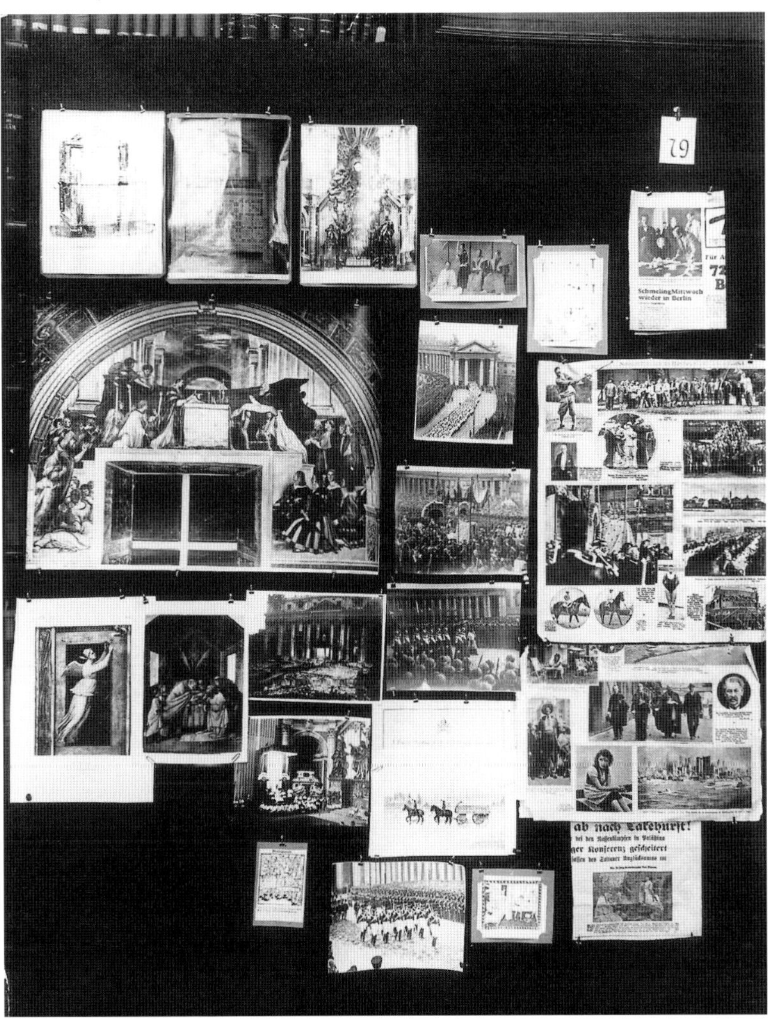

Aby Warburg, *Mnemosyne Atlas*, Plate 19. Courtesy the Warburg Institute.

charting the series of recurring motifs of gesture and bodily expression that he had identified in his notorious term as "pathos formulas". But the *Atlas* according to its author's intentions should also achieve a materialist project of constructing social memory by means of the photographic reproductions of a broad variety of practices of representation. Warburg's *Atlas* thus reiterated his lifelong challenge to the rigorous and hierarchical compartmentalisation of the discipline of art history, it attempted to abolish its methods and categories of exclusively formal or stylistic description, and, equally important, it eroded the disciplinary boundaries between the conventions (and the study) of high art and mass culture. Most crucially perhaps, Warburg's project constructed a model of the mnemonic in which, under the threat of its extinction, Western European humanist thought would once more, perhaps for the last time, recognise its origins and trace its latent continuities into the present.

Kurt Forster, the editor of the forthcoming English edition of Warburg's writings, describes the arrangement as follows:

> There, cheek by jowl, were late antique reliefs, secular manuscripts, monumental frescoes, postage stamps, broadsides, pictures cut out of magazines, and old master drawings. It becomes apparent, if only at second glance, that this unorthodox selection is the product of an extraordinary command of a vast field.[7]

Moreover, we encounter in Warburg's project an almost Benjaminian trust in the universally emancipatory functions of technological reproduction and dissemination, those of the photographic image in particular. Thus, the extreme temporal and spatial *heterogeneity* of the *Atlas's* subjects is juxtaposed with the paradoxical *homogeneity* of their simultaneous presence in the space of photographic reproduction – a 'photographic condition' anticipating the subsequent abstraction from historical context and social function in the name of a universal aesthetic experience by André Malraux in his *Le Musée Imaginaire*. This condition alone seems – at first sight at least – to situate the

Mnemosyne Atlas in a peculiar parallelism to artistic practices of the historical avant-garde of the 1920s. Not surprisingly, this argument is in fact made by numerous Warburg scholars, notably by Wolfgang Kemp, Werner Hofmann and most recently and most emphatically by Forster himself, in his two essays on Warburg's methods. Thus he states for example that in

> ... terms of technique Warburg's panels belong with the montage procedures of Schwitters and Lissitzky. Needless to say, this analogy implies no claim to artistic merit on the part of the Warburg panels; nor does it invalidate that of Schwitters' and Lissitzky's collages: it simply serves to redefine graphic montage as the construction of meanings rather than the arrangement of forms.[8]

It is this remark (and many similar ones by the Warburg scholars mentioned), in particular its intriguing and surprisingly clear-cut opposition between a "construction of meanings" (supposedly Warburg's) and an "arrangement of forms" (supposedly that of Kurt Schwitters and El Lissitzky) which poses another question: namely, whether any aspects of Warburg's *Atlas* can be productively compared to the collage and photomontage techniques of the 1920s or whether we could understand more about either side of this problematic comparison by differentiating its two parts more rigorously. Or, more importantly for our project, whether it would be potentially productive to compare Warburg's *Atlas* with the structural organisation of Richter's *Atlas*, as another mnemonic project, while recognising first of all that both projects obviously address the problematic conditions of mnemonic experience under dramatically different historical circumstances – the former at the onset of the most devastating cataclysm of human history brought about by German Fascism, the latter looking back at its aftermath from a position of repression, disavowal and an attempt to reconstruct remembrance from within the space of trauma.[9]

Wolfgang Kemp had been the first to point out that Warburg's project of an organisation and presentation of vast quantities of historical information without any textual commentary could remind us of surrealist montage procedures.[10] Thereby, Warburg's *Atlas* inevitably also enters into a comparison with another extraordinary and unfinished montage-project of the late 1920s, a *textual* assemblage which had attempted to construct an analytical memory of collective experience in nineteenth-century Paris. Benjamin had associated his *Arcades* project with the montage techniques of the surrealists and had explicitly identified it in those terms when he wrote that the "method of this work is literary montage. I have nothing to say, only to show."[11] And Theodor Adorno's description of the *Arcades* project could just as well be addressing the essential features of Warburg's *Mnemosyne Atlas*:

> [Benjamin] deliberately excluded all interpretation and wanted to have the actually existing conditions to be foregrounded through the shocks that the montage of the materials would inevitably generate in the reader .... To bring his *anti-subjectivism* to the point of culmination, Benjamin envisaged that the work should only consist of accumulated citations.[12]

Again, several terms stand out in this discussion that deserve our attention, both with regard to the accuracy of the description (and the potential differences) of Benjamin's and Warburg's model and with regard to the accuracy of their definition of the epistemes of collage. First of all, *the exclusion of interpretation* in favour of *actually existing conditions* in the discursive construction of the textual memory. Secondly the *anticipation of shocks* as an inescapable and intended result of the montage technique, presumably occurring most vividly in the interstices of discursive fields (such as the pictorial versus the photographic; the mass-cultural clutter versus the structural distillation of the avant-garde strategy; the artisanal artefact versus the technically reproduced; the scriptural versus the painterly; to name but a few

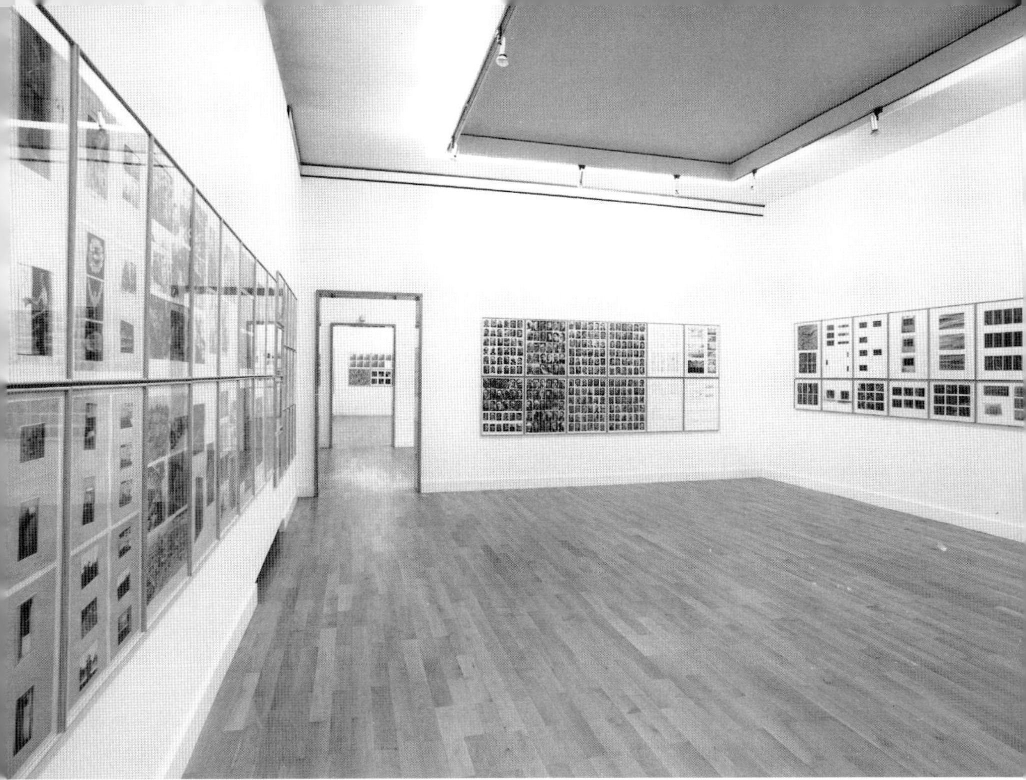

Gerhard Richter, *Atlas*, on-going since 1969.
Installation view. Courtesy of the artist.

of the classical topoi and tropes of collage and montage aesthetics). Thirdly, and crucially, it is Adorno's observation that 'anti-subjectivism' is the driving force of the collage aesthetic, that presumably initiates the articulation of a systematic critique of what would later come to be called "the author function" of a text. Lastly, and directly connected with the preceding term, Adorno's emphasis on the "accumulation of citations" as a newly emerging structuring device of montage aesthetics: first of all, in photomontage itself, where it displaces the homogeneity of the conception and execution of painting, and then in its transformation of literary or filmic aesthetics (those of the Soviet Union in particular) as, for example, in the factographic novel where it will displace authorial omniscience, narrative and fiction.

Simultaneously, one could argue, montage emerged even within the new models of written historical accounts such as Warburg's, or those of the Annales historians. In all of these projects, literary, artistic, filmic or historical, a new post-bourgeois subjectivity is constituted and the telling of history as a sequence of events and as an account of its individual agents is displaced by a focus on the simultaneity of separate, but contingent social frameworks. The process of history is now conceived as a structural system of perpetually changing interactions and permutations between economical and ecological givens, class formations and their ideologies and the resulting types of social and cultural interactions specific to each particular moment.[13]

If Warburg's *Atlas* was in fact part of a newly emerging cultural paradigm of montage as a new process of writing decentred history and constructing mnemonic forms accordingly, it could ultimately also have served as a precursor – even if unbeknownst to the artist – to Richter's development of a photographic archive of post-war history. It could have paradoxically served simultaneously as the model for the principle of heterogeneity and for that of homogeneity. Therefore, if we consider only the structural arrangement of the photographic source materials in Richter's photo collection we could be even more tempted – as were Forster and Kemp – to construe yet another case of continuity or similarity, or rather, a case of pseudo-morphism relating Richter's cumulative, not to say statistical, photomontage aesthetics, to Warburg's *Atlas*. I hope to elucidate in the following, however, that any comparison between Warburg and the montage techniques of the artistic avant-gardes, let alone the neo-avant-garde, will remain highly problematic if it does not recognise first of all the actual *discontinuities* of the collage/photomontage model itself.

These internal shifts and breaks in the paradigm emerge in the late 1920s, and these changes will become especially decisive in the paradigm's rediscovery in post-war practices. Furthermore, any attempt at a comparative reading of the structurally comparable projects will have to develop an equally differentiated understanding of the contradictions and changes which emerge already in the 1920s in defining photographic functions, both in the *theoretical approaches* to photography in Weimar Germany and the Soviet Union as much as in the artistic practices deploying photography in both countries. More specifically, and particularly important for our discussion of Warburg's project, is the fact that at the very moment of its elaboration opposite theorisations of photography had collided precisely on the question of the impact of the photographic image on the construction of historical memory.

This dialectic is evident in the positions articulated in 1927–1928: on the one hand we have to confront Siegfried Kracauer's epochal essay on photography, arguing that photographic production devastates the memory image, a position which implies (most likely unbeknownst to both) a severe critical challenge of Warburg's project to conceive of the *Atlas* as a model of the construction of social memory. At the opposite end of the spectrum, one would have to consider the famous photography debate of the Soviet Union as it emerges around 1927, primarily in the writings of the Soviet theorists and artists Ossip Brik, Boris Kushner and Alexander Rodchenko. Thirdly one would have to consider what remains probably the most important essay on photography of the first half of the twentieth century, written shortly after Warburg's project was interrupted, Walter Benjamin's "A Short History of Photography" of 1931, which argues against the media pessimism of Kracauer's essay in favour of a new media culture of politically motivated montage.

To sketch out these oppositions only in the briefest terms one would have to point first of all to the latent dichotomy operative in collage and montage aesthetics from their inception: the poles of opposition could be called the order of perceptual shock and the principle of estrangement on the one hand, and the order of the statistical collection or the archive on the other. The structural emphasis on discontinuity and fragmentation in the initial phase of Dada-derived photomontage introduced the subject's perceptual field to the "shock" experiences of daily existence in an advanced industrial culture. While the metonymic procedures of photomontage and their continuous emphasis on the fissure and the fragment – at least in their initial appearance – operated to dismantle the myths of unity and totality that advertising and ideology consistently inscribe on their consumers, photomontage paradoxically collaborated also in the social project of perceptual modernisation and its affirmative agenda. But this revolutionary effect of the semiotic upheaval of poetic shock and estrangement was short-lived. Already in the second moment of Dada collage (at the time of Hannah Höch's *Meine Haussprüche* of 1922) for example, the heterogeneity of random order and the arbitrary juxtapositions of found objects and images, and the sense of a fundamental cognitive and perceptual anomie, were challenged as either apolitical and anti-communicative, or as esoteric and aestheticist. The very avant-garde artists who initiated photomontage (e.g. Heartfield and Höch, Klucis, Lissitzky, Rodchenko) now diagnosed this anomic character of the Dada collage/montage technique as bourgeois avant-gardism, mounting a critique that called, paradoxically, for a re-instating of the dimensions of communicative action and instrumentalised logic.

What we are already witnessing in fact in the mid-1920s, becoming more decisive later in that decade, is a gradual shift towards the order of the *archival and mnemonic functions* of the photographic collection

Gerhard Richter, *Atlas*, detail shot of '48 Portraits'. Courtesy of the artist.

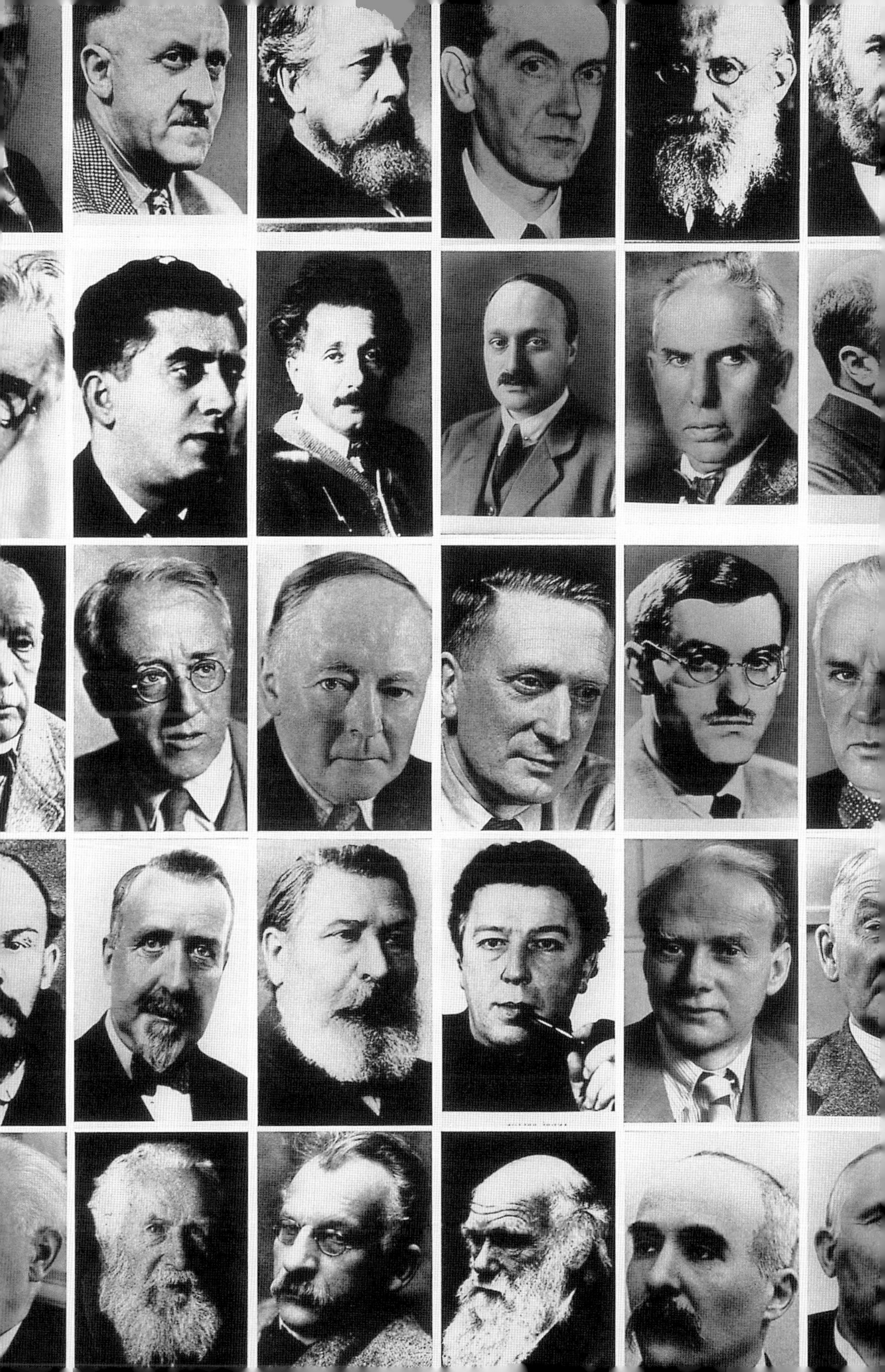

as the underlying episteme of a radically different aesthetics of photomontage. In terms of its conception of the photographic, it is a shift that originates in a celebratory trust in photography's versatility, its authenticity as empirical document, and the radical emancipatory power of the egalitarian effects of photographic reproduction. The photographic image in general was now defined as dynamic, contextual and contingent, and the serial structuring of visual information emphasised open form and a potential infinity, not only of photographic subjects eligible in a new social collective, but equally an infinity of contingent, photographically recordable details and facets that would constitute each individual subject within perpetually altered activities, social relations and object relationships. Once again it would be worthwhile to investigate the parallels of the Soviet model of the photographic with the radical reconception of the historic process emerging simultaneously in the work of the French Annales historians Marc Bloch and Lucien Febvre. These parallels between the conception of the historical process and the construction and ordering of the photographic representation become obvious when we read Ossip Brik's argument suggesting that,

> ... to differentiate individual objects so as to make a pictorial record of them is not only a technical but also an ideological phenomenon. In the pre-Revolutionary (feudal and bourgeois) period, both painting and literature set themselves the aim of differentiating individual people and events from their general context and concentrating attention on them .... To the contemporary consciousness, an individual person can be understood and assessed only in connection with all the other people – with those who used to be regarded by the pre-Revolutionary consciousness as background.[14]

This argument implies a radical redefinition of the photographic object itself. It is no longer conceived as a single-image print, carefully crafted by the artist-photographer in the studio, framed and presented as a pictorial substitute. Rather, as was the case already for Rodchenko's definition, it is precisely the cheaply and rapidly produced snapshot that will displace the traditional synthetic portrait. The organisational and distributional form will now become the *archive*, or as Rodchenko called it, the *photo-file* – a loosely organised, more or less coherent accumulation of snapshots relating and documenting one particular subject.

Rather than plotting the future models of participatory photographic experience under Socialism, Siegfried Kracauer analysed the actually existing usages of the photographic image in the Capitalist media practices of Weimar Germany, specifically those governing the illustrated weeklies. Linking the capacity of the formation of memory images to an actual relationship with material and cognitive objects, Kracauer's extreme media pessimism recognises that it is precisely the universal presence of the photographic image that will eventually destroy cognitive and mnemonic processes altogether. Thus he argues:

> Never before has an age been so informed about itself, if being informed means having an image of objects that resembles them in a photographic sense .... In reality, however, the weekly photographic ration does not at all mean to refer to these objects or ur-images. If it were offering itself as an aid to memory, then memory would have to make the selection. But the flood of photos sweeps away the dams of memory. The assault of this mass of images is so powerful, that it threatens to destroy the potentially existing awareness of crucial traits. Artworks suffer this fate through their reproductions .... In the illustrated magazines people see the very world that the illustrated magazines prevent them from perceiving .... Never before has a period known so little about itself.[15]

Now, we have to at least sketch an outline of the profound discrepancy of these photographic legacies of the historical avant-gardes and the positions assumed by post-war artists. We can easily recognise that Richter's choice of amateur photography inverts the utopian aspirations of the avant-garde model on every level: if the avant-garde practices assumed a teleological perspective of enactment and empowerment, of articulation and of self-determination, Richter's work assumes an attitude of critical negation; if the agitational dimension of photomontage originated in an attitude of radical transcendence of the given socio-political conditions that determine authorship and production, Richter's work departs from this attitude of absolute affirmation; if the Workers' Clubs photographic movement aspired to the potential of photography as a weapon of self-definition, Richter identifies with the advanced conditions of amateur photography within consumer culture, where the mere acquisition of minimal photographic skills has long become the basis for yet another domain of rigorously enforced and muted consumption.

From a position quite typical for post-war German artists, primarily oriented toward the New York and Paris activities of the moment rather than toward the overshadowed legacies of the historical avant-garde of the 1920s, Richter credits the work of Robert Rauschenberg with having provided his introduction to the collage/montage aesthetics. This paradoxical historical and geo-political shift poses a number of additional questions in the reading of Richter's photographic archive.

First of all, it poses the question of how the principle of random accumulation operates under substantially different historical circumstances, that is at a moment when randomness and arbitrary juxtaposition are not only functioning as established aesthetic procedures, but also as socially enforced legitimation of anomie disguised as an advanced state of individual independence. Collage aesthetic in Rauschenberg's hands had re-inaugurated the elimination of authorial choice and artistic authority by intrinsically linking authorship to the actual conditions of experience within advanced consumer culture, where the formation of exchange-value residing in the sign itself determines the constitution of the identity of the consuming subject.

Clearly, in the post-war moment, techniques of decentering the subject and dismantling authorial claims had changed once again in the transmission from Duchamp to John Cage, one of the formative figures for Rauschenberg's collage culture.[16] It is not easy to determine whether, in what was now the period of the neo-avant-garde, the radically subversive decentering of the (bourgeois) subject had just become a principle of affirmative indifference towards subjectivity altogether (for example, Cage's *Zen* approach); or whether, in the post-war recurrence of these strategies, the politically enforced elimination of subjectivity necessitated this aesthetic recourse to structural, perceptual and cognitive anomie, since this model alone seemed to enact the decreasing validity of concepts of communicative action, self-determination and transparent social organisation. The demonstrative 'de-skilling' of photographic practice – the manifest neglect of the criteria of the craft and conventions of the medium – is but one of the consequences at the centre of Richter's choice of amateur and journalistic photography.

What, in turn, differentiates Richter's arrangement of found photographs structurally from the traditional modes of collage aesthetics and what has made the reading of the *Atlas* difficult, is once again precisely their emphatic denial of all of the visual and spatial codes that determined collage and photomontage. If collage had been structured spatially according to latent or manifest principles of shock, estrangement and dynamism, then Richter's accumulations are distinguished by their serial, almost didactic organisation. If collage aesthetics had emphasised perceptual, material and spatial discontinuity, Richter homogenises his materials both structurally and iconographically. What one could call the essentially *syntactic* character of avant-garde collage aesthetics from cubism to the early collage work of the Soviet avant-garde in the mid-1920s, is countered then in Richter's *Atlas* in a model that one could call *paratactic*. In the former model, in spite of its emphasis on disjunction and fragmentation, on disparity of materials, textures and surfaces, an integrating reading is suggested precisely to generate the mimetic effect of structural difference, of shock and simultaneity. In the latter model by contrast, with its emphasis on a relative homogeneity of sources and materials and its ostentatious de-dramatisation and de-spatialisation of collage dynamics, collage is defined as a mere collection of image-quotations, ordered according to the principles of archival alignment, with its lapidary and monotonous positioning of one thing next to, or after, another.

The paratactic structure of Richter's *Atlas* then has to be positioned at the opposite end of a spectrum of avant-garde positions. Neither the semiotic revolution of an aesthetics of structural difference that governed cubism, nor the mimetic internalisation of an aesthetic of shock and mechanical dynamism that governed the futurist and constructivist model, nor the sudden juxtaposition of images and objects that would call up oneiric configurations and the logic of reification in the unconscious in the projects of the surrealist collage, can be quoted here as predecessors. Instead, what governs the photomontage aesthetic of Richter is precisely the mechanical alignment found in the order of the statistical aesthetic of passive administration, the aesthetic of a lapidary *archive*. Against the gesture of rebellion and political agitation, against the posture of utopian political claims articulated by the avant-garde, against the infliction of the viewer with the shock of the uncanny, Richter proposes the repetitive litany of reproduction, presented in an administrative display, a pictorial order that is always already mired in the very power structure against which avant-garde gestures still claimed to rebel. Thus Richter's aesthetic reflections on the question of technical and photographic reproduction are at the opposite pole of the photographic dialectic, rather different from Benjamin's theories on the subject of technical reproduction developed in the early 1930s.

It had been one of Benjamin's arguments that mechanical and photographic reproductions function primarily to reduce size and scale and that reduction allows for the establishment of a relationship of domination between the contemporary viewer and the works of art from the past. This interaction would otherwise cease to exist altogether for a mass audience since the reproduced image – unlike the cult image – is no longer experienced as an image of overwhelming power.[17] As this process is inextricably entwined with the loss of the aura, photography makes the experience of exhibition value all the more important. In fact, the latter will eventually displace cult value altogether and exhibition value will become part of the public sphere where the image – now reduced, reproduced and multiplied – can be controlled and manipulated.

Thus Richter's argument is in fact closer to Kracauer's concerning the dialectic of representation and memory, exhibition value and historical object experience, as developed in the essay from 1927, from which I have already quoted earlier:

> What the photographs by their sheer accumulation attempt to banish is the recollection of death, which is part and parcel of every memory image. In the illustrated magazines the world has become a photographable presence and the photographed present has been entirely eternalised. Seemingly ripped from the clutch of death, in reality it has succumbed to it.[18]

Richter (as had Kracauer before him) opposes the media optimism and its radical egalitarian and emancipatory aspirations associated with the rapid rise of a culture of photographic reproduction in the avant-garde of the 1920s. By contrast, as an artist of the neo-avant-garde, Richter sees the erosion of avant-garde positions and practices paradoxically embodied in the loss of the (painterly) object and corroborated by the degree to which photographic reproduction enacts the intrusion of mechanisms of the culture industry within the traditionally exempted sphere of avant-garde culture itself. In this regard Richter's position on photography and painting as the lost object is comparable to the mourning of the loss of the object and the loss of the real articulated by Jean Baudrillard:

> In the exact duplication of the Real, preferably by means of another reproductive medium – advertisement, photography, etc. – and in the shift from medium to medium, the real vanishes and it becomes an allegory of death. But even in its moment of destruction it exposes and affirms itself, it will become the quintessential real and it becomes the fetishism of the lost object.[19]

Footnotes

1 Maud Lavin has given us the most comprehensive description and discussion of Höch's *Scrap Book* in her monographic study *Cut With the Kitchen Knife*, Yale University Press, 1993, pp. 71–121. Yet Lavin does not even attempt to address the contradictions that become apparent in her own discussion when she continuously refers to the scrap book as a photomontage project only to assert at the same time that in fact it differs in many unfathomable ways from photomontage proper. This unresolved ambiguity becomes most apparent in Lavin's final statement on the *Scrap Book*: "... but the strongest impression one gets from looking through Höch's *Scrap Book* is that it is a collection compiled for her own intense visual, sensual and spiritual pleasure. This private view differs from the representations in Höch's public and more critical photomontages, and as such the *Scrap Book* can be considered as a mediation between the presentations of the Weimar mass media and the exhibition displays of one avant-gardist." (p.120).

2 Communication would in fact have been particularly difficult, if not downright impossible for the family of a "deserter of the Democratic Republic," as refugees from East Germany were termed in official party language, and to travel back across the border would have meant imprisonment for Richter after the construction of the Berlin Wall in 1961.

3 See Richard Semon, *Die Mneme als erhaltendes Prinzip im Wechsel des organischen Geschehens*, Leipzig, 1904.

4 See Richard Terdiman, *Present Past: Modernity and the Memory Crisis*, Cornell University Press, 1993.

5 Aby Warburg, "Introduction to Mnemosyne Atlas", Warburg Archive, No.102.1.1, P. 6; quoted in Matthew Rampley, "Mimesis and Modernity: Aby Warburg and Walter Benjamin", unpublished manuscript. Also see Rampley's contribution to this volume.

6 See Walter Benjamin, "A Small History of Photography", in *One Way Street*, trans., Edmund Jephcott and Kingsley Shorter, NLB/Verso, 1985, pp. 240–257. (translation modified by the author).

7 Kurt Forster, "Die Hamburg Amerika Linie oder Warburg's Kunstwissenschaft zwischen den Kontinenten", in *Aby Warburg: Akten des Internationalen Symposiums*, eds., Horst Bredekamp, Michael Diers and Charlotte Schoell-Glass, Acta Humaniora, 1991, pp. 11–37.

8 Forster, "Hamburg", p. 31.

9 Joseph Koerner has suggested, in a moving essay on Warburg, that the rise of Nazi Fascism in Germany at the time would in fact have had a tremendous impact on the orientation (or disorientation) of Warburg's personal and professional life, as early as the outbreak of his illness. See Joseph Koerner, "Aby Warburg among the Hopis: Paleface and Redskin", in *The New Republic*, 24 March 1997, pp. 30–38.

10 Wolfgang Kemp, "Benjamin und Aby Warburg", in *Kritische Berichte*, vol. 3, no.1, 1975, p. 5.

11 Walter Benjamin, *Das Passagenwerk, Gesammelte Schriften*, eds., Rolf Tiedemann and Hermann Schweppenhäuser, Suhrkamp Verlag, 1972–1989, vol. V, p. 574.

12 Theodor W. Adorno, "Charakteristik Walter Benjamin", in *Prismen: Kulturkritik und Gesellschaft,* vol.10/1, 1977, pp. 238–253.

13 Not surprisingly then, the parallels between the Annales historian Marc Bloch and Aby Warburg have been discussed. See Ulrich Raulff, "Parallel gelesen: Die Schriften von Aby Warburg und Marc Bloch zwischen 1914 und 1924", in *Aby Warburg: Akten des Internationalen Symposiums*, eds., Horst Bredekamp et al, Acta Humaniora, 1991, pp.167–178.

14 See Ossip Brik, "From Painting to Photography", in *Photography in the Modern Era*, ed., Christopher Phillips, 1989, pp. 231.

15 Siegfried Kracauer, "Photography", *The Mass Ornament*, ed. and trans., Thomas Y. Levin, Harvard University Press, 1995, p. 58.

16 The consistent decay of the dialectical potential of the procedures of fragmentation, aleatory order, and arbitrary relations already evident in the first instances of their post-war rediscovery in the work of Rauschenberg and Paolozzi leads ultimately to their deployment as mere strategies of domination in contemporary advertising.

17 This paraphrase of two crucial ideas from Benjamin's 'Artwork' essay is quoted from an excellent paper by Horst Bredekamp, "Der simulierte Benjamin", in *Frankfurter Schule und Kunstgeschichte*, eds., Andreas Berndt et al., Reimer Verlag, 1992, pp. 118–119.

18 Kracauer, "Photography", p. 59.

19 Jean Baudrillard, *L'Echange symbolique et la mort*, 1976, p. 86.

A different version of this essay will be published in a future volume of October.

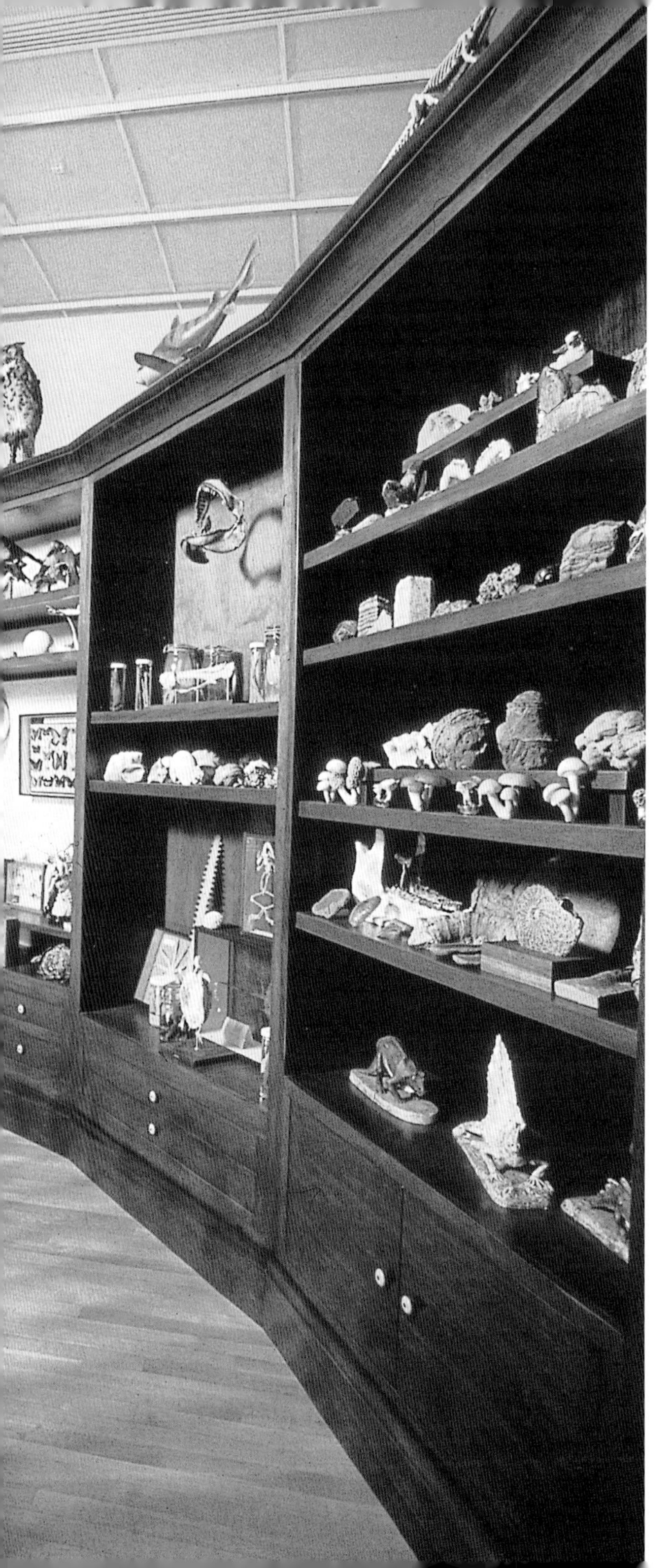

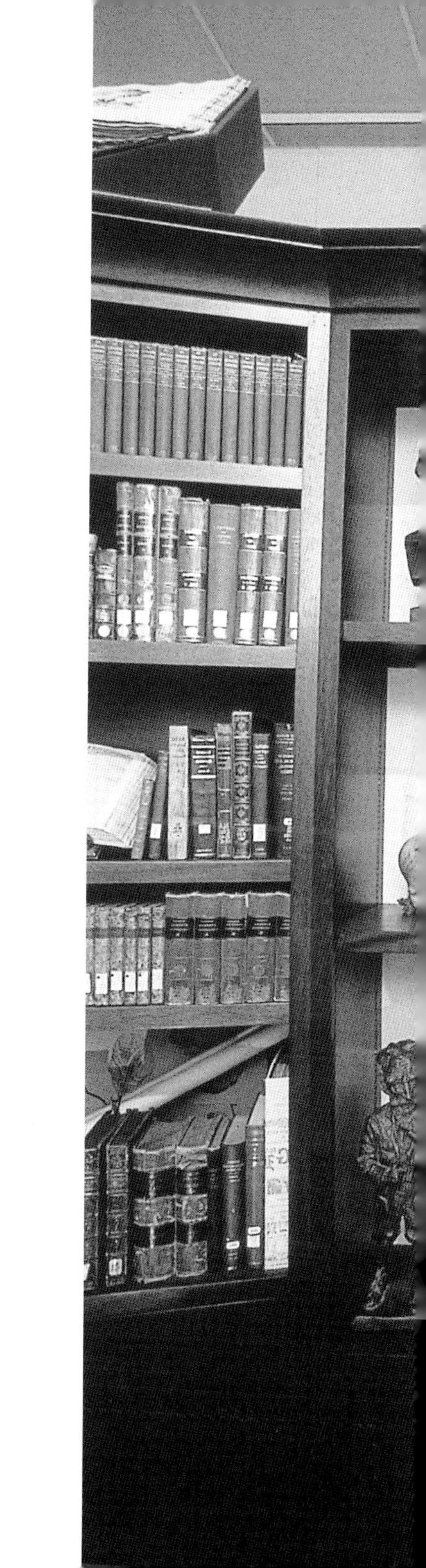

Field Work and The Natural History Museum

Mark Dion Interview

Reading Walter Benjamin in the 1980s

Alex Coles Initially I want to take you down memory lane. Did your work on the Whitney Program in the mid-1980s – with visiting lecturers such as Craig Owens, Hal Foster and Douglas Crimp – expose you to recent reworkings of Benjamin in terms of contemporary art practice? It seems that these have been very important – particularly Crimp's work on Broodthaers and Benjamin, the collector and the museum; Owens' work on Smithson and Benjamin, the site and the ruin; and Foster's more recent work on yourself and artists such as Fred Wilson, Andrea Fraser and Benjamin, on the theme of 'the artist as ethnographer' (invoking Benjamin's "The Author as Producer").

Mark Dion You should be cautious when walking me down memory lane because it is a twisted road, bristling with narrow blind alleys, dead ends and detours which could take us far afield from your question!

The works of Walter Benjamin were introduced to me long before the Whitney Program of Independent Study. The early 80s were an exceptional time to be in art school, at least for the things I am interested in. The period was dynamic. All three schools I attended – the Hartford Art School, the School of Visual Arts and the Whitney Program – were places one could find a commitment to art-making as an intellectual process. While at HAS and SVA not every faculty member shared the notion that art was about ideas, in fact it may have been a minority who had that view. However, they were a powerful cadre. At SVA I studied intensely with Craig Owens and frequently on Benjamin Buchloh's course. At the Whitney, Foster, Crimp, Buchloh, Owens and Ron Clark were all seminar leaders or advisors. It would be wrong to frame these critics as the only people who taught and were engaged with Walter Benjamin or other theorists, since numerous artists who lectured and led courses were also directing a critical inquiry into the Frankfurt School. Tom Lawson, Yvonne Rainer, Joseph Kosuth, Barbara Kruger, Martha Rosler and numerous others were all fluent in the language of critical theory, but spoke differently from the academics. It is important to try to understand the difference between how art historians and literary critics use what used to be called philosophy, and is now called critical theory (or even cultural studies), and how artists use these ideas.

On one hand, the demands of form and conventions of distribution often necessitate academic rigour for writers, while on the other artists tend to use critical theory in a pragmatic mix-and-match method. They use what works and discard the contradictions. One very real reason for this is that as students we were studying contemporary critical theory without having had a background in philosophy. We were reading Foucault, but had never read Kant, reading Jameson without having studied Hegel. Most of us who survived this trial by fire later went back to fill in the gaps. In fact, Craig Owens once took a seminar to walk Gregg Bordowitz, Jason Simon and I through Marx's *Das Kapital*.

There are other, more important reasons why an artist's relation to reading theory is different from an academic's. Artists are not interested in illustrating theories as much as they may be in testing them. This is why artists may choose to ignore contradictions in a text, or may choose to explode those contradictions. The artwork may be the lab experiment which attempts equally as hard to disprove as prove a point. The artist may not be terribly interested in the object of an experiment but merely in learning the method. For artists, reading philosophy is like acquiring new tools for your tool chest – some tools you need every day and others are required only for specific jobs. Critics improve the tools, artists improve their application.

There was a low point in the 1980s when you could walk into an exhibition in New York and actually construct the artists' reading list. All across the US many artists were reading the same material. This resulted wonderfully in a shared discourse, a language which allowed artists all over the country to communicate comprehensively. But it also came very close to producing a new academy. This was avoided by the impact of critics and artists like Stephen Dillemuth and Christian Philip Müller from Europe.

There were staple texts which were read in almost every seminar each semester. They would be examined in the way a pathologist examines a corpse. Some of the most persuasive were the introduction to *The Order of Things*, some essays from the 1970s British film theory – works by Roland Barthes, Edward Said and Walter Benjamin. I don't know how many times I read "The Author as Producer" but I do recall reading "The Work of Art in the Age of Mechanical Reproduction" in three courses at the same time. Rather than exhaust the text, the experience revealed the extraordinary depth and richness it had. It expanded continually. At times, however, we would joke about what a cliché it became to start an essay with a Benjamin quote; wondering whether, since a Benjamin quote was obligatory, maybe we could put it in the middle or the end, instead of at the beginning! It is the expansiveness of Benjamin's work that made him so appropriate for then and now. Benjamin, as an intellectual, seemed orientated in a production way to the emergence of what, at the time, was called a postmodern practice. What made him attractive was the bond between

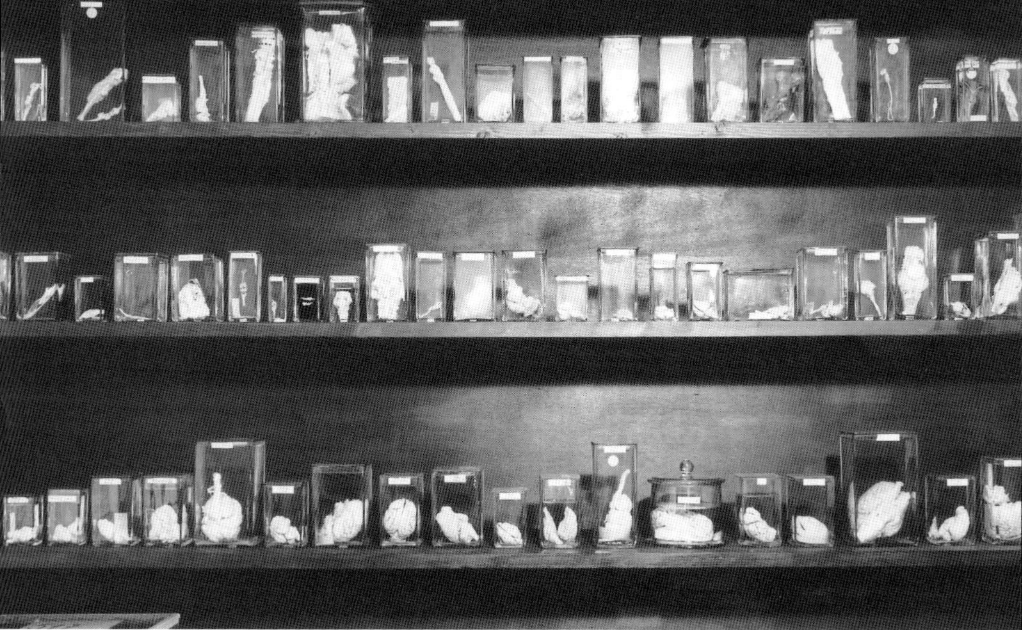

Mark Dion, *Adventures in Comparative Neuroanatomy*, 1998, Deutsches Museum in Bonn (detail). All images Courtesy of London Projects and American Fine Arts, Co., New York.

an intellectual critical response and a political commitment – anti-fascism which seemed very relevant in the Regan/Thatcher years of the 1980s. Likewise, Benjamin's interest in history and what happens under repressive governments also seemed relevant in the 1980s. This was very much the topic of the film I made with Jason Simon in 1988 – *Artful History: A Restoration Comedy.* Lastly, it is easy to see how Benjamin's interest in the contradictions of collecting influenced artists of my group, like Andrea Fraser and Renée Green.

Could you unpack the link with *Artful History: A Restoration Comedy* by explaining a little bit about how it came together? This piece seems very important in relation to much of your subsequent practice, especially in terms of your tactic of surfacing/discussing fictional structures whilst producing yet more absurd ones.

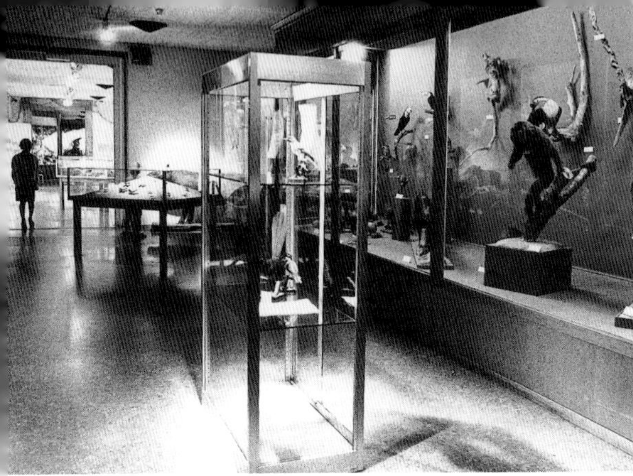

Mark Dion,
Nos Sciences Naturelles,
Installation view,
Fri-Art, Fribourg.

You could not be more right in perceiving the importance of this project. *Artful History: A Restoration Comedy* marks the break from my student work with everything I would do afterwards. It also taught me how a project develops – growing like a tree with branches going in different directions, with deep roots and shoots, with buds and seeds which sprout other ideas. You see, *Artful History* had many different incarnations. It began as an installation of fragments of an altered painting on a salmon-pink wall with labels. This was exhibited at the Whitney ISP and later at its sibling downtown Museum Branch. It was also in the exhibition *Rooted Rhetoric* curated by Gabriele Guercio in Naples, and the exhibition *Transitional Objects* in Lyon. But the installation also became a performance in which I told horror stories of abuse from the art restoration studio where I worked. This was at Four Walls in Hoboken, New Jersey in 1985. Susan Morgan and Thomas Lawson commissioned the work as a piece for the *Real Life Magazine*. Lastly, Jason Simon and I made a thirty-minute, broadcast-quality, pseudo-documentary out of the work. In the film we could explore the issues with incredible complexity. We examined how history is constructed through fragments like painting, which are subject to external factors like economics, labour conditions, chance. We were interested in how history seemed to become destabilised and unhinged, subject to contemporary whims.

The film is remarkably impure, which is what I still love about it. It is unclear, even to Jason and I, if I am in character or a real art restorer; if this is a fictional work or a documentary; which stories are true and which are fiction. This lack of any firm anchorage for truth is what I have built much of my work on since then. My foundations are built on this shifting ground. The humour and absurdity of the film is cut very close to the seriousness of the documentary form. I remember Jason and I would show the film to some audiences where the irony and comedy were just lost; other audiences would see the entire work as a fiction – as a tongue-in-cheek film. Sometimes we achieved comedy and other times tragedy with the same work.

As I mentioned, we really saw the film as a metaphor for the way the conservatives were re-writing history in the mid-1980s: how Hollywood and the White House were perfecting 'doublespeak', raiding history and dismantling the opposition. We were interested in using art restoration as a model because it has such a powerful status in the ideology of disinterest and beneficence, just as I would later find in the natural sciences.

The Natural History Museum

Your work falls into two main categories of site: the museum work and the field work – both of which are in constant dialogue with one another, and both of which mobilise strategies of fictional address. Let's look at the museum first: in what specific ways do your tactics work with, or fight, these fictions of 'Nature' and 'History', for example in the Natural History Museum? Fictions which are, in linking back to Benjamin, forms of propaganda. (Incidentally, this nicely corresponds with a comment Broodthaers once made: "Fiction enables us to grasp reality and at the same time that which is veiled by reality.")

I always like to say that the reason I like the Museum of Natural History is that it really is this very unself-critical site of the production of 'truth'. It shows how society tells the 'truth' about nature and it is a very elaborate construction of an official story reflecting the changes in that story: new obsessions, new economic demands, and so on. I always see nature as a fantasy, as a refuge, a site of savagery or an Eden, or as an economic structure; all of this is very much reflected in how the museum organises itself. As an artist who works with things, I am drawn to the museum itself, for the museum is where you tell that story through things, through a very particular type of representation. A representation that is not a text the way a book is a text, not photographs, not film, but is actually the specimen, which is a very particular kind of representation: for it is both the thing itself and a representation of it. This is what brings it into the orbit of what I and others do as practitioners. In many ways, much of my work involves producing elaborate fictions that parallel – and so call into question and destabilise – the 'true' fictions that the museum tells. It gives you an option that is not present. This often takes the form of providing characters that are not present, including the fiction creator. The museum always attempts to speak in a kind of normal propagandistic way from a unified position. All sense of behind-the-scenes dispute is concealed. There are many tactics I use to get at this strategy: one is fabricating fictions, another a cunning use of humour. This is crucial when most museums are chronically humourless. In a way I'm fighting dirty!

What is also interesting about the museum is that you can, with a lot of travel, collect the experience of these places, obsessions and previous museum ideologies, because they still exist. This also allows you to compare and contrast such ideologies, and to see how they have evolved. Amidst all this, over time, sometimes particular museums become museums of museums. This has happened here in London with the British Museum. A museum tells us how particular people at a distinctive moment in time thought about their relationship with the natural world.

I'm interested in your Broodthaers quote, because it both affirms the importance of an interrogation of material conditions, while at the same time casting doubt upon the affirming of the truth value any such discovery would have. It is exactly the kind of approach one needs to counter the approach of popular science.

In the 1980s, interest in the conceptualist critique of the museum shifted its point of focus with the work of Benjamin Buchloh and Douglas Crimp et al. This is most evident when thinking of the shift away from Hans Haacke towards Marcel Broodthaers (to use two paradigmatic artists). Often Benjamin's work informed these shifts and likewise they often reposition Benjamin. For like him, these artists and critics were interested in forms of 'institutional critique' that create, instead of just expose, fictions through deploying particular strategies of collecting, display, and anti-commodification. (This has led to the recent outpouring of titles from book factories, such as Routledge, on the museum.) Similarly, in the mid- to late-1980s, your conception of a type of institutional critique shifts, from works like *I'd Like to Give the World a Coke* (1986) – which are slightly more dependant on these earlier forms of 'institutional critique' – to the *Extinction Series* (1989) and on to more recent work, whereby a new language of address is assembled: a language consisting of elaborate fictions. What motivated this shift towards the Natural History and Ethnographic Museum?

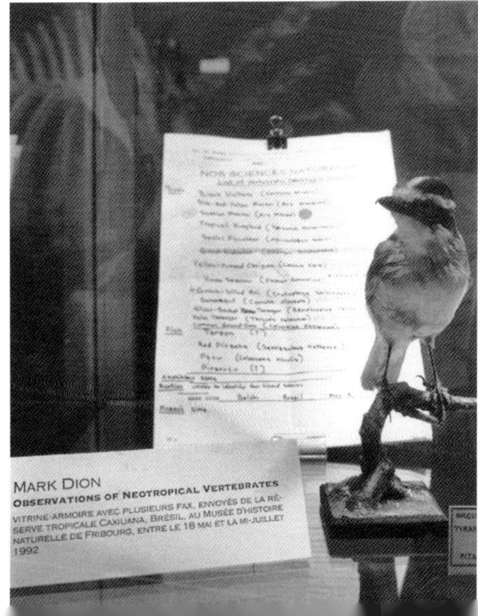

Mark Dion,
Nos Sciences Naturelles,
Installation view,
Fri-Art, Fribourg.

One of the things that motivated this shift for me was the situation of 'endgameness' in which many conceptualist critiques of the gallery found themselves. Because of their repetitive type of game play, at one point it seemed as if these practices were heralding a new kind of formalism. I remember talking to Gregg Bordowitz about this, at the point when we were both really looking elsewhere: he was very involved in the foundations of queer politics, I was at that time trying to catch up and learn about the basics of biology. So we were both pondering over this when he said: "Look, I have no more questions for white walls!" Neither of us found the museum/gallery system (the way patronage works, etc.) very complex. Already, artists like Haacke were art history by the time we were studying (he had also moved on from these critiques), and it became a question of looking at other sites and asking 'bigger' questions. While the art world is considerably fucked-up because of its relationship with archaic systems of patronage, we are all dying of boredom, waiting for a more modern development of this system to kick in. So it was not that interesting at that time to continue talking about the corruption of the museum. With its abuse of power, cowardice and dull witlessness on such a petty and obvious level, it's hard to get up the energy to critique it. Life is much too short to waste time on investigating the collusion of the art market and the museum structure.

Did the dryness of much conceptualist practice also contribute to your fatigue of it?

Sure. As much as I identify with some of it, it really apes a scientific sociological proceeding without any type of criticality towards its methods; or even the basic notion that asking a very particular question is going to direct your methods of finding out the answer to that question. It is also not very self-reflexive about just producing another 'truth'. This transformation in my practice was also a result of my desire to bring together my own personal passions, which comes from

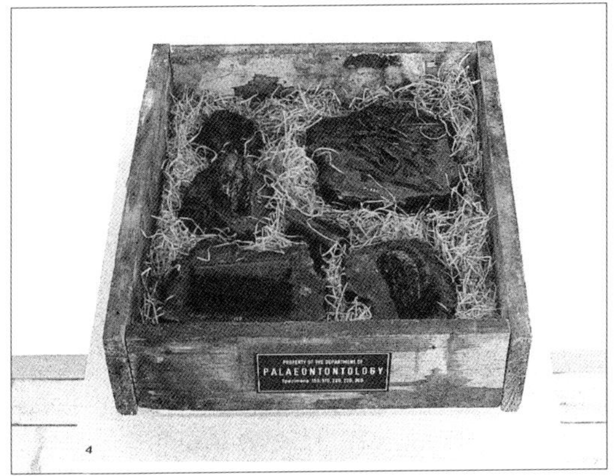

Mark Dion,
Nos Sciences Naturelles,
Installation view,
Fri-Art, Fribourg.

a place too complex even for me to necessarily get entire control over it. On the one hand, I was living the life of someone who has a great passion for interacting with nature, and a great passion for its forms of representation, whether that be the Natural History Museum, television, or the apparatus of collecting, and on the other, I was living the life of an artist who was almost disinterestedly pursuing the methodology of institutional critique, something I didn't necessarily give a damn about, one way or the other. The important thing was that I was able to bring together something I did give a damn about, with the same conceptual tool box I had developed to take apart these other things. For me, this makes the strongest art in some way: where there is a level of conviction that comes from another place, not internal to art, that cannot be taught as an academic procedure.

I have heard you talk about this before and it often comes over as a sort of 'small bang theory', whereby one day you woke up to find that at last the two parts of your life were in dialogue with one another. As this is such an important moment in your development, can you be more specific?

Yes, things *are* more complex here. I can trace a couple of points out for you. One is that at the time I was working for Ashley Bickerton, and his way of being able to work as an artist, and be a surfer, along with his passion for going out into the wilderness in an off-road vehicle – his having a relationship with nature that was a pleasurable one – rekindled my interest, because I did not have access to that outside of the city, outside of Central Park and the Museum of Natural History. At the same time, I started to find the kind of things I was interested in critically, in cultural studies, for example, in people who were interested in biology. Stephen Jay Gould's writing allowed me to see how the methodologies of critique I was interested in could actually be applied to the things I was concerned with. This included problems of extinction, conservation, etc. These were things I did not have access to: for at this time there was either critical work in cultural studies or extremely uncritical natural history writing. Of course, now things are very different. But at the time I couldn't orientate myself towards these things alone – I didn't have the signposts: so Stephen Jay Gould provided one, Ashley Bickerton another. Also, in addition to these, at that time I began taking trips to South America and getting involved with the beginnings of tropical conservation ideas. That experience kind of cinched it for me.

This is great to hear, because what you have are three very different things that suggested to you this new direction: your work with another artist, your reading of a theoretician, and your actual field experience.

But in addition to these, I realised I needed to go back to basics regarding my study of natural history – I had only received a little at this point. So, I had my work cut out for me!

In what ways have your strategies developed from the first negotiations with the museum in the early 1990s to the present?

There are a lot different shifts involved here. But one important thing for me was to redevelop the idea of installation. This primarily comes from being interested in documentary, but not wanting to make a film. The way this kind of documentary seems to exist is in museums like the Smithsonian, whereby you can actually produce knowledge from a particular arrangement of things that is in some way very similar to the desire in documentary to tell the 'truth'. My 'truth' is always in quotations and in squiggles. Early incarnations of installation were about transporting the viewer to an environment you stepped into, whereas I was interested in making a site that was on a stage and in brackets already. With this comes an attempt to try and deal with the problem of realism, or the decentering of experience that 1970s installation was about.

This notion of the stage is particularly enhanced when you have a cuddly toy or a stuffed animal standing in for an explorer, or even hybridised versions of explorers.

Right, this is another important dimension: I never wanted to make a kind of total art work that gave you the illusion you were not in a gallery. For instance, *Frankenstein – in the Age of Biotechnology* (1991) was the first time I was able to construct a space entirely that fabricated a character as an allegory. So this is a very important piece.

In one of your lectures, "The Natural History Box: Preservation, Categorisation and Display", you begin and end with a familiar Benjamin quote from the "Theses on the Philosophy of History": "A Historical Materialist views (cultural treasures) with cautious detachment. For without exception the cultural treasures he surveys have an origin which he cannot contemplate without horror .... There is no document of civilisation which is not at the same time a document of barbarism. And just as such a document is not free of barbarism, barbarism taints also the manner in which it is transmitted

from one owner to another.". This seems key to the development of your critical strategies we have been discussing. Within the context of the museum, what does this quote mean to you?

First of all, it is a mildly comical throwback to something we discussed earlier, a little 'in-joke'. I wanted to start an essay/lecture with a quote since that was a late 80s convention, and also to finish the lecture with one, so the quote appears at both ends of the lecture.

More seriously, Benjamin here articulates, with precision, the conflict and ambivalence that anyone working with the museum feels today. The quote is powerful to me because I doubt Benjamin's "cautious detachment", or rather I feel it disguises a distressing attraction to things, and an uncertainty about how to both love them and be critical of the situation which produced them. This quote also expresses the problems the museums have when they become somewhat self-reflexive and politicised. Museums today have this problem of being

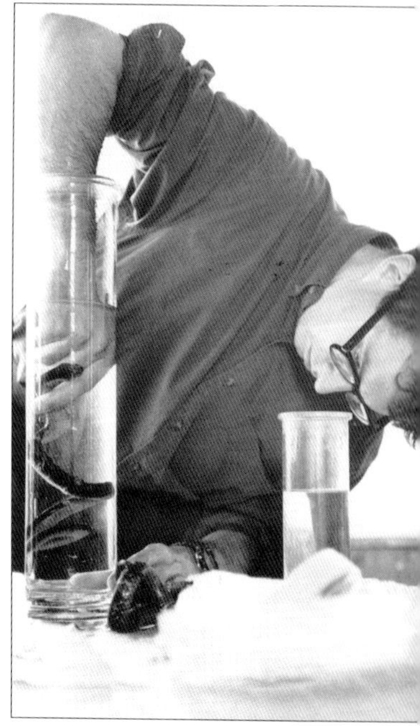

Mark Dion, *Four Experiments in Abiogenesis*, 1994, from the exhibition *Pro-Creation?*, Fri-Art, Fribourg.

filled with this 'stuff' which has been gathered through means now recognised as barbaric and unethical. The question is what to do about it. How do you organise this material in a way which does not implicate the institution? Is there a way to use these specimens differently? There is a subjective history to every artefact in every collection – Who shot it? Who bought it? Who dug it up? Who painted it? This is perhaps more obvious in the art museum which highlights the differences between collecting and how they reflect the predilections of the patrons, rather than the scientific aspects of archaeology or natural history collections. There has to be a 'why' to recontextualise material culture, to discuss its conditions of acquisition. Museums have to be honest with themselves and with the public, it's the only way to move on. Rather than try to hide the colonial practices and racist tendencies of the past, the museum must implicate itself and come clean. This is where perhaps artists can be of assistance, since some of the most brilliant work on this situation has already been constructed by Hans Haacke, Fred Wilson, Renée Green, Andrea Fraser, and Christian Phillip Müller. These projects are not just footnotes, they actually provide a model for a productive relationship to the horrors of the past. Not that I expect museums to really come clean.

Non-Site/On-Site: Field Work

A further question about fiction – this time from a slightly different angle. Popular representations of the model of the ethnographer /explorer are extremely problematic: whether this be Tintin in the Congo, or Indiana Jones reclaiming lost arks for natural history museums. In both cases, the fictional hero acts as a kind of coloniser. There are many photographs of you taken during field work in heroic guise: braving the weather, unearthing new categories of (insect) life, and so on. With its strategies of fictional address, how does your work treat these problematics associated with this model? What forms do the critical strategies take here? (You have been asked this on previous occasions, but I have not been completely satisfied with your replies.)

This is an interesting question and we could easily spend an entire interview just trying to unpack it. One aspect of the question I've tried to discuss before is that not all colonisers are the same. Alfred Russell Wallace, H.W. Bates or Charles Darwin were remarkably different from a garrison commander, plantation farmer or colonial administrator. Likewise, today, someone researching termites in Venezuela is remarkably different from a Shell Oil geologist in the same tropical jungle. This does not mean that they are not all part of the same colonial process, but it does history a great disservice to crush difference so dramatically.

When I take on the role of the tropical naturalist in those photos (and believe me I'm very careful about which photos I release), it is quite similar to when I put on a lab coat in works like *The Great Munich Bug Hunt.* A simple gesture becomes shorthand for a larger network of ideas and a frame of reference. In the same way as the institutional performance related work, there is a blurring between myself as the artist and myself as a character.

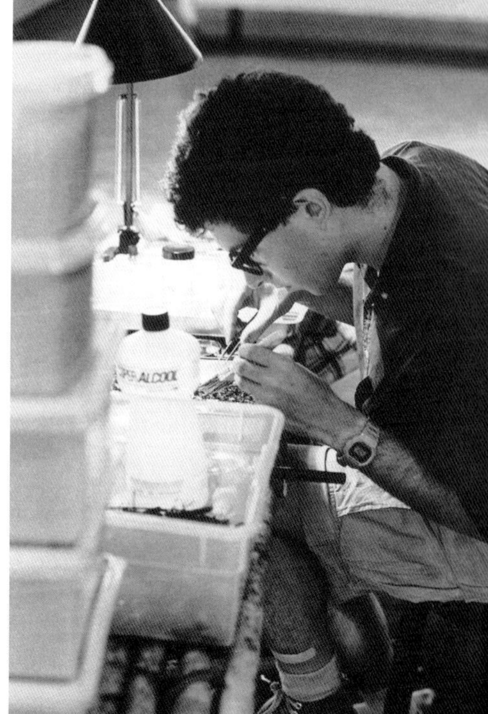

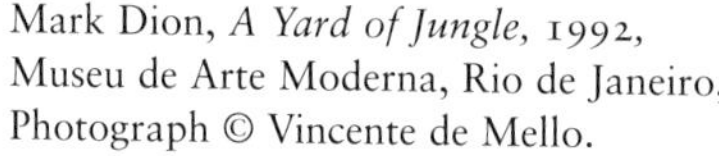

Mark Dion, *A Yard of Jungle,* 1992, Museu de Arte Moderna, Rio de Janeiro, Photograph © Vincente de Mello.

'The jungle', the tropical forest, is no less an institution for me than the museum. My taking on of a persona reflects a process of the colonisation of my (and many others') consciousness, the construction of a body of ideas which precedes and directs my sense of the jungle before I've ever set foot there. I had so much knowledge about tropical forests before I ever saw one. I knew in a very approximate way what to expect as far as an image goes. It is interesting that senses other than sight were more likely to be surprised – smell, the sense of heat, the pain of insect bites, the silence. Of course, once you are in a place there is an intense experience of unlearning the expectations you arrive with. Knowing how the image of the jungle is constructed I have a great deal of control with the images I produce of myself in the jungle. (The images are almost always taken by my friend and frequent collaborator, Bob Braine.)

The images, and in fact the experience, is very much about implicating myself in a vast array of fantasies about the natural world. While not entirely blinded by the constructions of the European in the bush, be that Tintin or Darwin, I cannot express Benjamin's "cautious detachment". I'm not interested in standing back and wagging my finger at the bad colonialists of the past and their misguided beliefs. It's too easy, too distant to really learn anything from. I need to be a little closer to the flame even if it means getting a bit burnt. In this way, the project (the artwork) can function as a lightning rod for contradiction and argumentation not merely as a cool, distanced critical appraisal. I don't believe one can ever dismiss desire and self from the process of analysis.

In every work where I use the strategies of placing myself in the 'explorer' role, I find ways of frustrating the expectations of that logic. For example, the materials collected in Venezuela end up being archivally protected, thus destroying the 'show and tell' logic of the expedition: rather than seeing rarities from the deep, dark jungle, one can only witness a series of numbered plastic containers. Or in the *Yard of Jungle,* all that results from the research in the Amazon is a collection of invertebrates, almost all too small to be seen with the naked eye. Some projects reverse the collection impulse, looking more at what is brought into the sight rather than what is removed.

For Benjamin, collectors present a critical model because of their resistance to the demands of capitalism – they render as useless the objects they form in a collection; thereby enabling them to unravel the secret historical meaning of the things they accumulate. While this tactic is put into play in your work, one can also recognise the more directly interventionist tactics of "The Author as Producer", reflected in the way many of your projects are a direct activist intervention into a very particular context. Are these two strategies of critical address in friction or co-ordination with one another in your practice? (One seems more passive than the other.)

For me, making a project is an extremely situational endeavour. The result is affected by so many factors, some visible to anyone (location, network of assistance, budget, energy level, identification or animosity to the hosting institution, political climate) while many of the factors are not entirely visible to everyone (how a project responds to what I did last; how homesick I am; my secret five year plan, etc.). As I've said elsewhere, I think about what I do as a practice, which has multiple types of expression that are articulated in a variety of sites. This practice is bound by a theme which is the representation of nature and a belief that is a part of a political dialogue which is represented through the production of culture in any society. This dialogue has a concrete function in shaping social relations and in how we construct nature.

The use of these two strategies has evolved very slowly. In my early work, I tried to do everything, say everything. This made many of the projects unwieldy, overly information-packed, too ambitious. Stepping back, I can now see how works support each other, how an argument is slowly built. Each work is a battle in a longer war.

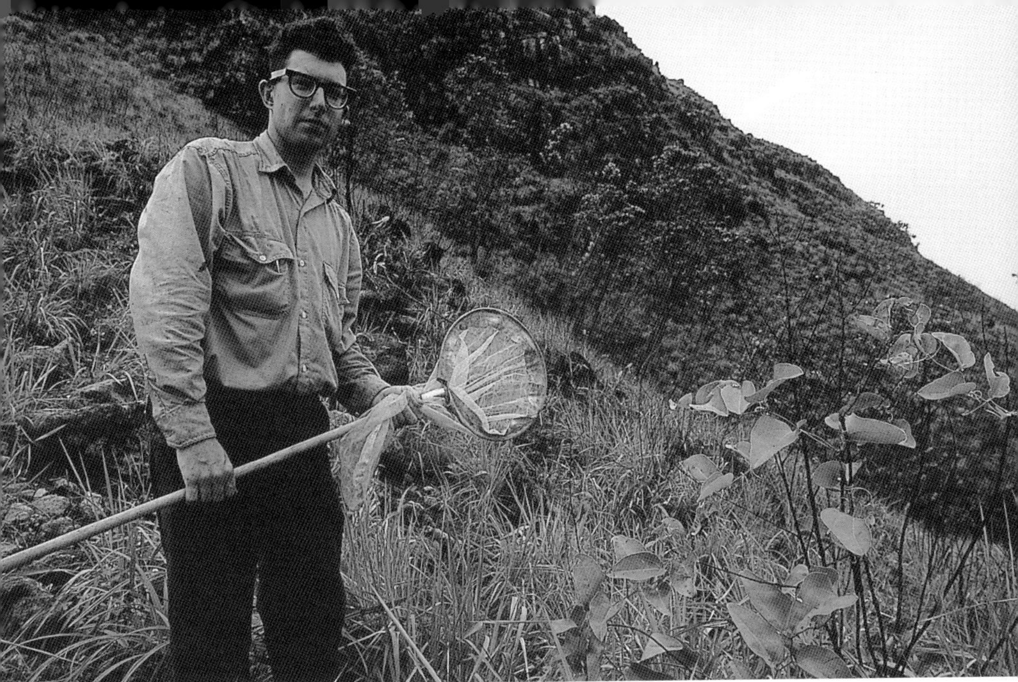

Mark Dion collecting insects in Venezuela, 1991. Photograph © Bob Braine.

Of course, context constructs a response and has very much to do with which form of address, which voice, one wishes to use. It's easy to make assumptions about who the audience is in a university gallery in the mid-western US but you may want to speak differently if your work is placed in a public venue in a city. Also, efforts have to be somehow co-ordinated to produce at least the illusion of satisfaction, if not satisfaction itself. After working too long in the ivory tower, it helps to clear the head by going into the streets, after the compromises of the streets, it's satisfying to return to the control of the ivory tower. It is an intense dissatisfaction with both modes which results in this hybrid method. It also seems extremely important as an artist to present a moving target, because once you become classified it's possible to place you on the shelf. And that is an extremely difficult location to speak from.

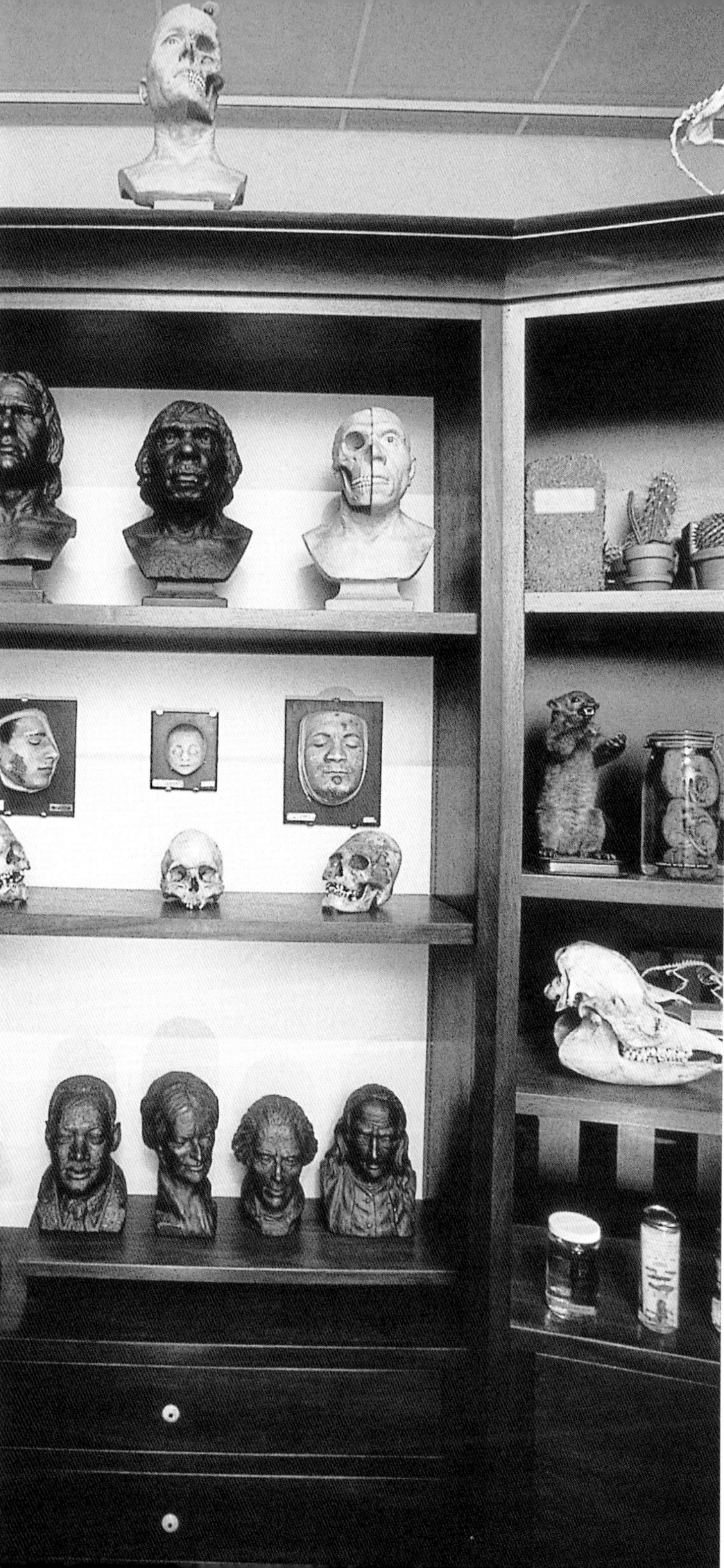

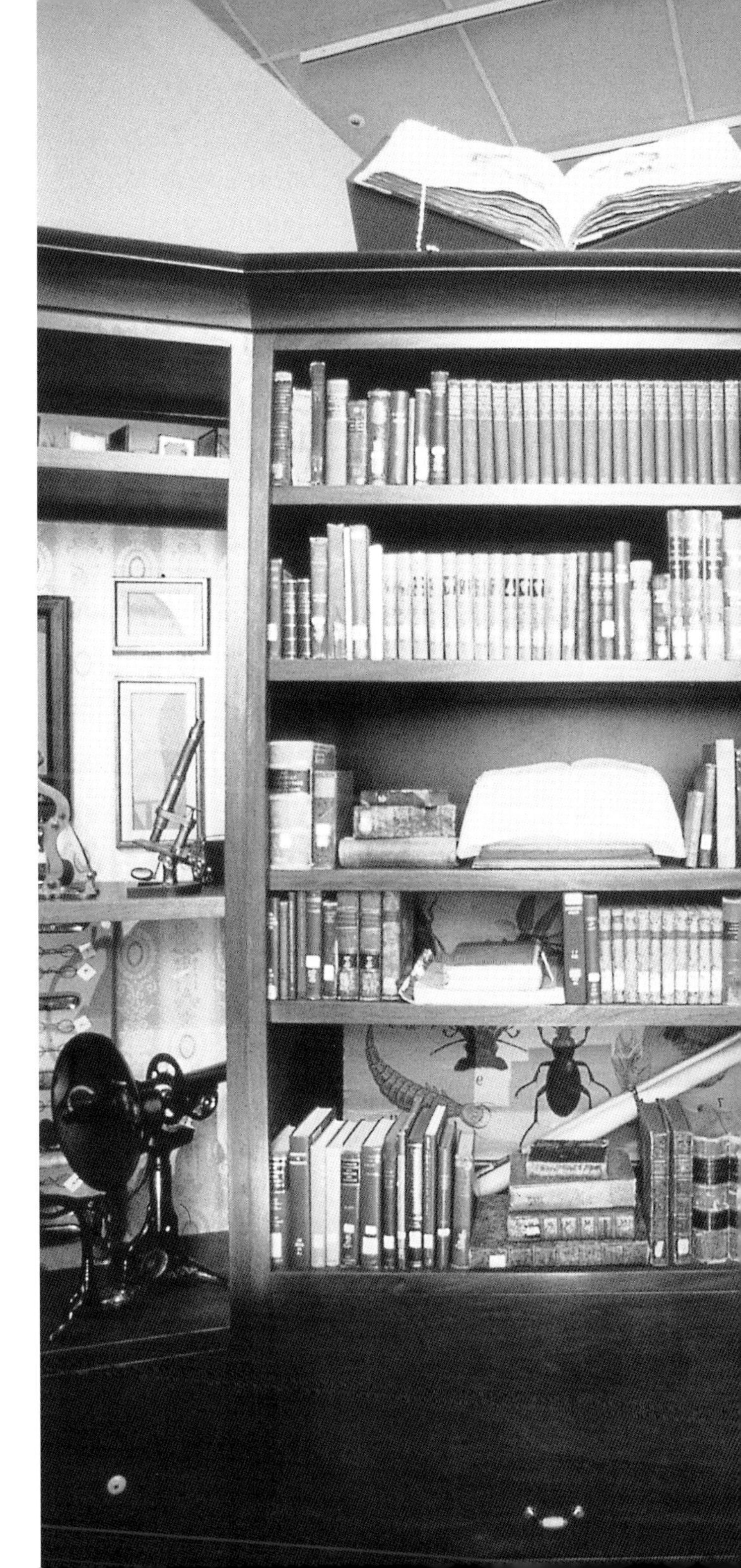

Telescoping the Microscopic Object: Benjamin the Collector

Esther Leslie

> Who amongst you has not, in the long hours of leisure, taken a delicious pleasure in constructing a model-apartment, an ideal home, a revision?
> — Charles Baudelaire, 1852
> Introduction to Edgar Allen Poe's *Philosophy of Furniture*

Irregular (Re)collections

In the late 1930s, having fled the Third Reich, Walter Benjamin collated a series of autobiographical snapshots, and gave them the title *Berlin Childhood around 1900*. The forty-odd vignettes are a collection of memories from his childhood, and at the same time, communicate recollections from the infancy of a new century. Some of these memories uncoil in the open spaces of the park, the market and the streets, but many describe remembered interiors and their objects. The interiors figured are those of schools, department stores, and, in particular, Benjamin's homes and the apartments of his aunts and grandmothers. In recalling them, Benjamin exhibits a quite delicious pleasure in constructing a model-apartment, an ideal home, a *revision* of the past.

A letter from 1935 introducing the "The Work of Art in the Age of Mechanical Reproduction" to a friend conjured up an optical device – a telescope – to figure this revisioning with its emphasis on seeing more closely and seeing anew. The revisioning entails a curious temporality. Benjamin's telescope has a line of sight that cuts through time itself, spying a fantastic image of the nineteenth century as a mirage seen through a bloody fog, in a future, liberated condition. The telescope was a well-chosen tool, for it, along with the microscope, found new uses in the nineteenth century, transferring from the realm of amusement to the realm of scientific and practical value.[1] In the letter to his friend, Benjamin notes that he will have to build the telescope himself, and his efforts so far have led him, as pioneer, to discover fundamental elements of materialist art theory. It is such a special, well-equipped telescope of memory – utopian, re-visioning, meddlesome – that Benjamin focuses on the minutiae of his past, cutting through time to detect as yet unredeemed utopian inklings.

In *Berlin Childhood around 1900* Benjamin returns to a social infancy that is impersonally concerned with spaces, places and objects. Evading sentimentalism or individualism, Benjamin attempts to transcribe a chronicle of social history rather than an autobiography. He dissolves himself into social spaces and speculations on things. He stumbles through the ruins and rubble of over-cluttered interiors in Berlin's West End, writing less of people and more of the objects there, and the spaces they inhabit. Benjamin scents out the 'thing-world' of his childhood. This thing-world is an assortment of spaces congested with the splinters of urban bric-a-brac: telephones, chocolate machines, trains and railway stations, postcards, cluttered plush interiors, optical toys, rebus puzzles, sewing machines, velvet-lined caskets, stamps, majestic stone and metal monuments that crown tree-lined avenues or nestle alluringly in Berlin's cultivated Tiergarten.

Of course, there are also dispatches from the world of amusements. The second scene in *Berlin Childhood around 1900* describes the *Kaiserpanorama*, the imperial panorama, a nineteenth-century contraption with viewing windows and stools, set in a circle. This construction allowed an automated, fixed-time viewing of hand-coloured, postcard-sized stereoscopic images of interiors stuffed with bric-a-brac, museum sculpture galleries and remote lands. By Benjamin's time, these optical devices, "aquariums of distance and of the past,"were going out of fashion, and so he was always guaranteed a seat. Staring at these vivid and miniaturised three-dimensional selections of landscape, with their curious tangibility, his desire for distant travel was kindled. He watched the images of mountains and railway stations rest awhile in the gaslight awaiting the bell that signalled their departure. Yet the desire awakened was not a hankering to thrust out into the unknown, but seemed rather to be a longing to return home.

Berlin Childhood around 1900 re-images the past from what Benjamin casts as a child's perspective – curious, utopian, non-conformist. Youth's experience is seen to be dreamlike, invested with possibilities and hope. Elsewhere Benjamin had written that, through children, each epoch maintains some stake in fantastic dreaming. Benjamin's own writing in the memoirs is wide-eyed, taken from the viewpoint of a novice. To be child-like is to be engulfed by the city, amalgamating with its glass and asphalt. The infant's unfamiliarity with objects makes all things novel. Emergent technologies are associated with the newly born. In one scene from *Berlin Childhood around 1900* Benjamin depicts his father as he executes business transactions on the telephone. Inside that telephone is incubated a newborn voice. Images of birth, technological birth, perceptual rebirth in the autobiographical fragments are matched by the attempted exclusion of dying from the scenes of childhood. At no. 12 Blumeshof, the good bourgeois home of Benjamin's maternal grandmother, Benjamin remembers that the cozy, seemingly built-to-last furniture radiated a trust in an eternity that has banished death. That denial of mortality was a precarious posture, for it was held by a generation soon to be involved in mass death. War was rumbling in the distance at the time of Benjamin's childhood, and again at the time of his writing the memoirs. For the first time, these twentieth-century wars were threatening the fabric of the safe European home.

Benjamin accumulates his remembered shards of the turn of the century for an antagonistic scuffle with history as it has been. The act of remembering, he says, involves the associative "capacity for endless interpolations into what has been."[2] His plushly remembered past is shown to contain in all its dusty, over-cluttered effects the first spoors of the historical decline of the bourgeoisie. Illustrations of upholstered chunks of luxuriance and depictions of moments of class-isolation fabricate a metropolitan topography that is lavishly kitted-out with decay. In representations of the years preceding the destruction of the city by war, the adult-child's mock-prophetic suspicions enable him to show how the city's foundations betray the fissures and the fractures of an accelerating decomposition. Using the construct of the child or the 'as-if' child is a way of returning to the past, in order to suggest a technique for envisioning and then breaking with that past. In writing and remembering, he envisages a possibility whereby the initial glimpse of a fresh, utopian, "mythic" relationship between child and new technological cosmos provides an impetus for change, a "hope in the past."

Writing from a position of knowledge of intervening events – and a shrewd grasp of those to come – Benjamin develops an odd gaze in which the role of memory signals a strategy for splicing historical continuity with political interpretation. In (re)constructing collective histories or collective memories, Benjamin proposes a "collective unconscious" and suggests a creative relationship between generations and their wish-investments in new technologies and new products. He accentuates the unredeemed promises of bliss that attended endless spectacular consumption and boundless technological production – and that outflows into war's military technology and propaganda. This childlike vision is broadcast not least to reanimate old and squandered social hopes that have fled, like Benjamin, into exile. His telescope of memory – built in exile – is a fantastic construct assembled to match the fantastic potential of modern technologies. It finds its complement in the figure of the optical unconscious roused by the new visional technologies of photography and film. This camera, unconscious partner of the viewer's analytical researches into the composition of the modern, displays a new nature for humans, and this new nature is endowed with utopian potential. Benjamin introduces the term 'optical unconscious' to describe a mode of perception made visible on celluloid and initiated by cameras. The first mention of an optical-unconscious appears in an article on Soviet film, "Erwiderung an Oscar A. H. Schmitz" (1927), where Benjamin identifies film as a place where there "arises a new region of consciousness" through which people get to grips with the ugly hopeless world, comprehensively, meaningfully and passionately. Photography and film, because of their indexicality to the world, reflect it; but in reflecting it, they also construct it as a world of stretched-out temporality and fragmented space, a universe of "synthetic realities." The optical unconscious assembles an exploratory way of seeing, a microscopic incursion that slices up the intricate configurations of natural and social life.

Mechanically reproductive technology operates such that it ruptures life's continual flow of images. A fragment that now figures as a representation of the real is blasted out of the incessant movement of experience by its reproduction. As representation, it is held up, made still for an instant of conscious reflection on its significance. The cognitive potential of the newly discovered celluloid realm relies on technical trickery to reveal new structurations of material. Montage in film, the normal filmic process of editing and montage in photography, an artistic and commercial practice, reflect back to viewers the world as experienced, but also, simultaneously, bring to view a world that is malleable and as yet unknown. Photography and film bring objects closer, exported across time, across space, available to microanalysis. It lays the world out for intimate inspection. For example, Benjamin is impressed by Blossfeldt's plant photography in *Urformen in der Kunst* (1928). These extreme close-ups reveal the forms of ancient columns in horse willow, a bishop's crosier in the ostrich fern, totem poles in tenfold enlargements of chestnut and maple shoots, and gothic tracery in the fuller's thistle. Nature is revealed as a wonderful zone of cultural activity. Film technologically stretches time and shrinks space, synthesising connections and disruptions. Film and photography, through the optical unconscious, tap transformative potentials embedded in actuality. Such a vision also turns out to be redemptory, for the uses to which the new technologies are put, in Nazi Germany at least, have little to do with social analysis and more to do with social power.

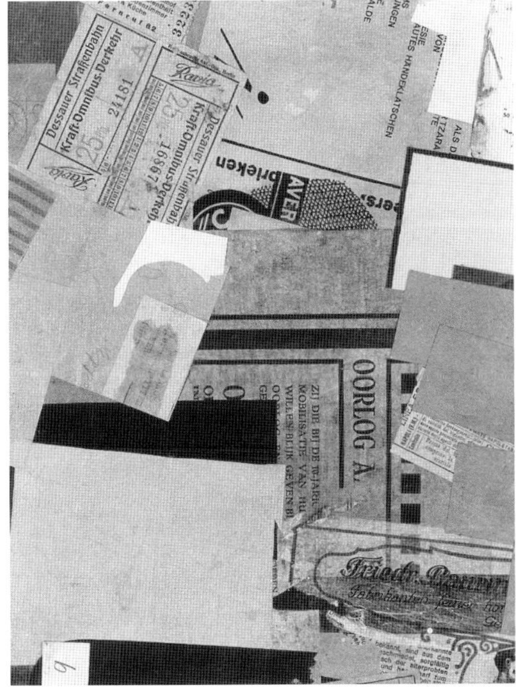

Kurt Schwitters, *Oorlog*, 1930. Courtesy of Donald B. Marron.

The motif of reanimation of energies now slumbering in objects, the latent contents of the actual, is acted out again and again in the small vignettes that Benjamin sketches in *Berlin Childhood around 1900*. For example, a sketch called "Hiding Places" (also in the 1926 collection *One Way Street*) describes children's mimetic relationship to a material world that encloses them at play, and in which, for example, a dining table transforms into a temple with columns, and the child becomes its wooden idol. Making itself like the world that encloses it, the child under the *portière* turns into a flapping ghost. Hidden behind the door the child mutates into a threshold, a force that can hex all who unwittingly enter. The segment "Death Notice" explores the idea of re-awakened meanings in objects and words through reflection on the idea of the *déjà vu*. *Déjà vu* signals the renascence of meaning in events that reach us – Benjamin grasps the acoustic, not the visual – like an echo awakened by a call, "a sound heard somewhere in the darkness of past life."[3] Benjamin ponders how words, thuds and rustlings may be endowed with the magic power to transport us into the tomb of long ago, and he also notes the effect of its counterpart, the sudden re-encounter with a word left over like a muff left forgotten in our room, a deposit from a future yet to come.

A sketch called "Cabinets" (1933) – on the assorted cabinets in his bourgeois childhood home – parallels the reanimating act of recollecting with the procedures of collecting. As the years passed his mother would present him with keys to more and more cabinets. Each time he received gifts he had to choose which was worthy of placement in the most recently accessible cabinet. He reasoned that things locked away stayed new longer, and yet he also knew that it was not the newness that he wanted to preserve, but rather he hoped "to renovate the old," in that, he, as newcomer, made it his.[4] Such renovation, he tells us, was also the feat of the collection that thronged in his drawer, where every little stone, every plucked flower, every pinned butterfly formed the basis of a specialist collection and the whole lot combined, everything he owned, was his collection. The same phrasing can be found in *One Way Street*, in a section titled "Untidy Child", where Benjamin affiliates the child, the researcher, the antiquarian and the bibliomaniac. All are hunters after spirits whose trail they scent in things. This collecting is no accumulation of inert objects, but rather an imaginative transformation of objects into desired deposits. To have cleared out the drawer full of treasured objects, he says, would have involved destroying a construction comprised of thorny chestnuts that were morning stars, tin foil that was a silver stockpile, building bricks that were caskets, cacti that were totem poles and copper pfennigs that were shields. A treasure trove accessible to touch, his miniaturised childhood assets grew and disguised themselves. Held in his hands, squinted at through his myopic vision, the collection became the locus of an imaginative enterprise. Such re-invention mirrors the way that Benjamin's recollection of this material also enacts a transformation of that past, into possible pasts, and so suggests alternative futures. Benjamin's collections paralleled (and parodied) his parents' connoisseurial collections – his father was, after all, an antique dealer, and proud of his clutter of silver terrines, Delft vases, bronze urns, glass goblets and the like, secreted in niches and under domes and baldachins – all forbidden to his young son's touch.

Blueprinted in the "Cabinets" anecdote is Benjamin's theory of collecting. The child-collector flaunts a charged, imaginative, romantic affiliation to objects, that is also seen to be exhibited by the collectors that Benjamin cherished and about whom he wrote: art collectors Wallraf and Boiserée, Von Stosch the gem collector, Marolles the print collector, and the Goncourt brothers, whose concern, notes Benjamin, was, unusually, with the housing of objects rather than the objects themselves. Eduard Fuchs, amateur of caricatures and erotic art, was subject of an essay, entitled "Eduard Fuchs, Collector and Historian" (1937), an unsurprising title given Benjamin's theory that the collector's affinity with objects is a form of historical research. Another collector mentioned is Pachinger, about whom Benjamin relates an anecdote concerning the search for a misprinted tram ticket that had been in circulation for only a few hours. Such dedication to transitory detritus is the quirk of amateur collectors, also dubbed by Benjamin the "true collectors." Benjamin affirms Fuchs's comment on how private collectors, committed to encyclopedism, systematicity and unswerving single-mindedness, do not indulge in procuring only those showpieces, such as turn the public collections into accumulations of things divested of their shabby, workaday clothes and dressed up in flashy Sunday best. Fuchs, a Marxist reformer, wishes to connect the collectible to its social provenance. Shrunk to mere merchandise it has been cut off from those who produced it and those who are best equipped to understand it. Benjamin agrees.

Benjamin was a collector. He collected children's books and toys, for reasons that are bound up with his anthropological-materialist concerns. Benjamin was a collector who made it his business to know his collections inside out, and he wrote expansively about those collections and his passions. For example, in "Cultural History of the Toy" (1928), a feuilleton piece written for the literary supplement of the *Frankfurter Zeitung*, he tracks the history of toys. Before industrialisation they were produced by artisans, wood-carvers, pewterers, made on the side as miniature reproductions of objects of daily life. As such they contained indications of the adult world. Later, in the epoch of industrialisation in the nineteenth century, toys become ever more distant from the adult world. But Benjamin's observations are not tied to the factuality of the object under scrutiny. Benjamin imagines the toy in a universe of handling. In a blow against naturalism, he makes the point that it is the imaginative act of play, culturally and class-determined of course, that makes the toy, not the toy that determines the play.

The study of toys was just one of a number of pieces on children's effects written through the 1920s. In these short articles – on alphabet books, rebus books, Russian toys, colour and monochrome illustrations – published in newspaper supplements, literary journals and illustrated magazines, Benjamin worked out ideas about play and the enchantment of objects. It is significant that his ideas about play, essentially ideas about the processes of cognition, are worked out for the pages of newspapers and journals, transitory forms of text, passing through on their way to becoming detritus. These articles catch spoors of what later blooms in the autobiographical memories: play as transformation, play as magical, play as mimetic and primitive. "Toys and Play" (1928), written for a literary journal, reveals how Benjamin, like the children he observed, was intrigued by fairy tales and toys' imprints of an animistic, primitive sense; the rattle, for example, he claims, is an instrument that wards off evil spirits.

Accompanying these socialising and supernatural facets is always a sense of the transformative aspect of play and childish perception.[5] An essay called "Insight into Children's Books" (1926), published in the same literary journal, acknowledges the materiality of transformation in childish things, particularly in the trick-books that Benjamin prized, with their shifting page-orders, where words appear in costume, and where hidden flaps reveal concealed figures, and ribbons or tabs are tugged to trigger or resolve episodes. These trick-books demonstrate how much seeing and knowing is tied to touch. Rebus puzzles, Benjamin informs us, were once thought to take their name from *rêver*, to dream, not *res*, for thing; conjuring up all dream-work's action of transfiguration, condensation and antithesis.[6] Such imaginative work of renewal of matter signals to Benjamin an originary impulse to revolution that exists in the child. It is in this sense that a child lodges inside each true collector. "The collector," writes Benjamin in 1935, "makes the transfiguration of things his concern": the collector, infantile, irresponsible, immune to the world of calculation and appliance, exists outside an economy of use, in a realm of desire.

To him fell the task of Sisyphus which consisted of stripping things of their commodity character by means of his possession of them. But he conferred upon them only a fancier's value, rather than use-value. The collector dreamed that he was in a world not only far-off in distance and in time, but which was also a better one, in which to be sure people were just as poorly provided with what they needed as in the world of the everyday, but in which things are free from the bondage of being useful.[7]

The visionary collector creates value by zealous imaginative projection. The desirability of release from exchange-value may go without saying, for a leftist. The release from use-value signals a release from a dull utilitarianism, emancipation from the inert and homogenising factuality of objects. Benjamin wants to hold on to the specificity of objects, and the possibility of an object's sensuous participation in a genuine life not dominated by exchange and functionalism. An essay from 1930, "In Praise of the Doll", characterises the genuine collector:

> The true, unrecognised passion of the collector is always anarchistic, destructive. For this is its dialectic: by loyalty to the thing, the individual thing, salvaged by him, he evokes an obstinate, subversive protest against the typical, the classifiable.[8]

The collector does not amass the hoard of objects as dead material. That is the debased attitude of the souvenir-hunter. Substituting for genuine experience, the souvenir attempts to generate intentional memory, voluntary memory, which is for Benjamin never true memory. True memory is involuntary memory, holds Benjamin, after Proust and his evocative crumb of madeleine. Involuntary memory summons up, in one flash, the narrator's past or a past ready for narration, out of the blue. For Proust, involuntary memory is impromptu, bouncing off objects encountered randomly. It is lucid, pre-verbal, and coupled with euphoria, which is why, in Proust as in Benjamin, such memories are often linked with childhood. Involuntary memory provides an unanticipated link between an experience in the present and one in the past. It confounds linearity, disrupts temporality – and it inclines towards discovering utopian potential. It is an agent of that action described in the epistemological section of the *Arcades* project: "telescoping the past through the present."[9] In the *Arcades* project, Benjamin draws on Proust to explain the peculiarities of voluntary and involuntary memory:

> The canon of involuntary memory, like that of the collector, is a kind of productive disorder. "And my life was already long enough, so that for every entity it offered me, I'd find in the opposite regions of my memory another entity to complete it .... Like an art-lover who is shown the wing of a triptych, recalling in which church, in which museum, in which collection, the others are dispersed (likewise in following sales catalogues or in visiting antique shops, he finishes by finding the twin of the object he possesses and makes a pair, so that he can reconstitute the predella in his head, the whole altar-piece)" .... Voluntary memory, on the other hand, is a registry, which classifies the object with a number, behind which the object disappears. "We must have been there." ("That was an experience.")[10]

Benjamin invokes Proust to knock over-commodified experience. For the true collector, material provides access into materiality, memory, history and knowledge of all kinds. Imaginative projection into the object is not a free-form rhapsody, but a reverie that is as determined and symptomatic as dreams. Benjamin explains how, for the collector, the whole world is present in each of his objects. The object focuses knowledge. Employing the collected material telescopically, the collector sees through the object into its whole past, its origin and manufacture, its uses, its value across time. In delineating collecting in this way Benjamin invokes the characteristics of a scholarly methodology that had long been his own. "Eduard Fuchs, Collector and Historian" augments an earlier thought from *The Origin of German Tragic Drama*:

> It is the dialectical construction which distinguishes that which is our original concern with historical engagement from the patchwork findings of actuality. "That which is original is never revealed in the naked and manifest existence of the factual; its rhythm is apparent only to a dual insight. It ... is related to its pre-history and subsequent development."[11]

All this detail that can be invoked – by looking, by loving, by touching – comprises a magic encyclopedia that relates the fate of each object. The collector handling his objects, notes Benjamin, appears as a magician who peers through them into a distance called history. Collectors, he proclaims, are "physiognomists of the thing-world," that is, they are skilled in foretelling character or destiny from the features and lines of the object's "face."[12] The object provides access into origin and past, but also into the future, into prospective worlds and future modes of dealing with objects. Typically for Benjamin, his musings occupy the interface of historical materialism and magical thinking.

These thoughts on collecting, voiced in "In Praise of the Doll", are also to be found in Benjamin's unwieldy assortment of quotations, aphorisms and commentaries, all ordered into note bundles and known as the *Arcades* project. The *Arcades* project is a practical example of collecting. One of the entries in a bundle of notes on 'The Collector' (in German: *der Sammler*) claims that "collecting is an ur-phenomenon of study: the student collects knowledge."[13] The *Arcades* project is Benjamin's treasure trove of archive findings. These notes on the theory of collecting record the decisive thing in collecting: that the object is dissolved from its original function, released from the "bondage of being useful," and is brought into the closest possible relationship with its equals. He states how for the true collector each single thing in this system becomes an encyclopedia of all knowledge from the epoch, the landscape, the industry, and the owners from which it derives. The collector magics the object into a charmed circle, where it petrifies, as a final shudder (the shudder of acquisition) brushes it. Everything remembered, thought and known about the object forms its podium, its frame, its seal, its context. "Collecting," writes Benjamin "is a form of practical remembering." Objects shelter a profusion of memories and histories – he is not keen to untwist the two things. This sheltering is especially resonant when it is acknowledged that, for the private citizen, the interior is required to support him in his illusions, in contrast to that separate zone called work, the site of reality, as Benjamin notes in the 1935 outline for the *Arcades* project. The reactivation of the "phantasmagorias of the interior," those of Benjamin's past, of his collections, and of the pasts he found detailed in the archives, awakens a political memory, such that Benjamin insists:

> Every smallest act of political reflection marks a new epoch in the antique trade. We are constructing here an alarm clock that calls the kitsch of the previous century to 'collect en masse'.[14]

Kitsch and Fossils: Matter in the Last Century

Benjamin had evoked the image of the alarm clock once before – at the close of his essay "Surrealism: The Last Snapshot of the European Intelligentsia" (1929) where he writes that the surrealists "exchange, to a man, their human expressions for the face of an alarm clock that in each minute rings for sixty seconds."[15] Surrealism was the century's wake-up call. According to Benjamin, only the surrealists had understood correctly the ways in which mass industrial society had technicised human existence, producing a collectivity, a technicised *physis*. And only the surrealists could circumscribe how that new technical reality was charged up on dreams and mythologies that needed to be interpreted. Surrealist methods bestow admittance to an underbelly of experience, discovered through a ransacking of the unconscious and the dreamworld. The surrealist take on objects coincided with Benjamin's concurrently unfolding methodology in studies of the Parisian arcades and elsewhere. The surrealists propose an anti-commodity poetical strategy of data collection from everyday life, from dreams and streetlife, and from the banalest environments. As such, they provide the artworld version of Benjamin's child-time collecting. In his first study of the surrealists, a newspaper article called "Dreamkitsch" (1926), Benjamin writes:

> The dream no longer opens onto a blue distance. It has turned grey. The grey layer of dust on things is its best part. Dreams lead straight to the banal.[16]

Turning their gaze from the genteel and the pretty, the surrealists fix their attention on the everyday, insists Benjamin, with an eye to the street, sexual relationships, fashion and commercial products. They focus on the everyday not in order to smother everything with a blanket of boredom, but to rediscover the eccentricity of the humdrum. Benjamin asks what side does the thing display in the dream? And answers that in the dream, the hand grasps the object at its most well-worn part, the side covered with cheap slogans. The thing that appeals to the dream is kitsch, and kitsch is,

> ... the last mask of the banal with which we cover ourselves in dreams and in conversation, in order to take the power of the extinguished thing-world into us.[17]

Kitsch, for Benjamin, means all that is sloppily put together: all the rubbish and mass culture and cheap commodity output of the nineteenth-century, all that should have been thrown away. From the late 1920s onwards, Benjamin devoted his energy to demonstrating how mythic drives continue to dally in modernity, even in those precincts where instrumental rationality is alleged to reign. Kitsch and clutter is where

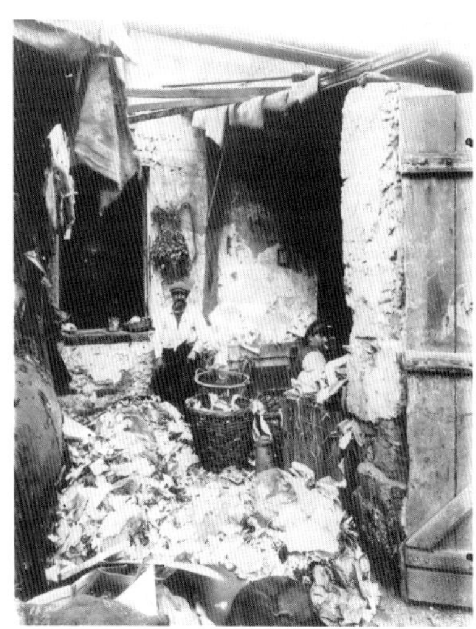

Eugène Atget, *Rag and bone men located on the seventeenth district of Paris*, 1913. Courtesy of Atget/Bibliotheque Historique de la Ville de Paris.

these dreams and unconscious impulses of a "dreaming collective" are to be found. The kitsch and clutter of the nineteenth century has soaked up myriad utopian fantasies and pledges of progress, abundance and the manifestation of a technical arcadia; it acts as a safe deposit of desire. Kitsch, especially antiquated, unmodish kitsch, confesses a collective psychoanalysis that can be tweezed out of things. Kitsch, because of its industrialised, formulaic mass-production, or its bogus pretensions, or its candid gushes of sentimentalism, enables an inquest into social desire, a social desire for fulfilment that Benjamin tags revolutionary. Once winkled out of the fashion circuit of commerce – that is, once it becomes passé – it can be viewed through telescope eyes.

This vision of objects marked by fossilised hints of collective wishes and fantasies is lashed in a special way to the particular mode of being of the bourgeoisie in the late nineteenth century. In "Experience and Poverty" (1933) he recounts how this century began with children still transported to their schools by horse-drawn carriage, but by the 1930s it housed adults who stood cut off from their ancestors and their own past by the technical experience of massive immolation in war, the speed-ups of ceaseless industrial innovation, and the social experience of a revolution that was obstructed. Benjamin is sure that these shifts – technical, political, social – affect the relation between memory and the past. Experience – *Erfahrung* – has vanished. In its place have flooded quackish ideas that seek to re-invent this missing wisdom. In an unpublished version of "Experience and Poverty", Benjamin remarks ruefully that it is most unlikely that "humanity will be able to get beyond the bottleneck before it is laden down with the baggage of a collector or antique dealer."[18] In the epistemological core of his *Arcades* project he notes an effect of the "accelerated tempo of technology" – the past quickly appears as if prehistoric, and as such its objects, its practices, its motivations, seem as mythic as ritual fetishes and acts. Registering both the rift with the past, and the speed-up effect in the present, Benjamin writes:

> The old prehistoric dread already envelopes the universe of our parents, for we are no longer bound to it by tradition. The remembered world breaks up more rapidly, the mythic in it surfaces more rapidly and more crudely.[19]

It is as if memory is always under threat, as technical change superimposes new layer upon layer of actuality. But, at the same time, what is "mythic" in those pasts juts forward more and more obviously. Thrilled by Marx's phrase – "the world has long possessed the dream of a thing that, made conscious, it would possess in reality," Benjamin's plot is to wake up the twentieth century from and to its dreams about the century just passed.[20] He hopes to track the myths that animated the dream worlds of the end of the last century, in order then to propel a "dissolution of 'mythology' into the space of history."[21] Benjamin asks what can be learnt about social worlds past, present and potential, if historically unfulfilled desires and fantasies – the stuff of mythology – are made manifest? The autobiographical writings contribute to this psycho-socialanalysis. Benjamin is true to his vision of the nineteenth century as the prehistory of a liberated humanity, as he fixes an image of a period of social paralysis and unconsciousness. He writes:

> When as children we received those great collected editions, *Cosmos and Humanity, New Universe or The Earth*, would our gaze not fall first of all on the tinted "petrified landscapes" or the "lakes and glaciers of the first Ice Age"? Such an idealised panorama of a scarcely past ur-epoch opens up when we gaze into the widespread city arcades. Here is housed the last dinosaur of Europe, the consumer.[22]

The idea of the consumer as dinosaur, as already seen from the perspective of its extinction, appears elsewhere in the *Arcades* project:

> Like places in the stones of the Miocene or Eocene Age that bear the impression of monsters from that geological period, so the arcades lie today in the great cities like caves with the fossils of ur-animals declared extinct: the consumers of the pre-imperial epoch of capitalism, the last dinosaurs of Europe.[23]

The consumer, as was, is en route to extinction. Benjamin pictures those consumers caught as in amber in the late nineteenth century, just before they bring about their own extirpation in war and in the class struggles of revolutions across Europe. After these events – that is, in Benjamin's moment of writing – consumers can no longer sleep easy in their beds, buffeted by dreams, illusions and the hope of a better order to come through the cosmic perfusion of capitalism.

The consumer-dinosaur inhabits a dark cave, where he hoards his objects, his possessions.[24] The cave is not bare, but crammed with fossilised vestiges. Benjamin notes that the bourgeois interiors of the 1880s, around the time of his birth, appear as casings for humans, padded cells of cushions and velvet and plush, themselves stuffed full of encased objects, of coverlets and linings, made of materials in which the imprint of things is easily left behind. This mark is called the trace, and it is left on stools, sofas and mantelpieces, and relatives leave theirs in photographs. In "Short Shadows", a sequence of 'thought-images' published in a Cologne newspaper in 1933, Benjamin observes that in the parlour:

> ... there is not one patch where the inhabitant has not left his mark: on the mantel piece with all its knick-knacks, on the upholstered seats with their tiny covers, embroidered with monograms, screens in front of the window panes, on the fire-guard in front of the stove.[25]

Indeed the casings, the coverlets, the linings that cover the objects in the interior are safeguards to catch traces and keep them. And, notes Benjamin, they make the bourgeois parlour the perfect setting for a detective story, and for the manoeuvres of the new science, forensics – a science related in a way to Benjamin's historical materialist research. The traces betray an ideology: for even the twee slogan – "just forty winks" – embroidered on the cushion cover reveals, says Benjamin, that the bourgeoisie did not dare to think about the future development of the order of production that they had set in motion.

Its textual counterpart is found in Nietzsche's idea of eternal return as spoken by Zarathustra. Eternal return, in turn, is however itself a dream – of the huge discoveries to come in the field of mass reproductive technology. In "Central Park" (1939) this mass of matter that absorbs traces is envisaged more sinisterly as part of an attempt to humanise the commodity, in a sentimental way; to give the commodity, just like the person, a house. Marx describes such humanising of material as commodity fetishism. Benjamin goes so far as to remark on the sex appeal of the inorganic. The traces indicate that something is trapped, calcified – but that it can be resuscitated, that is to say made conscious. Such resurrection is, of course, easier once the object has passed away, once the object has been discarded, thrust out of the home to turn up in junk shops or archives or dreams.

In the essay on surrealism, Benjamin pursues further the revolutionary energies that are stuck in the "antiquated" or "outmoded". The ruin hatches a revolutionary potential. His notes for this essay relate the following:

> In the first iron constructions, the first factory buildings, the earliest photos, objects that are starting to become extinct, pianos, umbrellas, clothes from five years ago, chic meeting places once fashion begins to withdraw from them. In short, just like the solar power machines man has built to draw massive energies from the atmospheric warmth. Just as man has turned the differing levels of water courses into sources of energy, so the enormous state of tension of the collective, which fashion expresses, should be made serviceable for the revolution.[26]

The surrealists persuade Benjamin to be interested in the world of obsolete things, remaindered not least by technological change. Technology participates in history by casting things into obsolescence. Or at least the external image of things transforms, even if things remain in essence the same, as fashion forces new superficialities of difference. "Dreamkitsch", once more raising the spectre of ephemeral tokens whose use-value and exchange-value is to be discontinued before banked, suggests that:

> Technology cashes in the external images of things, which, just like banknotes about to lose their currency, are never to be seen again.[27]

Fashion's permanent churning out and its adjustments of styles and types endlessly remainders products, dispensing novel modes of presentation, new images, new needs and wants. The surrealists instruct Benjamin that there are few things more socially poignant than these two: a once much-desired beauty from another epoch who now appears embarrassingly unfashionable; and a kaput gramophone, catapulted into uselessness. Like the surrealists, Benjamin's interest in the technological is directed not just at the new possibilities of hi-tech – the promises of utopias to come – but also at the revealing psychic reverberations and historically resonant energies of the passé – the uncashed utopian tokens of the past. Benjamin conceives of his remembered objects as the surrealists conceived of the bric-a-brac they found in Parisian flea markets.

Benjamin proposes the liberation of such dreams or energies from the past, stored up in objects – or remembered objects – like power in a battery. This liberation occurs through the removal of objects, labelled by Benjamin "enslaved and enslaving," from the circuit of fashion, releasing them, in order, in turn, to release the energies of the past in them.[28] Again he hopes "to renovate the old," proposing a withdrawal of objects from the cycle of exchange-value replacing exchange-value, a being in hock to fashion. He presents a redemptive religio-democratic vision – all objects come into their own – all have a place again – like the resurrected dead. Benjamin sets the revival of the unfashionable against the myth of progress, a myth that constructs a permanent present oriented to the promise of an ameliorated future. For progress-mongers the past is mobilised only to show that it is a place that we have, thankfully, left behind to move on to somewhere better. For Benjamin, the past is mobilised to show how the dividends it promised have not yet been doled out.

In the arcades, preferred hunting ground of the nineteenth-century collector, objects of industrial capitalism's commodity pile-up had entered into the most surreal and aberrant amalgamations in 'rebus' shop displays. On the walls of the cave-like arcades, the commodity grows like unforeseen flora, and, says Benjamin, like the tissue of an ulcer, they grow into the most irregular connections. A universe of cryptic connections emerges where palms jostle feather dusters, hair-driers and the Venus de Milo. Prostheses are flung next to letter-writing manuals. Players in a de-familiarised modernist mythology, odalisques skulk by inkpots while vestal virgins raise aloft bowls for burnt offerings in the form of cigarette tips.[29] Relations between objects compelled by commerce in the nineteenth-century find a form in modernism: inaugurated by Lautréamont's chance encounter of a sewing machine and an umbrella on a dissecting table, an image that galvanised surrealism. Like the transformed objects in Benjamin's childhood chest of drawers, the commodity is renovated in metropolitan modernism. Its renovation breaks the normal parameters of use-value and exchange to produce this imagination-value: a refusal of exchange and utilitarianism.

Come Closer

In his study of the Viennese satirist Karl Kraus, written in 1930, Benjamin quotes from the architect Adolf Loos's *Ornament and Crime* (1908):

> On reading the words with which Goethe censures the way the Philistine, and thus many an art connoisseur, runs his fingers over engravings and reliefs, the revelation came to him that what may be touched cannot be a work of art, and that a work of art must be out of reach.[30]

Loos divides the work of art from the article of use according to whether the object under consideration may be touched. Benjamin quotes this passage once more a year later in a jotting on those ships, mineworks and crucifixions that miraculously appear inside bottles. And he asks, perhaps ironically, whether things in bottles are artworks precisely because they are inaccessible to touch. Loos's remark on art and touch strikes Benjamin profoundly, and, on its basis, he draws consequences for a new, emergent spatiality that takes its cue from the image of the collector with his collectible in his hand. In "Dreamkitsch" Benjamin emphasises that technology also participates in a modern bridging of distances, noting that what counted as art in former days began at two metres distance from the body, but through mass-production the thing-world seems to edge towards the person. If, as Henri Bergson suggests in *Matière et Mémoire*, perception is a historical phenomenon, then the modern experience of the "new person," is one of objects thrusting themselves forwards, jostling for attention in cluttered environments. Objects' kitschiness, their cheap availability, their being at hand, compels a re-evaluation of ideas of closeness and distance between objects and people. It is a renovation of the relation between objects and people that the collector had seemingly already established, for things approach him, and each new thing that is acquired changes the meaning of all the other pieces. The true method of making things present to us, advises Benjamin, is to imagine them in our space, as does the collector. Indeed, Benjamin goes so far as to claim that the collector is the figure of the future:

> Possession and property are related to the tactile, and stand in a certain opposition to the optical. Collectors are people with a tactical instinct. By the way, recently, with the turn away from naturalism, the primacy of the optical, that dominated the previous century, has ceased.[31]

He concludes this note with the observation: "*Flâneur* optical, collector tactical." The age of the collector has begun, but it must be a democratic one. Tactility, *taktisch* were notions purloined from the art historian Alois Riegl. Riegl delineated a new organisation of perception in the ornamental forms of late Roman art and decoration, forms not included in the classical canon. His writings concentrate on a history of perception that moves between the tactical and optical, recognising how touch supplements the eye in the pursuit of material knowledge of objects. Benjamin translates this tactility of space and objects into the childhood experience of an empathetic touching, an intensified perception, bound up with shock, impact and curiosity. Tangibility is the thing, a visual tangibility, perhaps akin to that provided by the stereoscopic panoramas where objects seemed so three-dimensional the viewer felt able to reach out and touch them. Riegl is encountered in Benjamin's Berlin memories. In an antique dealer's in Berlin, at the beginning of the 1914–1918 war, Benjamin, "under the impression of Alois Riegl's *Late Roman Art Industry*, examines objects from antiquity, some breastplates, some bracelets.[32] He visits the shop because his friend wishes to buy friendship rings. Benjamin's recollection of these rings is an object lesson in tactile knowledge. He describes "the most fascinating ring" he has ever seen. It is a ring from the Roman imperial period:

> Worn on the finger, the ring seemed merely the most perfect of signet rings. You only entered its secret by taking it off and contemplating the head against the light. As the different strata of the garnet were unequally translucent, and the thinnest so transparent that it glowed with rose hues, the sombre bodies of the snakes seemed to rise above the two deep, glowing eyes, which looked out from a face that, in the purple-black portions of the cheeks, receded once more into the night.

The ring is picked up, examined against the light. It cannot be seen without being touched, and it is designed for wearing on fingers that feel. The ring is known through its being touched.

Benjamin registers the aesthetic advantages of mass production, imaged in the collectors who lovingly handle their pickings – without thereby approving of the fashion system that threatens to render it all obsolete. The sensory outfitting of the collector-type prototypes the perceptual apparatus of the new masses. And they will get the culture they deserve – a culture that juts into their space and demands manipulation. Here the idea of seeing meets the idea of touching in the notion of the close-up. The close-up enlarges the miniature, focusing attention on the particular, but at the same time it closes the gap, bringing nearer the desired object for intense scrutiny. The close-up takes up its place in the world of film and photography. So, of course, it is in the mass-reproduced that culture meets its viewer halfway. Contemplative and distanced observation is vetoed. Tactility and closeness mark out a new potential culture for and by the masses. Tactility and shock – forces that act on the body – form part of the new perception. This perception dislocates from a bodiless idealist aesthetic based on illusion, the imaginary and fictitiousness. Bourgeois idealist conceptions of art are seen to be wound into a narcissistic ideology that argues art is born from itself. Benjamin's approach retreads the ground of aesthetics sensuously. But closeness, tactility and sensuousness need not be interpreted as presence. In some ways, corporeal disappearance is precisely what is at stake in technological art. The copy is what is at hand. For Benjamin, the mass appropriation of culture signals literally a manhandling of cultural products. The mass-reproduced copy can be manipulated. It is "tactile." Exhibition, the ability to see and be seen, and tactility, the ability to touch, are sensuous concepts that relate new art to the physical presence of the collective receiving body. The most conspicuous example of tactile culture was architecture. Benjamin shifts his gaze from the velvet-lined casings in which nineteenth-century objects nestled to casings for humans, their places of habitation.

Benjamin argues for art as an embodiment of corporeal, material nature, and is not seduced by the ideal of artistic autonomy. It was Eduard Fuchs's insistence on the same principles that Benjamin recognised in him as collector and as art historian. Fuchs, he notes, attends to technologies of reproduction and the creation of mass art. Such attention in turn raises the question of reception and shifts analysis away from focus on the creator and his genius. Fuchs's concerns, non-connoisseurial ones, are appropriate for a new age of the masses.

Benjamin heralded Fuchs as one of the first to derive implications from the constellation of *Masse* and *Technik*. And just as Fuchs detects a new epoch marked by mass-reproduced art, so Benjamin registers an epochal shift in interiors. The new architects with glass and steel make rooms in which it is difficult to leave a trace in the old way. The padded cells of the nineteenth century give way to a twentieth-century translucent but shrunken space. It is a space for a new type of seeing. In "Experience and Poverty", while discussing Le Corbusier and Loos, Benjamin mentions their co-inspirator of modern beings, the science-fiction author and theorist on glass architecture, Paul Scheerbart. Scheerbart imagines suitable inhabitants of these new spaces, people who have been altered, for the better, by our aeroplanes, skyrockets and telescopes. The traces deposited by lives in their shiftable, hypervisible glass homes have not disappeared, indeed in our world we can see that they have multiplied. But they may adhere not so much to the furniture and baubles, as crystallise administratively in the archives of the expanded bureaucratic apparatus. Or these traces may nestle in the fragments of photography and the label and ticket debris of commercial intercourse. The collector, a figure who scoops up objects in the hope of discovering history and augury, must not be averse to taking in hand all this most degraded trash of city life.

Benjamin's collector assumes various guises. There is the collector as enthusiast, childlike in his relationship to the material world that he observes as an excuse for his burrowing, his tactile cognition, his imaginative revisioning. Such a figure may be a collector of objects; or a collector of memories – a recollector, such as Benjamin is in his autobiographical sketches, where he is set loose in a 'thing-world' that demands to be read politically. Such a collector of memories and recollector of the histories encoded in objects renovates the material that comes his way. This mode of seeing, piloted by the collector, is a mode of seeing that has much in common with the technologically enhanced vision of mechanical reproduction – reconstructive, synthetic, micrological, telescopic. An unpublished version of "A Short History of Photography" (1929) discusses the way that photography's miniaturisation of objects is a productive act because thereby old works are newly valorised, that is renovated.[33] Renovation and reconstruction form part of the mode of seeing another type, a composite of artist and street-person who in collecting this commercial debris, picking it out of the rush of everyday life, renovates it. He reworks the refuse of everyday life as a refusal of designated value. This is the particular business of one collector who features in Benjamin's studies of Paris and commodity culture: the *Lumpensammler*, the rag picker.

Object Art: Metro-Modernism

The rag picker makes his living from picking through metropolitan refuse. He is a man of the street (or the arcades), out in the public zone, away from the interior. The rag picker plays a role in Baudelaire's *oeuvre*, and it was there, in the poem *Le vin des chiffoniers,* that he sparked Benjamin's imagination. Baudelaire spliced the rag picker and the poet, and thought of both as types who collected the day's refuse in the big city. Everything that the city threw away, everything it lost, everything it despised, everything it crushed underfoot, all that they catalogued and collected, collating the annals of intemperance, the capharnaüm (stockpile) of waste, sorting things out and making wise choices, producing value out of trash, an alchemical act. The surrealist André Breton also styled himself as rubbish sifter, in search of the *trouvaille*, the lucky find, the trash picked up at the flea market or junk shop. The *trouvaille* finds its avant-garde form in the ready-made, the found objects attributed from 1912 to Picasso, Braque or Gris – these things are unmade by the artist, though the same cannot be said of the anonymous designer who first conceived them. Ready-mades refuse illusion, refuse representation, or at least confound it. The artistic experience is cut back to the object alone – and seen from the perspective of criticism, this very mimeticism forms a critique of object-merchandise.

With these motifs, the avant-garde game had kicked off, its movements succeeding one another according to the law of industrial production, and continuous technical revolution. From *l'art pour l'art* to assemblage, dada and surrealism, under the microscope is the status of the object in industrial commodity capitalism. To find out about objects in commodity-culture demands a lack of preciousness. For Benjamin, hand-dirtying is intrinsic to modernism with its lyricism of the everyday. Just as his theory of modernity had taken its energies from the interpretation of kitsch, so too modernist culture erupts from the kitsch and trash gathered off the streets, defiantly unresponsive to the eternal values of art or the high-minded quest for a purity of form and materials, and the assertion of an abstracted truth. Benjamin singles out Dada as proponent of the tactile culture of the future. The theses on the work of art in the age of its technical reproducibility note that it hits the spectator like a bullet: "It happened to him, and so acquired a tactile character." However full of high spirits, dada was also deadly serious because it learnt from the First World War that spawned it – get into your victims, hit them where it hurts, get up their noses.

While the ready-made or found object had challenged representation, asserting the engaging nature of objects in and of themselves, another way to confound representation and to hold on to the objectivity of culture was developed through montage's disruption and tearing. Sometimes this happened quite literally, as, for example, in the case of Kurt Schwitters's *Merzbau*. This was Schwitters's name for his series of collages and it derives from a word fragment torn off an advertisement for the Kommerz- und Privatbank. The name acknowledges and assaults the commodity-relation of art and anti-art, and it is also the art of the rag picker. Schwitters had a habit of foraging in garbage cans for scraps to use in his collages. One memorable ripe cheese paper spoilt a night at a first-class hotel in Switzerland. *Oorlog* (*War*), from 1930, is one of his many scrap collages. Its title comes from a torn scrap just off the image's centre, a news report on war –

while invoking the recent past, it hints at a dark future. Layered around this core are labels, wrappers, and tram tickets, from Dessau, home of the Bauhaus, and a Naples tram ride. The name Tzara peeps out by the word applause. The cubists, too, curated the arcana of labels, brand-marks, posters, and newspapers. Café life and cabaret provide the stimuli and the cubist collages deploy tear-outs and strips of newspaper, bottle labels, cigarette papers, handbills from department stores, bargain wallpaper – all carefully juxtaposed to allow puns, interplay between components and the emergence of symbolic meanings. The collector's eye for trash, for tokens that slip almost unconsciously through our hands, is the eye of the metro-modernist. The rag picker arranges himself and his junk in his modernist anti-home. He lives publicly, like his neighbour the *flâneur*, as Benjamin had learnt from Franz Hessel's Berlin study, *Spazieren in Berlin*. The *flâneur* was back, as the title of Benjamin's 1929 review insisted – "The Return of the *Flâneur*". And this *flâneur* was not just one man in the crowd, but was part of the crowd.

> For the mass – with which the flâneur lives – gleaming enamel sign-plates are as good or better a wall decoration as the oil paintings in the bourgeois salon. Firewalls are its writing desk, newspaper stands its libraries, postboxes its bronzes, benches its boudoir and the café terrace its oriel from where it observes goings-on.[34]

If the *flâneur* can be bothered to translate his viewing into reviewing, or his thought into theory, then this street furniture provides a bureau and drawing desk on which he can assemble the pieces of litter, the fragments of city lives, into images and narratives. The trash of the everyday metropolis is re-valued in the artwork. It is re-valued socially – that is to say, it gains an aesthetic value, and it is redeemed.

Benjamin wanted to collect art by Paul Klee, and, if he had been wealthy in later years, he would have acquired several items. In April 1921, Benjamin went to a Klee exhibition in Berlin, and at the end of

NEUER LEHRSTUHL AN DEN DEUTSCHEN UNIVERSITÄTEN

VÖLKISCHE TIEFENSCHAU

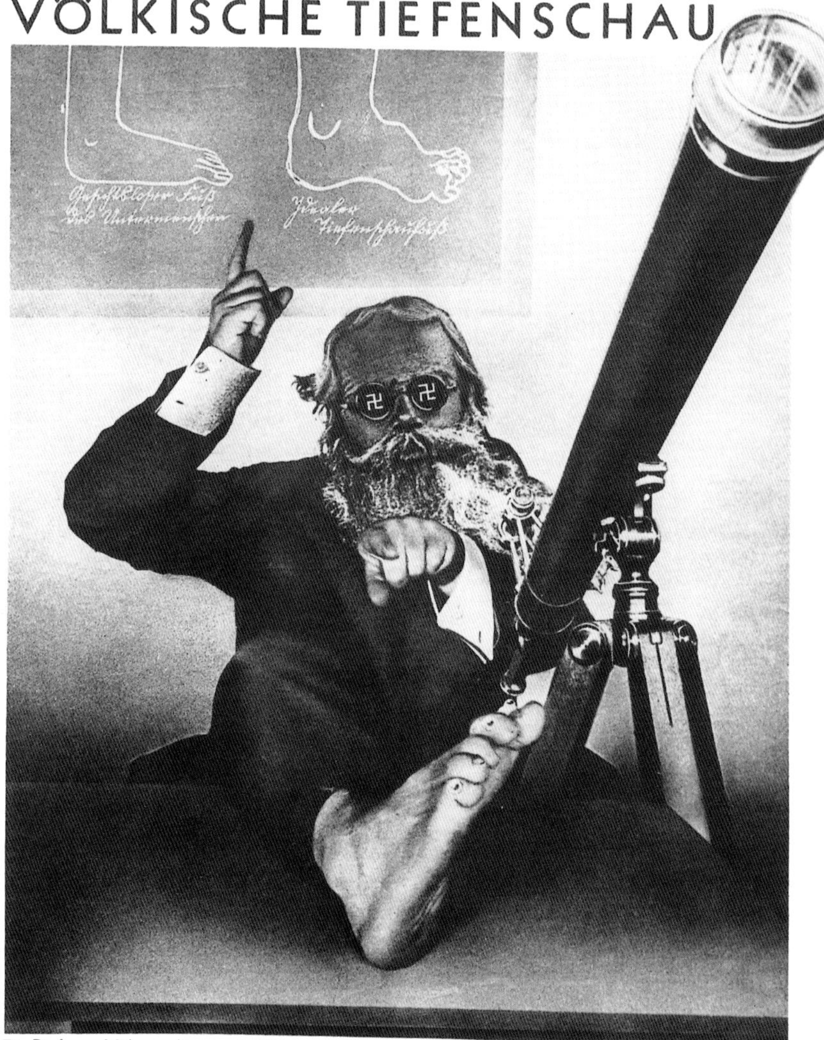

Ein Professor Vitlawopsky von der Universität Heidelberg hat festgestellt, daß das menschliche Hühnerauge, allerdings nur das germanische, befähigt ist, in die Zukunft zu schauen. Hitler hat sogleich nach Bekanntwerden der Entdeckung des genialen Forschers die Überführung von 1300 Hühneraugenoperateuren ins Konzentrationslager angeordnet.

Original-Aufnahme aus dem teutonischen Busch von John Heartfield.

John Heartfield, *New Chair at German Universities*, 1933.
Courtesy of Stiftung Archiv der Akademie der Künste, Berlin.

May he went to Munich and bought a watercolour by Klee, called *Angelus Novus*. The New Angel, affixed above his desk wherever he lived, fluttered through his life, until the exigencies of exile meant he had to abandon it. The angel provided the name for a critical journal he wished to found. He wrote about the angel as example of the child-like aesthetic at the core of the modernism he prized. It was the subject of the famous vignette in his final piece of work, "Theses on the Philosophy of History" (1939–1940).[35] The angel stares at the skyward-growing junkpile of debris, dreadful historical events, wasted lives, futile objects. The angel, like Benjamin, wants to gather up the rubbish and the rubble on the ever-growing junkpile. But the angel's optic – his eyes are staring, his mouth is open – is one of impotence. Touch, intervention into the catastrophic unfurling is what he cannot achieve. Collecting the rubbish together, repairing it all would be the act that could renew the hopes for progress through technology, raised in the nineteenth century and so horribly betrayed by two world wars. It marks that "hope in the past," hope encapsulated in the arc between past and present, caught by the telescope eye, or the "weak messianic power" with which each generation has been endowed. Benjamin insists on that possibility in his practice as historian and as collector. He insists on that possibility in the cruelest hours of the century, when Nazi rule is in place in Germany. His utopian telescope that pierces through time to witness the hope deposited in the past was invented for a humane optical science. It finds a demonic counterpart in a photomontage from the 31 August 1933, *A.I.Z.* by John Heartfield, published in Prague. Heartfield was the master of the art of revaluing scraps of everyday life and re-accenting words in common currency to produce destruction of dominant values. A professor with swastika spectacles obscuring his vision places a corn (in German *Hühnerauge*, literally 'hen's eye') at the eyepiece of a telescope. Heartfield's text reads: "New Chair in German Universities; Racial Depth Seeing: Professor Vitlawopsky of the University of Heidelberg has discovered that the human corn, that is to say, the Germanic corn, is capable of seeing into the future. Straight after the announcement of the discovery by the brilliant researcher, Hitler ordered the transportation of 1300 corn surgeons to the concentration camps." Heartfield was responding to the official acknowledgement on 29 August 1933 of the existence of concentration camps in Germany. The camps were built to house leftists and Jews. Many of the first inhabitants were the third of all university teachers who had recently been purged from the profession. Heartfield satirises Nazi pseudo-science, not least the pseudo-science of race, perpetrated by the Nazi-friendly professors in their new posts. Their telescopes are useless. Their vision is corrupted. The Nazi 'science' of seeing into the future by using German defects will lead them nowhere, and is just another example of the bankruptcy of their ideas. All intelligence, it would seem, had been sent into the camps or into exile. Like Eisenstein and Rodchenko, Heartfield's photomontages self-consciously evoked the theme of looking, of perspective and view-point. The corn looking through the telescope and the view through the swastika spectacle lenses will not achieve a true vision of the present or the future.

Heartfield was one of Benjamin's author-producers who perfected dada's meddling with the deployment of "authentic fragments of daily life." His montage-criticism, converting signs as found into portents of what was to come, proposed a new optics, an interventionist, hands-on optics of modernist engagement. This was precisely the optics that Benjamin proposed. It was an optics oriented to action, and it did not shy away from cutting up the fragments ripped off the world. The modern artist, here a photo-monteur, has become the (re)collector and preserver of sanity now banished. Benjamin comments on Heartfield in his lecture "The Author as Producer" (1934). Heartfield is one of those who confirms that:

> ... the tiniest authentic fragment of daily life says more than painting. Just as the bloody fingerprint of a murderer on the page of a book says more than the text. [36]

The "authentic fragment" is the clue to social actuality won from the busyness of the everyday and, "wrenched from modish commerce," it is preserved in a new setting, releasing new spins on its meaning. Heartfield's practice is playful, transformative, "re-functioning," surreal and critical, and he redeploys the cast-off materials of daily life – newspaper reports and photographs, current phrases and the tics of today's political rhetoric – in just the ways demanded by Benjamin's profiles of the collector who has a special eye for things – in its various guises as child, memoir-writer, researcher, antiquarian, *flâneur* and modernist. These collectors with their scavenger sensibilities promote a profoundly democratic attitude to the world of material that can function only as a critique of what is.

Footnotes

1 This is the argument put by J.D. Bernal, in his 1971 study Science in History, and is cited in Jonathan Crary, *Techniques of the Observer*, MIT Press, 1990, p. 131.

2 This appears in "Berliner Chronik" *Gesammelte Schriften* (hereafter *G.S.*) VI p. 476/"A Berlin Chronicle", *One Way Street*, trans., Edmund Jephcott and Kingsley Shorter, NLB/Verso, 1979, p. 305.

3 *G.S.*, IV.1 pp. 251–252.

4 *G.S.*, IV.1 p. 286.

5 Benjamin was keen to underscore the beastly nature of childish play. In "Old Toy" he criticises kid-glove pedagogy: "While pedagogues, pious as lambs, still cling to Rousseauesque dreams, writers such as Ringelnatz and painters like Klee have grasped the despotic and dehumanised aspect of children. Children are world-distant and immune to the cold." *G.S.*, IV.1 p. 515.

6 See *G.S.*, IV.2 p. 611. The Oxford English Dictionary notes that the word rebus derives from the ablative Latin of res, thing - as used in the phrase de rebus quae geruntur, concerning things that are taking place. This was the title given by the guild of lawyers' clerks of Picardy to satirical pieces containing riddles in picture form.

7 *G.S.*, IV.1 p. 53/*Charles Baudelaire; A Lyric Poet in the Era of High Capitalism*, trans. Harry Zohn and Quitin Hoare, NLB/Verso, 1973, pp. 168–169.

8 *G.S.*, III p. 216.

9 *G.S.*, V.1 p. 588/"File N", *Benjamin: Philosophy, Aesthetics, History*, ed., Gary Smith, University of Chicago Press, 1989, p. 60.

10 *G.S.*, V.1 p. 280.

11 *G.S.*, II.2 p. 468/"Eduard Fuchs, Collector and Historian", *One Way Street*, p. 352.

12 *G.S.*, III p. 217.

13 *G.S.*, V.1 p. 278.

14 *G.S.*, V.1 p. 271.

15 *G.S.*, II.1 p. 310/"Surrealism, The Last Snapshot of the European Intelligentsia", *One Way Street*, p. 239.

16 *G.S.*, II.2 p. 620.

17 *G.S.*, II.2 p. 620 and 622.

18 *G.S.*, II.3 pp. 961–962

19 *G.S.*, V.1 p. 576/*Benjamin: Philosophy, Aesthetics, History*, p. 49.

20 Quoted by Benjamin in *G.S.*, V.1 p. 583/*Benjamin: Philosophy, Aesthetics, History*, p. 55.

21 *G.S.*, V.1 p. 571/*Benjamin: Philosophy, Aesthetics, History*, p. 45.

22 *G.S.*, V.2 p. 1045.

23 *G.S.*, V.2 p. 670.

24 See *G.S.*, V.1 p. 286. These caves form a counterpart to the workers' caves that Marx criticises. See *G.S.*, V.1 p. 295.

25 *G.S.*, IV.1 p. 427.

26 *G.S.*, II.3 p. 1031.

27 *G.S.*, II.2 p. 620.

28 *G.S.*, II.1 p. 299/"Surrealism, The Last Snapshot of the European Intelligentsia", *One Way Street*, p. 229.

29 *G.S.*, V.2 p. 670.

30 *G.S.*, II.1 p. 336/ "Karl Kraus", *One Way Street*, p. 259.

31 *G.S.*, V.1 p. 274.

32 "A Berlin Chronicle", *One Way Street*, pp. 320–321.

33 See *G.S.*, II.3 p. 1138.

34 *G.S.*, III p. 196.

35 *G.S.*, I.2 pp. 697–698/"Theses on the Philosophy of History", *Illuminations*, trans., Harry Zohn, Fontana, 1992, p. 249.

36 *G.S.*, II.2 p. 693/"The Author as Producer", trans., Edmund Jephcott, *Reflections*, Schocken Books, 1986 p. 229.

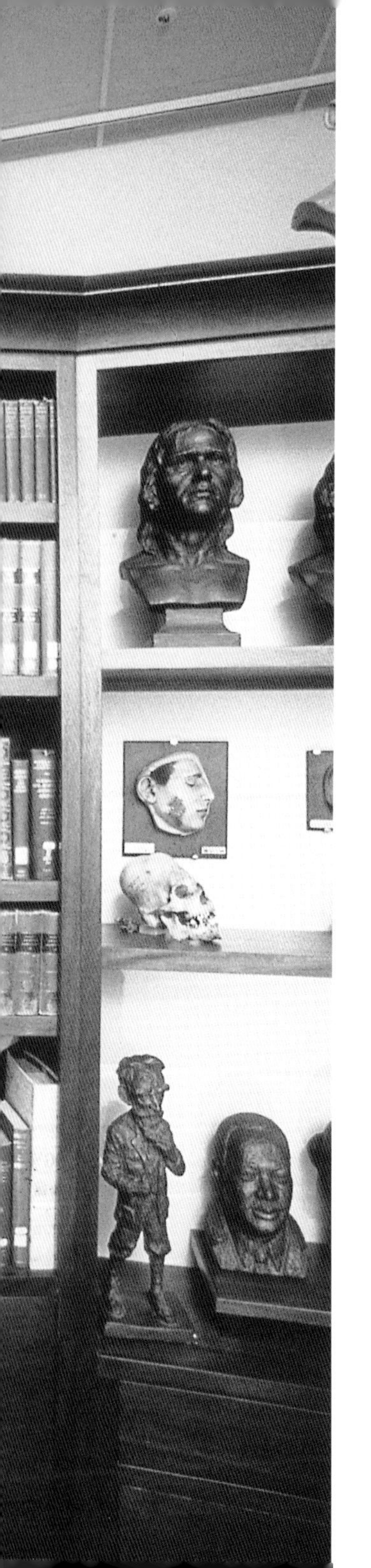

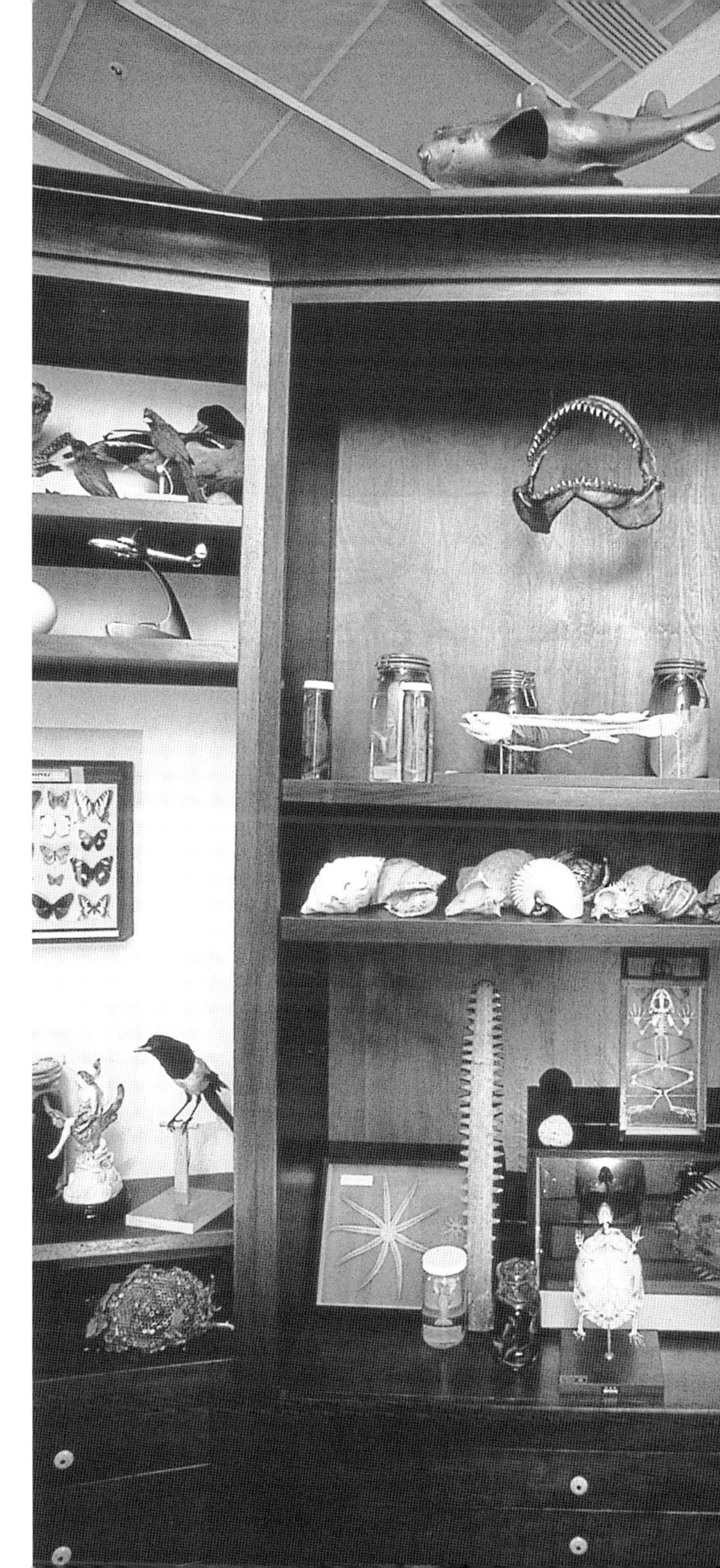

Archives of Memory: Walter Benjamin's *Arcades Project* **and Aby Warburg's** *Mnemosyne Atlas*

Matthew Rampley

In early September 1929 the airship *Graf Zeppelin* docked in New York en route to Lakehurst, New Jersey, where it began its second round-the-world flight promoted by the celebrated media mogul William Randolph Hurst. Although still a luxury mode of transport, the development of long distance passenger flight presented striking confirmation of the shrinkage of space in the modern world, and was the culmination of a process set in motion by the invention of the steam train nearly a century before. Of equal importance was the fact that the *Zeppelin*'s second visit to America coincided with the setting-up in New York of a station capable of the telegraphic transmission of images. Invented in 1792, the telegraph had been in general use since the 1830s and the invention of Morse code, but the ability to transmit images as well as text constituted a dramatic shift in its significance. More ominously, the installation of the telegraph station can be seen as looking forward to the much more dramatic case of the *Hindenburg* in 1936, which, on its arrival in Lakehurst, burst into flames. It was the first disaster in history to be caught by eyewitness photographers and, equally, was the first headline news photograph to be transmitted telegraphically.

The significance of the arrival of the *Graf Zeppelin* might be confined to the history of journalism, telecommunications and aeronautics, were it not for the interest taken in it by Aby Warburg. He had already expressed an interest in the airship some time before. In particular, his essay "Airship and Submarine in the Medieval Imagination" had analysed the meaning of the myth of Alexander the Great's flight in an airship drawn by griffons.[1] The dirigible also occupied Warburg's attention in the final year of his life; he included press photographs of the voyage of the *Graf Zeppelin* on one of the first plates of *Mnemosyne*, his unfinished pictorial atlas. The same plate included a diagram of the solar system from Kepler's cosmological text *Mysterium Cosmographicum* of 1596, and also an image of Mars from a medieval astrological manuscript in Tübingen.

The sense of this juxtaposition of modernity, Renaissance and the Middle Ages was multiple. First of all it could be read as tracing the transformation of the cosmos of zodiacal astrology into the astronomical universe of modernity. As has often been recognised, Warburg was thereby following well-established notions of the growth of Enlightenment rationality, in which a personalised mythical world order gives way to the rule of abstract logical thought. The arrival of the *Zeppelin* was thus a potent symbol of modernity's conquest of space which, no longer the domain of mythic demons, followed physical laws open to manipulation and control. It is clear, too, that Warburg took an interest in telegraphic transmission; he notes on one of the photographs that a telegraphic station had been set up. It is possible to discern a similar preoccupation with space, and the representation of space can be seen in the projected first plate of the *Mnemosyne Atlas*, which includes a sixteenth-century zodiacal map of the heavens, a map of Europe and the genealogical tree of the Tornabuoni family. Again the contrast between the personalised schema of the cosmos and the abstraction of modern cartographic representation is striking, and furthermore the inclusion of the family tree highlights the mapping of a chronological succession (the generations of the Tornabuoni) on to a set of spatial relations.

This shift in orientation towards the cosmos, beginning in the Renaissance, was also remarked on by Warburg's younger contemporary, Walter Benjamin. As he noted some four years before Warburg compiled the plates of his *Atlas*, "Nothing distinguishes the ancient from the modern man so much as the former's absorption in a cosmic experience scarcely known to later periods. Its waning is marked by the flowering of astronomy at the beginning of the modern age. Kepler, Copernicus and Tycho Brahe were certainly not driven by scientific impulses alone. All the same, the exclusive emphasis on an optical connection to the universe ... contained a portent of what was to come."[2]

Both Warburg and Benjamin recognised that the advent of modernity entailed a radical reorientation in the representation and experience of space and time, in which both material and conceptual shifts had brought about a collapsing of space (and time) into a visual simultaneity. For Warburg, it could be seen in the invention of the aeroplane or the telephone, which threatened to collapse the reflexive space he regarded as the principal achievement of civilisation. Most famously, in the conclusion of his study of the Pueblo Indians, Warburg claims, "the culture of the machine age destroys what the natural sciences, born of myth, so arduously achieved ... the modern Prometheus and the modern Icarus, Franklin and the Wright brothers, who invented the dirigible airplane, are precisely those ominous destroyers of the sense of distance, who threaten to lead the planet back into chaos."[3] This is of special significance for Warburg given that he regards "the acquisition of the sense of distance between subject and object" as "the criterion of progress of the human species."[4]

For Benjamin, the question of modernity was framed by the discourse of "aura." Modernity heralds the demise of auratic distance, and this occurs most noticeably in the aesthetic sphere in the growth of the reproductive technologies of the photograph, film and the record. The decline of aura can be registered in the decline of distance marking out the work of art as something apart. The authoritarian relation of the pious spectator to the venerated relic or image, which persists in the cult of aesthetic beauty, is gradually replaced with a "sense of the universal equality of things," a dispelling of aura intimately connected with the advent of mass society. As Benjamin notes, "Every day the urge grows stronger to get hold of an object at very close range by way of its likeness, its reproduction .... To pry an object from its shell, to destroy its aura, is the mark of a perception whose sense of the universal equality of things has increased to such a degree that it extracts it even from a unique object by means of reproduction. Thus is manifested in the field of perception what in the theoretical sphere is noticeable in the increasing importance of statistics."[5]

The shared discourse of spatial loss in Benjamin and Warburg might easily be read against the background of many other contemporary accounts of modernity, were it not for the centrality of spatial metaphors to their conceptions of history and of cultural critique. In particular, while both recognised that shifts in the material conditions of contemporary life were leading to a profound change in the perception of space, this recognition also led to a change in the logic of cultural representation. As a consequence of the general preoccupation with space, culture itself came to be considered in primarily *spatial* rather than historical terms. The importance of this substitution cannot be overestimated. For both Benjamin and Warburg the inherited dominant model of cultural history was governed by the Enlightenment notion of linear progress. The significance of a cultural formation was read in terms of its place within a genetic development, an interpretation which Darwin had even extended to the supposedly ahistorical domain of nature. In contrast, both Benjamin and Warburg were attempting to transform this dominant notion of history. Instead of the narrative of historical development one finds the idea of a cultural space, in which metaphors of vision become prominent. That both Benjamin and Warburg were working towards a similar notion is, of course, more than coincidence. Benjamin was acquainted with the work of Warburg; indeed, wished to gain access to the Warburg circle. This desire remained unfulfilled. Benjamin's friend Hugo von Hofmannsthal sent a copy of the manuscript of *The Origin of German Tragic Drama* to Warburg's former student Erwin Panofsky, whose response was distinctly unenthusiastic.[6] This effectively put an end to Benjamin's hopes, even though subsequently Fritz Saxl, Warburg's successor as Director of the *Kulturwissenschaftliche Bibliothek Warburg*, bought a copy of the work for the library when it was published. It is ironic, therefore, that the return of critical attention to the work of Aby Warburg owes more to the continuing prominence of Benjamin, than to a resurgence of interest in Warburg *per se.*[7] At the same time, the significance of such parallels should not be misread. Benjamin's concerns originated in the effort to visualise the dialectic of history, a process leading up to his embrace of Marxism and avant-garde montage. For Warburg, on the other hand, the telescoping of history stemmed from his engagement with psychology, and in particular his Nietzschean recognition of the persistence of the "primitive" irrational. Hence the possibility of recidivism undermined the neat linear model of progress. In this regard one should also avoid too hasty an identification of the pictorial montage of the *Mnemosyne* with Benjamin's interest in montage. The idea for the *Atlas*, a visual archive of the processes of sublimation and de-sublimation, was actually suggested by Fritz Saxl, who had used the technique when an educational instructor in the Austrian army.

Such reservations notwithstanding, the most inviting parallel to be drawn between Warburg and Benjamin lies in a comparison of the *Mnemosyne Atlas* and Benjamin's *Arcades* project. The former, in many respects a summary of all of Warburg's interests, was envisaged as a series of between 60 and 70 plates, each of which consisted of a montage of images of classical motifs and their reappearance and transformation in the Renaissance and also during Warburg's own

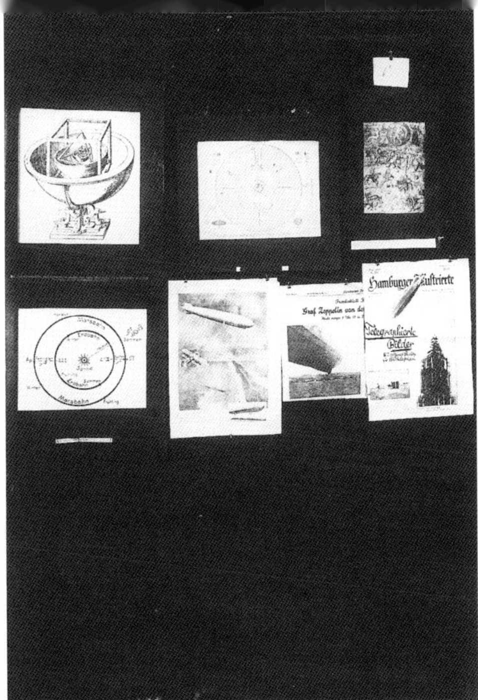

Aby Warburg, *Mnemosyne Atlas,* Plate C. All images courtesy of the Warburg Institute.

lifetime. They included cosmological maps, classical myths such as the legends of Heracles or the Judgement of Paris, and the integration of classical forms into Christian narratives. These plates were to be accompanied by a textual commentary on each plate, a general introduction and other texts the precise function of which remains slightly unclear. At the time of his death in 1929 it remained unfinished; having embarked on the project in 1927, Warburg could never decide on a definitive layout or order of plates, and consequently a number of versions of each plate exists, and in addition the texts remained fragmentary. The only substantial texts were an introduction and an essay on Manet's *Déjeuner sur l'Herbe*. However, the general logic of the work and its form is clear.[8] The use of photographic montage was to enable Warburg to offer a graphic presentation of his project of an "iconography of the interval," in which iconography was less a process of identifying visual texts than of mapping out their transformation and sublimation – from primitive mythic symbols to abstract allegories. The *Atlas* thus functions as a visual archive of European cultural history. Of this the juxtaposition of the *Zeppelin* images with the astrological manuscript offers a prime example. An even more dramatic example can be seen in Plate 64, on which are juxtaposed classical representations of Helios, Renaissance reworkings of the same motif, and contemporary images including stamps, advertisements encouraging the consumption of fish, and a poster for the Schneider Trophy. As in the Zeppelin plate, so here the plate outlines the metamorphosis of the chariot of Helios into the Supermarine seaplane, classical myth into modern technology. In his introduction, Warburg refers to the *Mnemosyne Atlas* as "an inventory of pre-coined classical forms that inform the stylistic development ... of the Renaissance", but it is clear that his interests extended beyond the Renaissance to include the present.[9] This is evident both in the *Mnemosyne Atlas* fragment on Manet's reception of classical myth[10] and also, as Charlotte Schoell-Glass has recently shown, his recurrent interest in contemporary anti-Semitism.[11]

Parallel to Warburg's pictorial *Atlas*, Benjamin's *Arcades* project aims to undertake the same visualisation of history. The *Arcades* project remained even more incomplete than the *Mnemosyne*; while the amount of material Benjamin gathered for the *Arcades* project far exceeds that associated with Warburg's Atlas, its eventual form is far less certain. Benjamin's account of nineteenth-century Paris consists of a vast collection of texts, painstakingly filed and documented, from 1928 until his death in 1940. They consist of a wide range of literary sources, ranging from his own notes on the various topics included, quotations from primary sources, quotations from contemporary critical literature and also personal correspondence. In addition there are various more substantial texts, such as "Paris, Capital of the Nineteenth Century",[12] two pieces entitled "Paris Arcades"[13] and finally a short essay on "The Rings of Saturn or Something about Iron Construction".[14] The *Arcades* project appears to have been formulated in three stages, each of which was distinct in character.[15] However, despite such internal heterogeneity, the material as a whole is organised according to one overriding method. Benjamin notes in a well-known summary of the work, "Method of this work: literary montage. I have nothing to tell. Only to show."[16] An earlier note in the same folio states that "It's a matter, in other words, of attempting to grasp an economic process as a visible [*anschauliches*] originary phenomenon from which stem all of the features of the life of the arcades (and to this extent of the nineteenth century)."[17]

Benjamin's choice of literary montage as the vehicle for his account of the Parisian arcades can be viewed in a number of ways. Most obviously, perhaps, it can be placed alongside his interest in the role of montage within avant-garde practice since the First World War, and his recognition of the loss of auratic distance takes up the theme of spatial disruption in the collages of Picasso and Braque, or the poet Blaise Cendrars' paean to modernity, *La Prose du Transsiberien.*[18] One can triangulate this relation by including Warburg's actual use of photographic montage plates in the *Mnemosyne Atlas*. In addition, one can point to the affinity between the *method* of representation and the substance of the *Arcades* project, namely, the process of the transformation of Parisian capitalism into spectacle. In this regard the method of this work invites comparison with the methodological considerations of *The Origin of the German Tragic Drama*, according to which "the total elimination of the problem of representation" as a *mediating* process, "is the sign of genuine knowledge."[19] Benjamin's use of montage thus mirrors the generation of phantasmagoria in the capitalism of nineteenth-century Paris, and constitutes one such attempt to overcome the problem of representation. Benjamin was aware of the attendant difficulties of this project – in particular one can cite his well-known correspondence with Adorno over his putatively undialectical and untheoretical method.[20] Yet Adorno crucially misunderstood the problem with which Benjamin was wrestling, namely "in what ways it is possible to hold to a heightened sense of the visible while pursuing a Marxist method."[21] The solution to this problem lay in the abandoning of a key tenet of Marxist theory; it lay in "a historical materialism ... that has annihilated the idea of historical progress."[22] It is clear that Benjamin recognised in this process an important shift in the spatial metaphors used to describe history. Presenting history as montage involved "Telescoping the past via the present,"[23] whereby the linear notion of history was replaced by the idea of the dialectical image. As Benjamin noted, "While the relation of past and present is a purely temporal one, that of the 'has-been' [*das Gewesene*] to the 'now' is a dialectical one: it is iconic, not temporal in character."[24] Metaphors of narrating are replaced by ones of seeing; as Benjamin notes in the "Theses on the Philosophy of History", "It is only as an image ... that one can hold

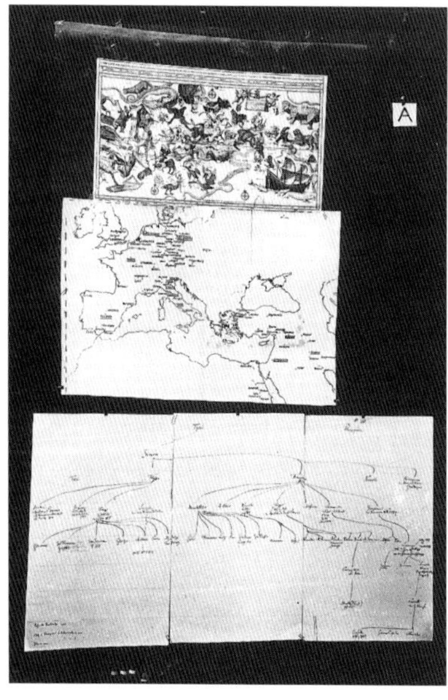

Aby Warburg, *Mnemosyne Atlas*, Plate A.

on to the past."[25] Instead of retelling the *succession* of events, historical knowledge for Benjamin compresses them into a semantically dense iconic simultaneity. Again the precedent of the study of *Trauerspiel* can be invoked in this context, specifically Benjamin's interest in the use of allegorical images such as that of the fragment or ruin to express the baroque idea of history.

Benjamin's contrast between the past and the "has-been," and between the present and the "now" introduces a distinction between the public abstract time of history as linear succession and an alternative temporality which, I shall argue later, throws up further significant parallels with Warburg. A fundamental part of Benjamin's exploration of the Parisian arcades is attention to the process of regression to archaic myth; the phantasmagoria of consumption and the resurrection of a dreamscape of primitive fantasy are opposites within a dialectic of modernity. As Benjamin notes, "Only the thoughtless viewer can deny that there are correspondences at play between the world of modern technology and the archaic world of mythic symbols,"[26] and in his essay on art and reproducibility he regards the cult of celebrity in cinema as an example of the reactivation of primitive fantasy.[27] At the root of this dialectic of the archaic and the contemporary is Benjamin's recognition of the role of recollection as a determinant of temporality. His model of materialist historiography aims to emulate such a dialectic of temporal experience: "The historical articulation of the past ... involves becoming master of a memory as it flares up at the moment of danger."[28] This conception of the past as a site of remembrance, and of history as a process of recollection, also informs Benjamin's notion of the meaning of tradition. Tradition no longer consists of the dead weight of events past; rather, "in every epoch one must make the effort to wrest tradition away from conformity."[29] Most immediately, Benjamin makes these comments in the context of class struggle and the appropriation of history, but it is clear that this informs his general conception of cultural critique. It informs his criticisms of the reactivation, in Hollywood cinema, of the archaic through the "fake" aura of movie stars, against what he saw, albeit naively, as the emancipatory potential of the medium of film.

At the root of Benjamin's account of the arcades is a spatial mapping of the culture of nineteenth-century Paris, which he describes with predominantly visual metaphors or simply *presents* as a dialectical image. Historical method consequently aims to reproduce the temporality of subjective experience, in which memory erases the gap between past and present. This linking of space and time is crystallised in the metaphor of aura. In his essay on the history of photography, aura is defined, in purely spatial terms, as "the unique appearance or semblance of a distance, no matter how close the object may be."[30] In contrast, the essay on technical reproducibility defines aura primarily in temporal terms: the aura of the work of art stems from its age and the indices of the passage of time, which function as the guarantees of its authenticity. Aura thus possesses a temporal and a spatial axis, and Benjamin's "auratisation" of history, his emphasis on the correspondences between the archaic and the contemporary, introduce the metaphor of history as a space of remembrance.

Benjamin's notion of history as recollection, indeed his picture of capitalism as a vast reactivation of auratic experience, echoes Warburg's account of historical memory. The latter's reading of the Renaissance as a cultural *space*, into which is telescoped chronological time, draws its force from his theory of cultural memory. At the heart of Warburg's theory of cultural memory are ideas drawn from Richard Semon's book *Die Mneme*.[31] For Semon, using a well-established metaphor, stimuli inscribe themselves on the memory and remain as traces, termed "engrams" by Semon, which can be reactivated under certain circumstances. Warburg adapts Semon's theory to explore the specifically *visual* forms of the engram, which he sees in visual representations. These he terms "dynamograms". The dynamogram is a visual inscription of primal experience; in keeping with nineteenth-century discourses of the primitive, particularly Tito Vignoli's *Myth and Science*, Warburg regarded these as essentially traumatic and laden with fear.[32] Fundamental to this originary experience is a primitive physics according to which natural events are motivated by personalised animating forces. The plate illustrating the flight of the *Graf Zeppelin* indicates how for Warburg this "primitive" theory of natural causation, manifest, for example, in the interpretation of natural disasters as acts of divine wrath, becomes transformed into the abstract world-picture of modernity, in which nature is governed by impersonal laws.

The symbol constitutes a visual imprint of primal trauma, and as such also preserves a memory of the experience that gave rise to them. Warburg notes in the Introduction to the *Mnemosyne Atlas* that "It is in the area of orgiastic mass seizure that one should look for the mint that stamps the expression of extreme emotional seizure on the memory with such intensity that the engrams of the experience of suffering live on, an inheritance preserved in the memory."[33] Following Semon, Warburg also held to the notion that exposure to such dynamograms constituted an unmediated encounter with the original phobic and irrational memories embodied in the representation.

In keeping with his Enlightenment sympathies, Warburg regarded it as the task of the artist to sublimate the primitive memories of inherited dynamograms through semantic transformation, a task parallel to the scientific disenchantment of nature. In his essay on Manet he regards *Déjeuner sur l'Herbe* as such a transformation of a motif from a classical sarcophagus, namely, the Judgement of Paris. The world of primitive violence, rape and war is transformed into one of contemporary urban leisure. One can only speculate, but the most significant reworking of this motif during Warburg's lifetime, Picasso's *Demoiselles d'Avignon*, would have been regarded unambiguously by him as an example of aggressive desublimation. Within this dialectic of sublimation and desublimation, Warburg appears to have accorded special significance to individual artists, who stand in contrast to the predominantly collective basis of primitive orgiastic experience. The influence of Nietzsche is at its clearest here, for in *The Birth of*

Tragedy the primal ecstasy of Dionysus is intimately connected with the loss of self. Against the regressive pull of collective memory, therefore, certain figures stand out as exemplars of the progressive appropriation of the past, prominent amongst whom are Albrecht Dürer, Sandro Botticelli and Piero della Francesca. Warburg's longest single essay consists of an analysis of Dürer's critical response to the widespread belief in astrology in sixteenth-century Germany, in particular his transformation, of what was widely held to be a demonic omen, namely, a pig born with eight feet, into an object of scientific observation, or his reworking of the zodiacal demon, Saturn, as an allegory of intellectual absorption and melancholy.[34]

The bulk of Warburg's scholarly work was devoted to the Renaissance, which he regarded as a liminal culture. It constituted for Warburg the threshold of modernity, a view he inherited from Jakob Burckhardt. But at the same time its "rediscovery" of classical antiquity potentially opened the way for regression to the originary violence of classical antiquity. In this he was profoundly influenced by Nietzsche's emphasis on the Dionysian undercurrents of ancient Greek culture, and mapped Nietzsche's dialectic of Apollo and Dionysus on to the Renaissance itself.[35] The Renaissance thus formed a cultural space for Warburg, in which were played out various conflicting impulses, and it is important to note that he also interpreted this quite literally in terms of geographical spaces. For example, a recurrent concern in his writings is the relation between the Florentine Renaissance, with its idealising recall of classical culture, and the culture of Flanders and Burgundy, which appeared so much more wedded to the late Gothic, pre-Renaissance, concern with naturalism.[36] This conflict between idealism and naturalism is interpreted as one of a set of mutually contradictory impulses within one cultural space; Warburg referred to the early Renaissance of the fifteenth century in particular as a "spatial totality [*Gesamtgebiet*] in the cultural history of Europe."[37] Moreover the naturalism of Burgundian and Flemish art, in which figures from classical legend are depicted in fifteenth-century costume, is seen as the expression of the lack of a sense of historical space on the part of the artists concerned. The construction of a linear chronology, together with a sense of the "otherness" of the past, are only achieved by the establishment of a space between "then" and "now."

However, it is important to note that while Warburg's primary interest was in the significance of the Renaissance, this was intimately connected to his concerns with the present. An example of this can be found in the materials he gathered for a lecture on the Death of Orpheus that he gave in 1905, subsequently published as "Dürer and

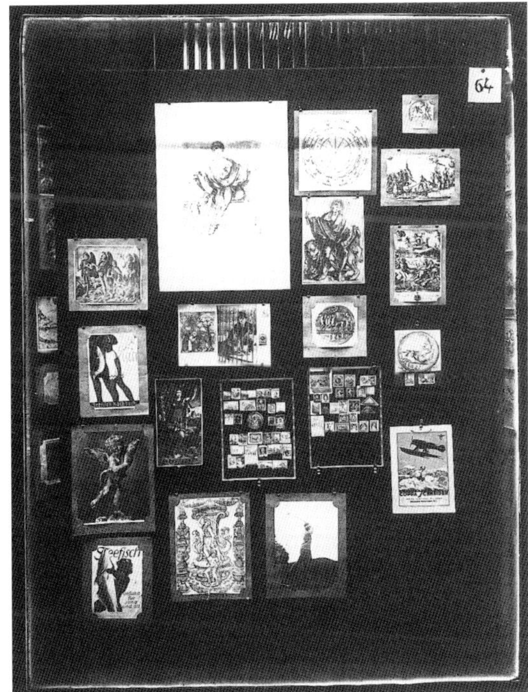

Aby Warburg, *Mnemosyne Atlas,* Plate 64.

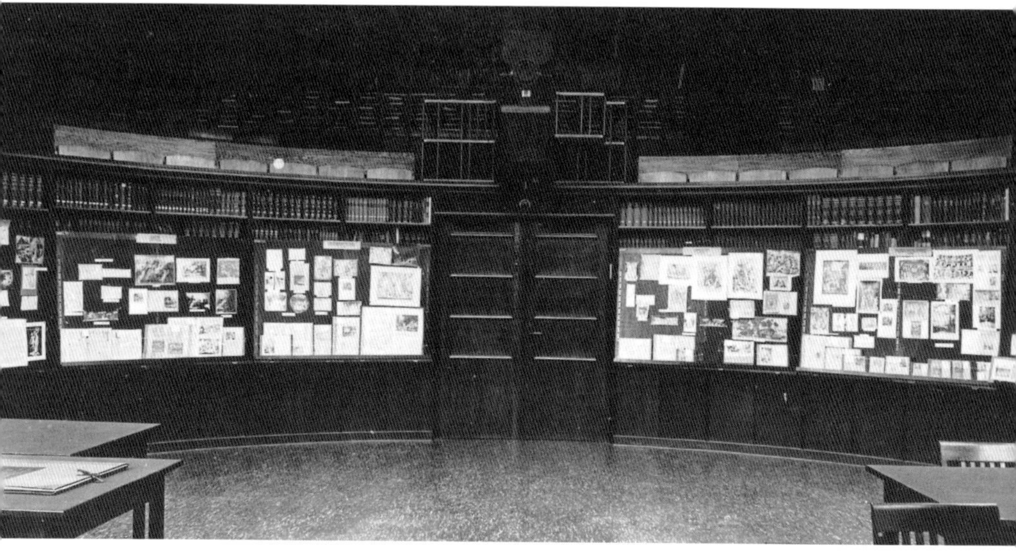

Aby Warburg's library in Hamburg, 1926. Many of the books are covered by the pin-boards that hold the images of the *Mnemosyne Atlas*.

Italian Antiquity".[38] The myth of Orpheus presents an exemplary case of what Warburg regarded as the violence at the root of Greek violence; he was torn to pieces by women who, according to one version, were jealous of his love for Eurydice, and according to another, were punishing him for his refusal to honour Dionysus. The recurrence of the myth in the visual culture of the Renaissance counted as testimony, for Warburg, of the persistence of primitive Dionysian memories amidst the putative "civilisation" of the Renaissance. Of equal significance is the fact that the archive material associated with this paper includes a cutting from the *Frankfurter Zeitung* from 1905, recounting a particularly brutal murder following the abortive revolution in Russia of the same year. It concerned a young teacher in Stavropol who, approaching a band of cossacks for protection from a mob led by the local priest, was trampled to death under the suspicion of being an anti-Tsarist intellectual "like the Jews."[39] Quite apart from Warburg's specific interest in the anti-Semitism apparent in the episode, it was also read as one more example of the general persistence of Dionysian violence. The newspaper cutting was annotated by Warburg: "The Death of Orpheus. The return of the eternally same beast, genus: homo sapiens."

The strikingly Nietzschean tone of Warburg's annotation indicates the wider meaning of this episode, for it invokes Nietzsche's doctrine of Eternal Recurrence, the primary aim of which was to counter the optimistic belief in historical progress. Underlying Warburg's observations therefore is a profound scepticism towards the legacy of the Enlightenment. Parallel to Benjamin's notion of history as a dialectical image, Warburg regards culture as the site of a dialectic of progressive differentiation (the establishment of reflective space) and regressive de-differentiation. Although he held to the *ideal* of cultural progression, and in this sense was a product of the Enlightenment, he also could not believe in the Enlightenment understanding of history. This is evident in his profound ambivalence towards the technologies of modernity. While the establishment of reflective space is the prerequisite of cultural progress in general, and science in particular, scientific "progress" has led to inventions such as the telephone, the aeroplane and others which he argues are in the process of breaking down the fragile space achieved since the Renaissance. Enlightenment is thus collapsing in on itself, a notion which Adorno and Horkheimer would later examine at much greater length.[40] It is because of his sense that modernity is introducing a regressive collapse of inversion that Warburg juxtaposes the contemporary seaplane with classical coins bearing the chariot of Helios. The brave new world of modern technology, specifically the air speed competition of the 1920s, is intimately connected for Warburg with a regression into myth. This sense of the evaporation of historical distance underpins his use of the deliberately anachronistic terms "airship" and "submarine" in his paper on the tapestry illustration of the legend of Alexander, and one can find contemporary parallels in Filippo Marinetti's mythification of the automobile in the *Futurist Manifesto* of 1909 or Charles Sykes's *Silver Lady* that has adorned the radiator of every Rolls-Royce since 1911.[41] Most immediately, it raises obvious parallels both with Benjamin's emphasis on the correspondences between modernity and the archaic dreamworld, and also with his well-known critique of Ernst Jünger's mythification of the First World War.[42]

Warburg's interest in collective memory, and in the role of dynamograms as the vehicles of cultural transmission can also be brought to bear on his concept of history, using, as an intermediary, Freud's work on repetition and recollection. In his paper of 1914 on "Remembering, Repeating and Working Through", Freud distinguishes between repetition-compulsion and recollection.[43] The compulsion to repeat, though it reiterates past experience, functions within a perpetual present; it thus cancels out the temporal basis of memory and acts in the place of what Freud regards as memory proper. This theme is taken up in the later essay "Beyond the Pleasure Principle", where Freud stresses the link between repetition-compulsion and death.[44] Recollection, in contrast, arises through the phenomenon of transference. This enables the individual to construct a narrative in which experiences are no longer isolated, iterable events, but instead take their place within a personal life history. I believe Warburg was struggling towards a similar view of collective memory, though using the completely inadequate vocabulary of Semon and Vignoli. Specifically, he distinguishes between the compulsive repetition of the primitive psychic engram, and its sublimation into the narrative of cultural progression. It is this set of concerns that frames his study of the Renaissance, for the latter is most commonly identified by its retrieval of classical antiquity, and as such it is caught between two contradictory impulses. One is the drive simply to repeat the primitive engrams and dynamograms of antiquity, and thereby to cancel a

Front page of the original edition to Walter Benjamin's *The Origin of German Tragic Drama* with Fritz Saxl's inscription to Warburg.

Walter Benjamin

Ursprung des deutschen Trauerspiels

1928

Ernst Rowohlt Verlag · Berlin

genuinely historical appropriation of it. The other is a reworking of antiquity and its dynamograms, a semantic transformation of their meaning comparable to Freud's notion of appropriative recollection. Tradition is thus a highly ambiguous phenomenon, and this recalls Benjamin's idea of an emancipatory critique that would wrest tradition "away from a conformism that is about to overpower it."[45]

Recent work on collective memory, in particular, that of Jan Assmann, has also drawn attention to its proximity to the process of repetition-compulsion outlined by Freud.[46] Specifically, collective memory, as opposed to the historical memory of a literary culture, relies on structures of repetition such as rituals and festivals that serve to secure the basis of a collective identity but which also telescope chronological history into an atemporal mythic past. As Assmann has argued, with the development of writing, repetition loses its function since cultural identity can be preserved and transmitted in the form of physical texts, such as inscriptions, tablets, manuscripts and so forth, whose meaning then becomes open to interpretative transformation.[47] Warburg's own analysis of the Renaissance can therefore be characterised as an exploration of the oscillation between repetitive collective memory and transformational historical recollection, as played out within the sphere of visual representations. Influenced by nineteenth-century empathy theory, he regarded visual images as particularly effective symbols of psychological states that could be recreated in the spectator. It is this conception of the role of memory and visual representations that underlies the format of the *Mnemosyne Atlas*. The method of pictorial montage reflects his understanding of culture as a memorial space, in which visual and other symbols function as an archive of juxtaposed memories. In this it can be compared with Benjamin's *Arcades* project, except that whereas Benjamin writes of the dialectics of vision in figural terms, Warburg is concerned with a dialectic of images in a very literal way; the most economic vehicle for exploring the process of sublimation is found in the actual juxtaposition of visual representations.

It has often been argued that the spatialisation of culture and history is to be linked with the rise of Saussurean methodologies in the human sciences. In particular, Claude Lévi-Strauss is often credited with the introduction of the spatial metaphor of culture as a structure, which he analysed through topological notions of spatial relations and structural transformations.[48]

This metaphor is carried through most consistently in the work of Michel Foucault, whose analysis of discursive formations speaks of mapping the "surfaces of their emergence" or of the "grids of specification" by which those various discourses are structured.[49] This is also paralleled by Foucault's interest in vision as a cultural determinant, from the panoptic surveillance of modernity analysed in *Discipline and Punish* to the disentangling of vision and language in the Classical Age explored in *The Order of Things*.[50] As I have indicated, however, the emergence of the notion of a cultural space, and the replacement of a concern with temporal diachrony by one of spatial synchrony can be traced back to Warburg and Benjamin. At the same time, however, it is important not to elide the enormous differences between Warburg and Benjamin on the one hand, and the more recent work of Lévi-Strauss and Foucault on the other. For Warburg and Benjamin, the central factor in the birth of the idea of a cultural space was the role of cultural memory and its residues, which contradicted the Enlightenment belief in unhindered historical progression and which could telescope linear chronology into a dialectical simultaneity. Memory plays no such role in the thinking of those later figures, which derives its force from the application of a particular linguistic theory to the study of social phenomena. Nevertheless it is of no small significance that their intellectual ancestry finds its origins in the work of a Swiss linguist approximately contemporary with Warburg himself. One can thus observe a striking parallelism, at the beginning of this century, between a material change in the experience of time and space, and an epistemic shift in historiographic method.

Footnotes

1 Aby Warburg, "Luftschiff und Tauchboot in der mittelalterlichen Vorstellungswelt", *Die Erneuerung der heidnischen Antike. Gesammelte Schriften*, B. G. Teubner, 1932, pp. 243–249

2 Walter Benjamin, *One Way Street*, trans., Edmund Jephcott, NLB, 1979, p. 103.

3 Aby Warburg, *Images from the Region of the Pueblo Indians of North America*, trans. Michael Steinberg, Cornell University Press, 1995, p. 54.

4 Aby Warburg, "Grundlegende Bruchstücke zu einer (monistischen) Kunstpsychologie", Warburg Archive, Warburg Institute, London, III No. 43.2, Section 328.

5 Walter Benjamin, "The Work of Art in the Age of Mechanical Reproduction", *Illuminations*, trans., Harry Zohn, Fontana, 1973, p. 217.

6 Walter Benjamin, *The Origin of the German Tragic Drama*, trans., John Osborne, Verso Books, 1985.

7 The volume of literature on Warburg has grown enormously since the late 1980s. See, for example, A. Meyer, "Aby Warburg in His Early Correspondence", *The American Scholar*, vol. 57, 1988, pp. 445–452; Carlo Ginzburg, "From Aby Warburg to E. H. Gombrich: A Problem of Method", Ginzburg, *Myths, Emblems, Clues*, trans., John & Anne Tedeschi, Hutchinson Radius, 1990, pp. 17–59; Edgar Wind, "Warburg's Concept of *Kulturwissenschaft* and its Meaning for Aesthetics", *The Eloquence of Symbols*, ed., Jaynie Anderson, Clarendon Press, 1993, pp. 21–35; Sigrid Schade, "Charcot and the Spectacle of the Hysterical Body. The 'Pathos Formula' as an aesthetic staging of psychiatric discourse – a blind spot in the reception of Warburg", *Art History*, vol. 18, no. 4, 1995, pp. 499–517; Kurt Forster, "Aby Warburg: His Study of Ritual and Art on Two Continents", *October*, vol. 77, 1996, pp. 5–24; Matthew Rampley, "From Symbol to Allegory: Aby Warburg's Theory of Art", *Art Bulletin*, vol. LXXIX, no. 1, 1997, pp. 41–55. The literature in German is even more extensive. For a comprehensive bibliography see Dieter Wuttke, *Aby M. Warburg-Bibliographie 1866 bis 1995. Werk und Wirkung*, Valentin Koerner Verlag, 1998; Christine Brosius. *Kunst als Denkraum. Zum Bildungsbegriff von Aby Warburg*, Centaurus, 1997; Jürgen Habermas, "Ernst Cassirer und die Bibliothek Warburg", *Vorträge aus dem Warburg Haus*, eds., Wolfgang Kemp et al, Akademie Verlag, 1997, pp. 3–29; Bernd Roeck, *Der Junge Aby Warburg*, C. H. Beck, 1997; Dorothea McEwan, *Ausreiten der Ecken. Die Aby Warburg – Fritz Saxl Korrespondenz*, Dölling und Gallitz Verlag, 1998.

8 A detailed account of the atlas can be found in Dorothée Bauerle, *Gespenstergeschichten für ganz Erwachsene. Ein Kommentar zu Aby Warburgs Bilderatlas Mnemosyne*, Lit Verlag, 1987.

9 Aby Warburg, "Introduction" to *Mnemosyne*, Warburg Archive, no. 102.1.1 p. 4.

10 Aby Warburg, "Manet's *Déjeuner sur l'Herbe*. Die vorprägende Funktion heid-

nischer Elementargottheiten für die Entwicklung modernen Naturgefühls", ed., Dieter Wuttke, *Kosmopolis der Wissenschaft. E R Curtius und das Warburg Institute*, Valentin Koerner, 1989, pp. 262–72.

11 Charlotte Schoell-Glass, *Aby Warburg und der Antisemitismus*, Fischer Verlag, 1998. See too Schoell-Glass, "An Episode of Cultural Politics during the Weimar Republic: Aby Warburg and Thomas Mann Exchange a Letter Each", *Art History*, vol. 21, no. 1, 1998, pp. 107–128.

12 Walter Benjamin, "Pariser Passagen I & II", *Passagenwerk*, ed. Rolf Tiedemann, Suhrkamp Verlag, 1991, pp. 993–1059.

13 Benjamin, *Passagenwerk*, pp. 45–59.

14 Benjamin, "Der Saturnring, oder Etwas vom Eisenbau", *Passagenwerk*, pp. 1060–1063.

15 The complete account of the genesis of the work can be found in Rolf Tiedemann's notes in *Passagenwerk*, pp. 1067-1205.

16 Benjamin, *Passagenwerk*, p. 574.

17 Benjamin, *Passagenwerk*, p. 574.

18 For a concise study of this theme, from early modernism onwards, see Margery Perloff, *The Futurist Moment. Avant-Garde, Avant-Guerre and the Language of Rupture*, University of Chicago Press, 1986.

19 Benjamin, *Tragic*, p. 27.

20 The correspondence in question can be found in *Aesthetics and Politics*, eds. Ronald Taylor and Fredric Jameson, Verso, 1979, pp. 110–41.

21 Benjamin, *Passagenwerk*, p. 575.

22 Benjamin, *Passagenwerk*, p. 574.

23 Benjamin, *Passagenwerk*, p. 588.

24 Benjamin, *Passagenwerk*, p. 578.

25 Benjamin, "Theses on the Philosophy of History", *Illuminations*, p. 247.

26 Benjamin, *Passagenwerk*, p. 576. Susan Buck-Morss has explored in depth the motif of the archaic dreamscape of modernity. See Susan Buck-Morss, *The Dialectics of Seeing*, MIT Press, 1989.

27 Benjamin, "Reproduction", pp. 211–244.

28 Benjamin, "Theses", p. 247.

29 Benjamin, "Theses", p. 247.

30 Benjamin, "A Short History of Photography", *Street*, p. 250.

31 Richard Semon, *Die Mneme als erhaltendes Prinzip im Wechsel des organischen Geschehens*, B. G. Teubner, 1904.

32 Tito Vignoli, *Mythus und Wissenschaft, eine Studie*, B. G. Teubner, 1880.

33 Warburg Archive, no. 102.1.1, 6.

34 Aby Warburg, "Heidnisch-antike Weissagung in Wort und Bild zu Luthers Zeiten", *Ausgewählte Schriften und Würdigungen*, [*ASW*], ed., Dieter Wuttke,

Valentin Koerner, 1992, pp. 199–304. This was later explored by Erwin Panofsky and Fritz Saxl in *Dürers "Melencolia I", eine quellen- und typengeschichtliche Untersuchung*, Bibliothek Warburg, 1923. Panofsky and Saxl's study informed Benjamin's account of *The Origin of German Tragic Drama*. See Benjamin, *Tragic*, pp. 149–50.

35 On Warburg's relation to Burckhardt and Nietzsche see Yoshihiko Maikuma, *Der Begriff der Kultur bei Warburg, Nietzsche und Burckhardt*, Hain bei Athenäum, 1985. See, too, Helmut Pfotenhauer, "Das Nachleben der Antike: Aby Warburg's Auseinandersetzung mit Nietzsche", *Nietzsche Studien* vol. XIV, 1985, pp. 298–313.

36 See, for example, Warburg's essays on "Der Eintritt des antikisierenden Idealstiles in die Malerei der Frührenaissance", Warburg Archive III 88.1; "Bildniskunst und Florentinisches Bürgertum", *ASW*, pp. 65-102; "Flandrische Kunst und Frührenaissance", *ASW*, pp. 103–24.

37 Warburg, *ASW*, p. 130.

38 Warburg, "Dürer und die italienische Antike", *ASW*, pp. 125–130. The illustrations for the lecture "Der Tod des Orpheus" are included as an appendix on pp. 132–135.

39 Warburg Archive no. 61. The entire article is quoted in Schoell-Glass, pp. 88–89.

40 Theodor Adorno and Max Horkheimer, *The Dialectic of Enlightenment*, trans., John Cumming, Verso, 1979.

41 Filippo Marinetti, *The Futurist Manifesto*, eds. Charles Harrison & Paul Wood, *Art in Theory 1900–1990*, Basil Blackwell, 1992, pp. 145–149. On the Rolls Royce see Erwin Panofsky, "The Ideological Antecedents of the Rolls-Royce Radiator", *Three Essays on Style*, ed., I. Lavin, MIT, 1995, pp. 129–164.

42 Walter Benjamin, "Theories of German Fascism. On the Collection of Essays *War and Warrior* edited by Ernst Jünger", *New German Critique*, vol. 17, 1979, pp. 120–128.

43 Sigmund Freud, *The Standard Edition of the Complete Psychological Works of Sigmund Freud*, Hogarth Press, 1953–1974, vol. XII, pp. 147–156.

44 Freud, "Beyond the Pleasure Principle", *The Standard Edition*, vol. XVIII, pp. 1–64.

45 Benjamin, "Theses", p. 247.

46 Jan Assmann, *Das kulturelle Gedächtnis. Schrift, Erinnerung und politische Identität in frühen Hochkulturen*, C. H. Beck, 1997. See, too, Peter Burke, "History as Social Memory", *Memory*, ed., Thomas Butler, Basil Blackwell, 1989, pp. 97–113; Paul Connerton, *How Societies Remember*, Cambridge University Press, 1989.

47 On the specific subject of writing and memory see eds., Aleida and Jan Assmann, *Schrift und Gedächtnis*, Willhelm Fink Verlag, 1983. See, too, eds., Jürgen von Ungern-Sternberg and Hansjörg Reinau, *Vergangenheit in mündlicher Überlieferung*, Teubner, 1988.

48 Lévi-Strauss has asserted that in general "we are concerned with the spatial

distribution of social phenomena." *Anthropologie Structurale*, Plon, 1958, p. 320. In *Tristes Tropiques* he notes of his intellectual development that "like a city-dweller transported to the mountains, I became drunk with space." *Tristes Tropiques*, trans., John and Doreen Weightman, Jonathan Cape, 1973, p. 59.

49 Michel Foucault, *The Archaeology of Knowledge*, trans., Alan Sheridan, Tavistock, 1974, pp. 41 and 42.

50 Michel Foucault, *Discipline and Punish*, trans., Alan Sheridan, Penguin Books, 1977; *The Order of Things*, Tavistock, 1970. On the role of vision in Foucault see Martin Jay, *Downcast Eyes. The Denigration of Vision in Twentieth-Century French Thought*, University of California Press, 1994, pp. 381–416.

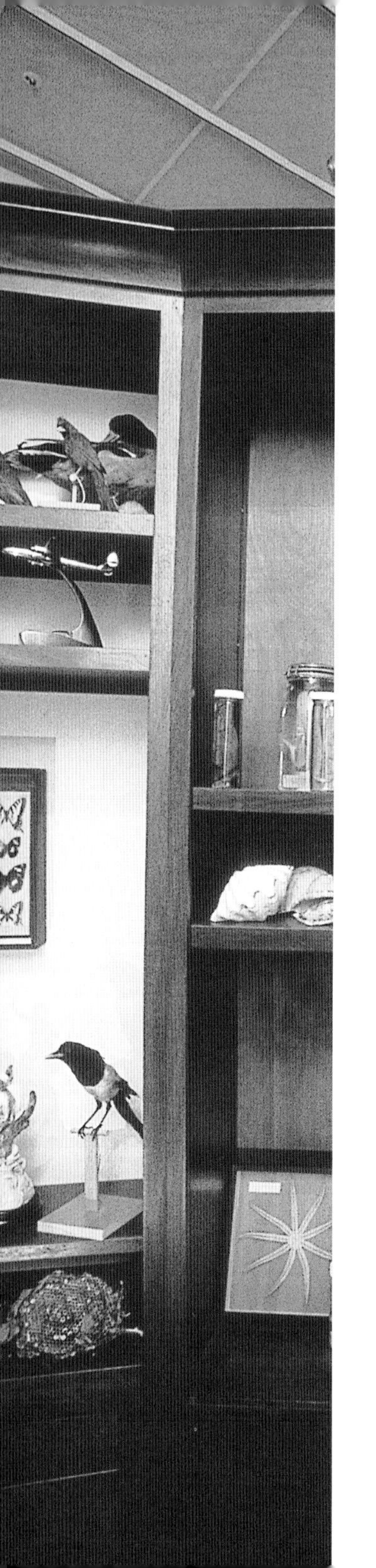

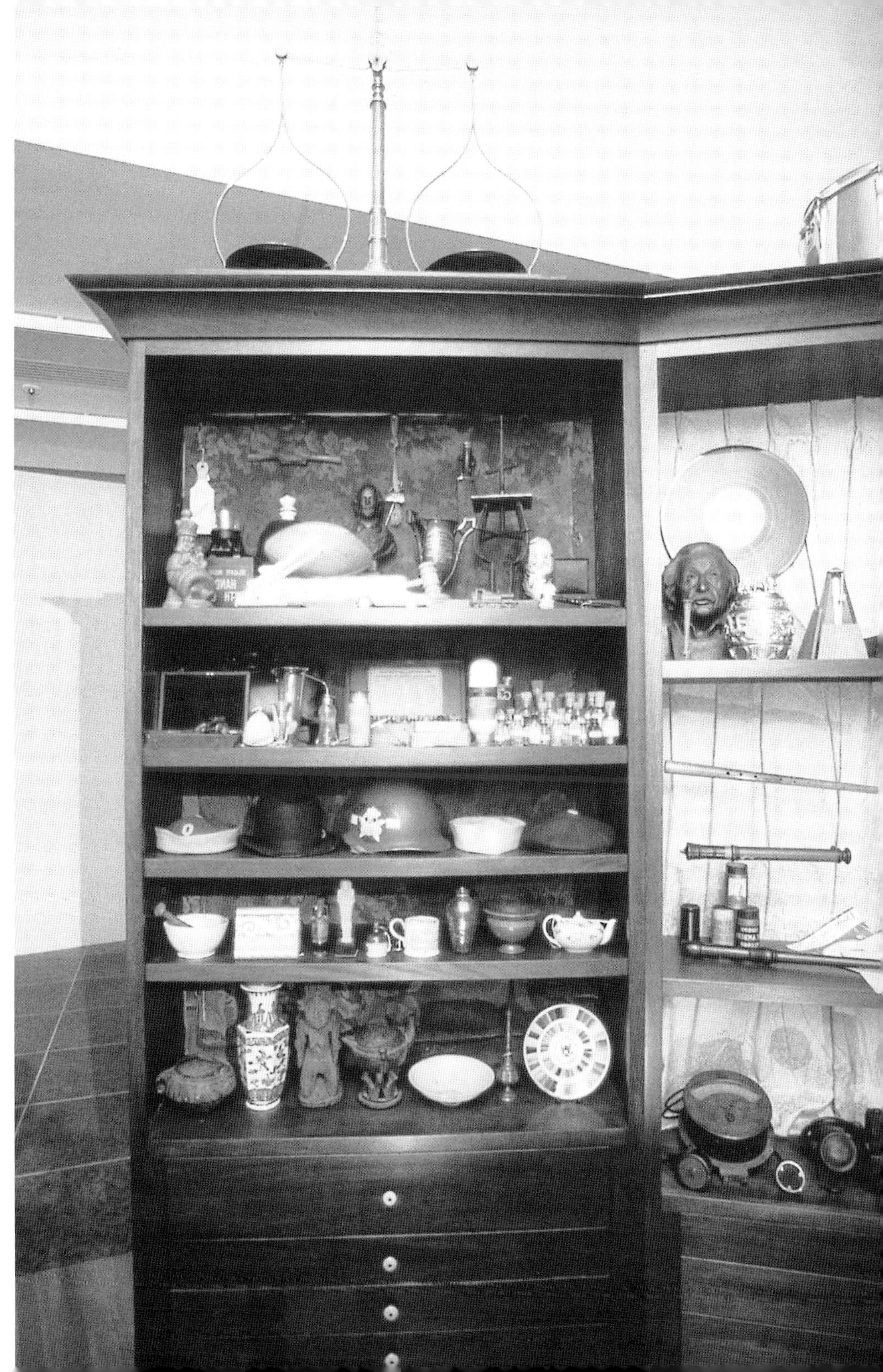

The Crystalline Veil and the Phallomorphic Imaginary: Walter Benjamin's Pantographic Riegl

Donald Preziosi

I, who late sang Belgravia's charms – and strove
To paint her beauties, and her merits prove,
Now sing the CRYSTAL PALACE! – theme sublime,
That shall astound the world throughout all time!
Aid me. Ye Muses! Aid! Your seat is here!
Ye murmuring fountains, charm my listening ear!
Fair sculptured forms, whose classic beauty bears
The spirit back to Rome's enchanted years,
Lend to my strains the power of art divine,
And let your soul poetic breathe in mine!

Lo! As I roam o'er this unequalled spot,
Earth and its drearier scenes are all forgot;
The mighty minds that with resistless will,
Raised the fair temple, seem to haunt it still!
A solemn glory shines along these aisles,
And in the violet-tinted distance, smiles;
And Peace, with dove-like pinions, seems to brood
Above this swarming, countless multitude.

Ah! Priceless boon! Ah, blessing unconfined!
All hail to thee! Benignant power of *mind!*
Where'er I turn, are wonders wrought by thee!
And still, in these, the *great First Cause* I see,
Whose mercy gave that spark of Heavenly fire
To light man here, and direct him higher.
I gaze around – and thousands meet my eye –
I look within – the smallest unit, I!
Yet, with that wondrous power – my living soul,
I soar above, and contemplate the whole;
Nor only through these various scenes I range,
But search the shadowy future, and its change,
Far times – when this assembled crowd shall rest,
"Dust unto dust," within earth's quiet breast,
And all the glory of our golden age,
Shall be a word – no more – in hist'ry's page!

Yet shall this crystal pile – this mighty plan,
An influence wield upon the mind of man,
Free as itself, as wondrous and as vast,
And lasting still – whilst time itself shall last.
No narrow views – no rights exclusive, bar
This brilliant scene – nor its enchantments mar!
The prince and serf, the peasant and the peer,
Alike may revel in the beauties here;
Alike must feel how feeble and how small,
Each man alone – how great, how glorious all!
And in this fairy world of labour, see
A type of what the actual world should be.

Here, in one Brotherhood, the nations greet
With but one heart – as 'neath one roof they meet.
How wide soe'er their home – uncouth their name,
Or wild their nature, *here* they feel the same.
The same bright visions glad their eager eyes,
The same strange marvels strike them with surprise;
Their bosoms beat with rapture, or with woe,
Whether from India's heat, or Russia's snow;
And each high work of art, or priceless gem,
Calls forth responsive, tear or smile from them.
They meet – as all in this cold world should meet,
(One Heaven above – one Earth beneath their feet),
In peace and simple faith – a quiet band
Of Brothers – greeting in a foreign land.
From East to West – from North to South they come,
As to a father's feast, a common home;
Partake with joy of all that varied store,
And part at last – to meet again no more.[1]

It has been customary for some time to believe that artworks are historically significant phenomena, and that art itself has a 'history', the astute delineation of which would provide us with significant insights into the (presumably parallel or complementary) histories of individuals and of peoples—insights which provide lessons for our own time. The modern institutions of art history and museology are, of course, founded upon this enabling assumption, one of whose several corollaries has been that changes in form are taken to correspond (directly or indirectly) to changes in beliefs, attitudes, mentalities or intentions, or to changes in social, political, or cultural conditions. This has always been a virtually irresistible fiction, and it has been one of the cornerstones of the edifice of the modernity into which we have built ourselves, the exits to which lead only to other, identical spaces.[2]

There was no more brilliant stage upon which modernity was to be delineated, and made factual than the *Great Exhibition of the Arts and Manufactures of All Nations* at the Crystal Palace in London in 1851.[3] This most radically translucent of nineteenth-century constructions may well have been modernity's most unsurpassable artefact. It embodied the principle of modern order itself: infinitely expandable, anonymous; transparently and stylelessly abstract. In the words of the poem, it was a "mighty plan," and "type of what the actual world should be" that is in fact "lasting still," everywhere in us and around us. The very diagram of the modern Symbolic Order, it was, "as wondrous and as vast" as "the mind of man" itself.

Simply put, it offered – as Freud was later to say of psychoanalysis – an "impartial instrument, like the infinitesimal calculus" for making legible both the differences and similarities, and the cognitive and ethical hierarchies amongst peoples by means of their juxtaposed and plainly seen products and effects.[4] All the world in a room: at once the modern apotheosis of the *Wunderkammer* (in which objects were catalysts for a fraternal intercourse bent toward making conversational sense of a jumble of things), and the implicit ideal of what were to become the arcades in Paris and other cities.[5] The Crystal Palace, erected four years after the opening of the British Museum across London in its present *faux*-classical form, was the system of modern museology (and art historicism) as such, stripped to the skin. A dream from which we have yet to awaken.

Alois Riegl (no less than Walter Benjamin and other notable pantographers of the late nineteenth and early twentieth centuries) cannot be appreciated or substantially understood apart from this "impartial instrument," this "father's feast." A feast, moreover, that was itself haunted by the presence of the greatest patriarch of them all, Queen Victoria, who was there (as a sort of permanent strolling exhibit) virtually every day of the building's *in situ* existence, and the mortal representative of that "great First Cause" seen behind all the "wonders wrought" here in this "common home" – the projective *Umwelt* ("one Heaven above – one Earth beneath") of a British Imperial Imaginary; a "fair temple" whose "classic beauty bears/The spirit back to Rome's enchanted years."

The modern disciplinary practices of art history and museology are both among the more powerful effects of this "mighty plan," and among its indispensible *modes d'emploi.* Art history was and remains the ghost in that crystalline machine, as it perpetually carries the memory of this "Muses' seat" as its innermost fixation. Bourgeois modernity's *stade du miroir*, the blinding quiddity of this "crystal pile," whose eidetic image is permanently imprinted on the art historical gaze. An art historical gaze that, in imagining itself as an eye on the world, is a ceaseless shuffling through a windowless slide collection growing faster than the eye can focus; the only art history, in fact, that we have. There is nothing outside its endlessly proliferating text.

The Crystal Palace's grand and 'styleless' system was replicated in countless expositions, museums and city plans created throughout Europe and the European dominated and influenced world (rapidly becoming, in the nineteenth century, coterminous with the world as such). Its exhibitionary order was the ideal horizon and the blueprint of patriarchal colonialism; the epistemological technology of orientalism as such.[6] It was the laboratory table upon which all things and peoples could objectively and poignantly be compared and contrasted in a uniform light, and phylogenetically and ontogenetically ranked. All this in relation to a Europe that had been learning to stage itself as the eyes and ears of the world; as the brain of the earth's body. The Crystal Palace – whose "bright visions" and "brilliant scene" were so profusely celebrated in the 150-page paean of 1852, the opening stanzas of which are quoted above – was the paradigm of the loom of modernity on which sexuality, capitalism and art have come to be woven together tightly into a sturdy, enduring fabric which has hardly frayed since (or which seems uncannily to weave itself back together after the occasion critical rip).

The pantographic enterprise of the modern discipline of art history prefigured by Winckelmann, Kant, and Hegel was lucidly figured in the 1851 *Great Exhibition* – itself a phallomorphic imaginary for rendering visible Europe's Others.[7] This visibility is both the proof and condition of the presence of the Other, whose existence is thereby guaranteed by its exhibitionary representation – which in effect precludes recognition of the Other's difference in favour of its phallocentric makeup: a covering-up of difference by a uniform visibility which 'de-Others' others and domesticates all difference. This universal lucidity (what our poem calls this "common home" and "father's feast") is thus a transparency which is opaque; a *crystalline veil*. The dream of a totally transparent society is the *hijab* of Europe's modernity.

The erasure of difference (this "abstraction") in favour of a "universal" and uniform "*fairy world* of labour" (my emphasis) endows everything (as the effective condition of their visibility in modernity) with a phallicised, commodified and fetishised value, making it evident that at the core of modernity (and perpetuated by the interlinked agendas of the museographic enterprises and disciplines) is precisely the conflation of aesthetics, ethics and sexuality in the commodity. This was the epistemological crux and midpoint of Benjamin's *Arcades* project, in Susan Buck-Morss's astute explication.[8]

It is perhaps fitting that (despite its material descendants on other sites, and even the incorporation of some of its actual physical members into these other 'crystal palaces') the Crystal Palace was a momentary, six-month phenomenon: a brief and blinding flash in mid-century that revealed, as would the quick shine of a torch in the night, an unexpected and uncanny landscape. The flash has remained imprinted on the European optic nerve now for well over a century; the uncanny landscape revealed is, in Benjamin's words, capitalism; that catastrophic "new dream sleep (that) fell over Europe."[9]

There is little in the work of Riegl, Wölfflin and Benjamin (except perhaps for Warburg, who at least knew where the problems lay) that can be said to escape this 'de-Othering' of others that had long been emblematic of the condition of visibility in modernity. An examination of the 'optic' of a Walter Benjamin who was blind to this, whose telescope was really a pantograph (a term I shall explain in a moment) may reveal why it may be about time, finally, to reassess those facets of Benjamin's aesthetic ideology (including what might be termed his 'art history') that have been revived by some of his contemporary re-readers to haunt us all over again. There is in fact nothing in Riegl or Benjamin which offers anything different, and certainly nothing that will derail us from our perpetual, recycling, or free us from a close cupboard of retrospective longing: our fixation with an illusory art historical wholeness will always be achingly felt just outside the door we are behind, or just round the next corner. As if, in finally reading Benjamin (or Riegl, or whomever), our disciplinary integrity and true trajectory might rightly be restored. I think our task must be different if we truly want to position ourselves at a distance from the realm of this Imaginary: rather than restoring the disciplinary train to the tracks from which some of its wheels have become derailed, we might instead take a look at the tracks themselves.

Let us turn the questions (explicit and implicit) of this volume back on themselves: rather than re-reading art history through the optic of Benjamin, it may be more useful, today, to re-read Benjamin through the optic of the nineteenth-century museography (whose most lucid European epitome was the Crystal Palace) of which his own pantographic messianic practice (at one with the art historicism of his time; see below) was the product.

In 1868, the linguist Michel Breal wrote that, in standing before a picture,

> Our eyes think they perceive contrasts of light and shade, on a canvas lit all over by the same light. They see depths, where everything is on the same plane. If we approach a few steps, the lines we thought we recognised break up and disappear, and in place of differently illuminated objects we find only layers of colour congealed on the canvas and trails of brightly coloured dots, adjacent to one

> another but not joined up. But as soon as we step back again, our sight, yielding to long habit, blends the colours, distributes the light, puts the features together again, and recognises the work of the artist.[10]

The masses of objects in a museum or exhibition came to be understood as analogous to the blobs of colour and the abstract dots and dashes described by Michel Breal as on a painted canvas. Only by taking up a proper 'perspective' and distance may these bits and pieces be seen as joining up to create the image, the figure, the physiognomy, of the character or mentality of a person, people, or period. It is precisely the pursuit of such a *perspectival position* that constitutes the modern discipline of art history as a politics of the gaze; an instrumental technology for fabricating genealogies of value, character, race, spirit, or mentality through the mediating fictions of style, intention, authorship and reflection.

It was the Crystal Palace that powerfully put this in the proper scale and perspective for all to see. In so doing, this supreme taxonomic and comparative instrument was arguably the first fully-realised modernist institution. The Crystal Palace is in fact the historical realisation and the implicit ideal, the ur-form and *Gesamtkunstwerk*, of what Benjamin's *Arcades* project was aiming to evoke, pantographically, from the Parisian arcades (and the Paris 1937 Exposition). Benjamin, however, quoting another verse about the Crystal Palace, saw the latter as an ur-form of the Exposition's 'Pavilion of Solidarity'.[11]

The key metaphorical conundrum of modernity is that the *form* of your work is (and should be *legible as*) the *figure* of your truth. Every object was to be framed as an object-lesson, and the art historical branch of the nineteenth-century enterprise of historicism was designed quite pragmatically to render the visible legible. Museological and art historical, theoretical, and critical practices (together comprising the core of the social matrix of what I am calling *museography*) were interlinked sites for the manufacture of the present, in particular the present that constituted Europe in its relation to all possible Others –

that 'modernity', that co-option of all possible ethnocentrisms, that has since come to cover the planet through its extensions, imitations and recapitulations everywhere. Art history is no less a factory for the production of the fictions that make up the load-bearing walls of that modernity – the phantasms of ethnicity, race, gender, nation, sex, indigenity, otherness, and of course the key enabling fiction, 'art' itself.

Art history has since its origins been the site of a modern semiotic and epistemological problem and paradox, one born out of a powerfully enabling set of assumptions: that the art object's visibility is a function of its legibility as a symptom of everything and anything that could plausibly be adduced as contributing to its appearance and morphology. A symptom of lack; of what is absent and lacking, in short. It became eminently reasonable to believe that the astute delineation of formal or stylistic genealogical relationships among artworks would provide significant insights into the (presumably parallel, complementary or homologous) histories of individuals and peoples. The modern institutions of art history and museology are, of course, founded upon this enabling assumption, where, as noted at the beginning, changes in form (or a lack thereof) are taken to correspond to changes (or a lack of change) in beliefs, attitudes, mentalities, and intentions, or to changes (or not) in social, political, or cultural conditions.

Simply put, the artwork (and perforce any palpable cultural artefact, object, or practice) is taken to bear a relationship of resemblance (a metaphorical – and hence substitutional – relationship) as well as a part-to-whole relation (a synecdochic – and hence metonymic or juxtapositional connection; an index) to its circumstances of production. This situation – this *synecdochic metaphoricity* – is precisely that of the pantograph, that horizontal, scissor-like artistic implement by which one can scale-up an image from a smaller to a larger size (or vice versa), thus retaining all the picture's features and qualities at an expanded size. As a pantographic enterprise, the analytic practice of the historian or critic may be justly said to comprise the projection of the object on to a larger screen – the social, cultural, historical, ethnic, racial or national horizon. In this regard, the artwork is a homuncular entity, whose *finality* is the horizon of its ideal, projected fullness – that "universal history" that Benjamin so admired Riegl's practice for evoking.

Such assumptions aid us in appreciating a deeper truth: the fact that 'art' and 'history' are co-constructed artefacts of the great enterprise of modernity; interdependent epistemological technologies linked to a larger matrix of practices and institutions, which I am calling *museography* (itself thus a species of pantography, which in turn is a dimension of allegory). Since the late eighteenth century, these co-implicative practices have functioned to render an object-domain called 'the past' synoptically visible so that it might operate in and upon 'the present'; so that this present might be seen as the demonstrable product of a specifically delineated past; and so that the past might be framed and illuminated as an object of genealogical desire in its own right, configured as that from which a properly disciplined modern subject (the citizen of the nation-state) might learn to desire descent (or, conversely, might learn to abhor and reject). In the most basic terms, 'art history' is a mode of disciplining thought – about nations, individuals, ethnicities, races, genders and classes, *on behalf of* social agendas or political desires projective of that *other* dimension of the present, that obverse of the past and its complementary fiction, 'the future'.

Art history is thus a pantographic instrument for the evocation and connection of two Imaginaries; for shunting an insatiable desire for wholeness between two poles – two Edenic realms of integrity (where might be projected, for example, an indistinction or commensurability between the subject and its objects). These are the Originary past and the future horizon of its imaginary rebirth, resolution, or reconstitution: that which the past is imagined to desire as its fulfilment, through the agency of us in the present who work to bring it about.

Everything that art history has been for the past two centuries follows from this theological dreamwork, and an appreciation of it is necessary to understand the history of art history both institutionally, as a professional, academic discipline, and more widely, as a component part of correlative institutions and practices (including, minimally, art criticism, history-writing, aesthetic philosophy, art-making, tourism, urbanism, museology and the heritage industry). In the long run, the very looseness of this overall museographical matrix, the opportunistic adaptability of its component practices, and the refracted echoes of one practice in another, have proven especially effective in naturalising the very idea of 'art' as an innate and 'universal' human phenomenon, with varying but navigable manifestations from one society to another. Once again, a condition of the very visibility of Others in modernity's "common home" and "father's feast."

All of which has served to legitimise art's – and art history's – principal function for modernity as a powerful instrument, measure, and frame for staging the social, cognitive, and ethical teleologies of all peoples: narrative emplotments linking the past and future, origins and ends. The principal disciplinary function of museography over the past two centuries has thus been the co-production of modern subjects and objects – and by extension the naturalisation of an entire nexus of dyadic concepts resonating with and framing many facets of modern life. Since concepts of the object within the horizons of the western metaphysical tradition are invariably deponent, being linked indissolubly to co-constructed framings and articulations of the subject, any attempt to understand art history's institutions should entail a certain stereoptical attention to the ways in which this dyadic opposition has functioned in and for the history of art history.

Understanding the larger social enterprise of modernity – and modernity's core problematic, namely the orchestration of disciplined, describable and predictable relations between subjects and between subjects and objects (the topologist's haunt) – is essential to any attempt to appreciate what art history was all about. In saying 'was', I don't mean that art history is now 'over', rather that it was *always already impossible*. Even in its perpetuation and contemporary indispensability: we live, in modernity, in and as that impossibility.

Such a project will also entail turning art history and its avatars 'inside out', so to speak, to delineate the kinds of subjects that art historical objects produce.

How, then, may we understand the practices of Riegl and Benjamin in light of the above?

As already suggested, art history arose historically as one of a series of practices and institutions aimed at addressing the central problem of modernity: the nature and status of the individual as a subject of newly evolving forms of community and fraternity.[12] This problem came to be expressed on two broad fronts – synchronically, and diachronically. Riegl's art history occupied a significant juncture in the playing out of this problem, and his theory of art and history constituted an attempt to articulate an organic historicism capable of addressing both facets of this problem.

For Riegl, a 'universal history' aligning together the stylistic features that might be seen at a given time and place (in everything from churches to tchochkes) was to be the "culminating point of all art historical research."[13] The will to form (*Kunstwollen*) is something that must be shown as manifested in all aspects of the social and cultural milieu of a time and place. The formational principle of *Kunstwollen* is imagined to be imposed with equal force and immediacy in every facet of the material culture of a time, place and people. In this immanentist organicism, Riegl is of course prefigured by Hegel; but he differs from the Hegelian romantic tradition that constituted so much of art historical theory and practice in the nineteenth century (and that provided the template for academic practice in Europe and America) in two respects. First, in his thesis that in principle all styles are of equal value – a consequence of his position that the significance of an object is a function of the standpoint of the observer. Secondly, in his articulation of a historicism without a teleology – a notion of the consistency and necessity of artistic development, in which any conflict between (as Henri Focillon would have put it) the timely, the premature and the superseded, is not resolved in favour of unilinear progress, as in Hegel's evolution of 'world spirit' toward ever more perfect manifestations in cultural form (for Hegel, the forms and format of worship in North German Protestant Christianity).[14]

For Hegel, the systems and structures of a culture had proximate sources (national geniuses or *Volksgeister*), individuals who were in effect mouthpieces of the deeper source, the unfolding world spirit. History becomes a genealogy of that spirit as its effects are manifested in the objects produced by societies through their national geniuses. Wölfflin's 'anonymous art history', or an art history without names, consisted of a genealogy of certain aprioristic aesthetic categories, such as 'seeing', in a manner that is perfectly consistent with Hegelian historicism.

Riegl's aims – though no less historicist and essentialist than those of his contemporary Wölfflin, or his progenitor Hegel – were somewhat more modest. For him, art's history was a history of solutions to aesthetic and material problems. In this, as Hauser rightly observed half a century ago, the work of art became just an illustration of formal problems.[15] The evolution of styles consists of questions to be decided. What art historians are faced with are solutions, answers to questions or problems which it is then necessary to reconstruct.

Art history, for Riegl, then, is fundamentally a pantographic practice of double-writing or double inscription: the art object (in Riegl's case, literally any material cultural formation, from salt-cellars to cities) is the occasion, the catalyst, for a larger articulation (the *Wollen*), which is imagined to pervade equally every cultural artefact at a given time and place. The object is the answer, and the art historian is charged with reconstituting the answer's question. In this regard, Riegl's art history is completely consistent with the historicist project of modernity as outlined above, representing a minor inflection of the immanentist romanticism of the Hegelian tradition.

Walter Benjamin's approval of Riegl's art history was as much a product of his negative reactions to Heinrich Wölfflin as a teacher as it was a signal of a certain theoretical and methodological affinity with what he understood to be Riegl's project. In his 1933 review of the first volume of the *Kunstwissenschaftliche Forschungen*, "Rigorous Study of Art", he argued that the true precursor of the new type of art historical scholar was Riegl (because of his underpinnings in the philosophy of history) rather than Wölfflin, whom he relegates to the position of mere formalist. For Benjamin, one of Riegl's most significant accomplishments was the replacement of a 'periodic' history of art, made up of advances and declines, with a vision of historical change which appeared to be devoid of such value judgments, and which valued equally all styles and forms of artistic expression in providing important information about the broader and deeper properties of a time, place and people.

He also devotes much of this text to justifying his view that Riegl's *Late Roman Art Industry* – which appeared at virtually the same time as Wölfflin's *Classic Art: An Introduction to the Italian Renaissance* – was one of the most significant advances in art historical scholarship, by aligning it with a tradition in various fields (particularly philology and literary study) of using the insignificant and minute to evoke universal principles and properties of cultural life. Benjamin, in an enthusiastic letter to Linfert in 1931, remarked on "numerous and profound affinities between our work."[16] Benjamin notes that Riegl's 1898 essay "Kunstgeschichte und Universalgeschichte" was "a penetrating interpretation of the individual work which, without in any way betraying its principles, uncovers laws and problems of the development of art as a whole."[17]

A paradigm, in fact, of Benjamin's own pantographic desire to redeem the meaningfulness of the past through certain *keys* that would decipher the broad topography of modernity, thereby releasing its utopian promise that had become buried under the lucid dream-land, the *Zeit-traum*, that was the nineteenth-century. Riegl in the end provided Benjamin with one epistemological blueprint for his *Arcades* project; the greater portion was supplied by his tragic attempt to articulate together Kabbalistic theologism with Marxist materialism, which like all such colloidal dispersions, time has settled back into its constituent solids and liquids. To say that would be to open up an occasion for a more radical re-reading of Benjamin, one which, whilst long overdue, must yet fall outside the frame of this walk.

> Long did I wander through that fairy place
> By quiet paths I oft had learnt to trace,
> Dwelling on beauteous forms, familiar grown,
> Yet finding still fresh marvels, all unknown –
> Till faint at last with gazing, I began
> To turn from Man's unequalled works – to *Man*
> Then on a quiet bench I sat – and found
> Food for fresh thought in all that passed around:
> Seeking – no hard nor thankless task – to trace
> The *Soul*'s unuttered thoughts on every face!
> In many a soft dilating eye, I saw
> Joy mixed with wonder – eagerness with awe!
> While sterner men, with philosophic thought,
> Mused on what labour, led by *Mind*, had wrought,
> And giddy fair ones gazed, but heeded less
> The works of *Art* around them, than the *dress*;
> Finding in gay capote, Parisian shawl,
> Or lace-trimmed robe, more powerful charms than all.[18]

Footnotes

1 Anonymous, *Recollections and Tales of the Crystal Palace*, 1852, pp.3–6. This remarkable 150-page poem by the unidentified authoress of *Belgravia, A Poem*, ed., 1852, is divided into six parts, devoted, respectively, to an overview of the year of the Exhibition from its opening on May 1st to its Autumn close, morning in the Crystal Palace (with the joyous arrival of the Queen), a discussion of the building's resemblance to great edifices of ice seen by Arctic mariners, the lamentation of a mother for her daughter lost in the crowds, a description of the progress of two anonymous persons through the Exhibition one day, closing with a discussion of "the ties that exist between a great Author and those of his Readers who appreciate his works" (p.137). See the excerpt quoted at the end of this essay. The Crystal Palace opened May 1st 1851, and closed October 12th, 165 days later.

2 These issues are taken up at length in my *The Art of Art History: A Critical Anthology*, Oxford University Press, 1998, especially in the essay "The Art of Art History", pp. 507–525.

3 The present essay is in part a synopsis of chapter III, "The Crystalline Veil and the Phallomorphic Imaginary", of *Brain of the Earth's Body: Museums and the Fabrication of Modernity*, 1999.

4 Sigmund Freud, *The Standard Edition of the Complete Psychological Works*, ed., James Strachey, 1953–74, vol. XXI, p.36.

5 See Tony Bennett, "Pedagogic Objects, Clean Eyes, and Popular Instruction: On Sensory Regimes and Museum Didactics", *Configurations*, vol. 6., no. 3., 1998, pp. 345–371, and Paula Findlen, *Possessing Nature: Museums, Collecting, and Scientific Culture in Early Modern Italy*, 1994, pp. 100–109.

6 On the history of art as a inescapably orientalist enterprise, see my 'The Art of Art History' cited above.

7 My perspectives here are indebted to the work of, and to work in the wake of, Luce Irigaray. See the special issue of *Diacritics*, vol. 28., no.1., Spring 1998, devoted to her work, and especially the article by Anne-Emmanuelle Berger, "The Newly Veiled Woman: Irigaray, Specularity, and the Islamic Veil", pp. 93–119, and see also Luce Irigaray, "The Blind Spot of an Old Dream of Symmetry", Luce Irigaray, *Speculum of the Other Woman*, trans., Gillian C. Gill, 1985, pp. 41–68.

8 Susan Buck-Morss, *The Dialectics of Seeing: Walter Benjamin and the Arcades Project*, MIT Press, 1989, p. 211.

9 Walter Benjamin, *Gesammelte Schriften*, eds., Rolf Tiedemann and Hermann Schweppenhausen, with the collaboration of Theodor W. Adorno and Gerschom Scholem, 1972– , vol V: *Das Passagenwerk*, ed., Rolf Tiedemann, 1982, p. 494 (K 1a,8)

10 Michel Breal, "Les idées latentes du langage", *Mélanges de mythologie et de linguistique*, 1887, p. 321. Regarding affinities between late nineteenth-century

linguistic and art historical theories (and theoreticians), see Donald Preziosi, *Rethinking Art History: Meditations on Coy Science*, California University Press, 1989, pp. 80–121.

11 Cited in Buck-Morss, *Dialectics*, p. 324.

12 On relationships between the origins of the modern museum movement in the late eighteenth-century and European freemasonry, particularly in Britain and France, see Preziosi, "The Pantograph of the Enlightenment", *Brain of the Earth's Body*.

13 Alois Riegl, "Kunstgeschichte und Universalgeschichte" (1898), *Gesammelte Aufsaetze*, 1929, p. 7.

14 Henri Focillon, *Vie des formes*, 1947, pp. 82–83.

15 Arnold Hauser, *The Philosophy of Art History*, 1958, p. 162.

16 Letter of July 18, 1931, cited in Walter Benjamin, *Gesammelte Schriften*, vol. 3, p. 653.

17 Quoted by Thomas Levin in his edited and translated version of Walter Benjamin's "Rigorous Study of Art", in *October* 47, 1988, p. 88, footnote no. 18. See also Levin's essay in the same issue, "Walter Benjamin and the Theory of Art History: An Introduction to 'Rigorous Study of Art'", pp. 76–83.

18 Anonymous, *Recollections*, pp. 34–35.

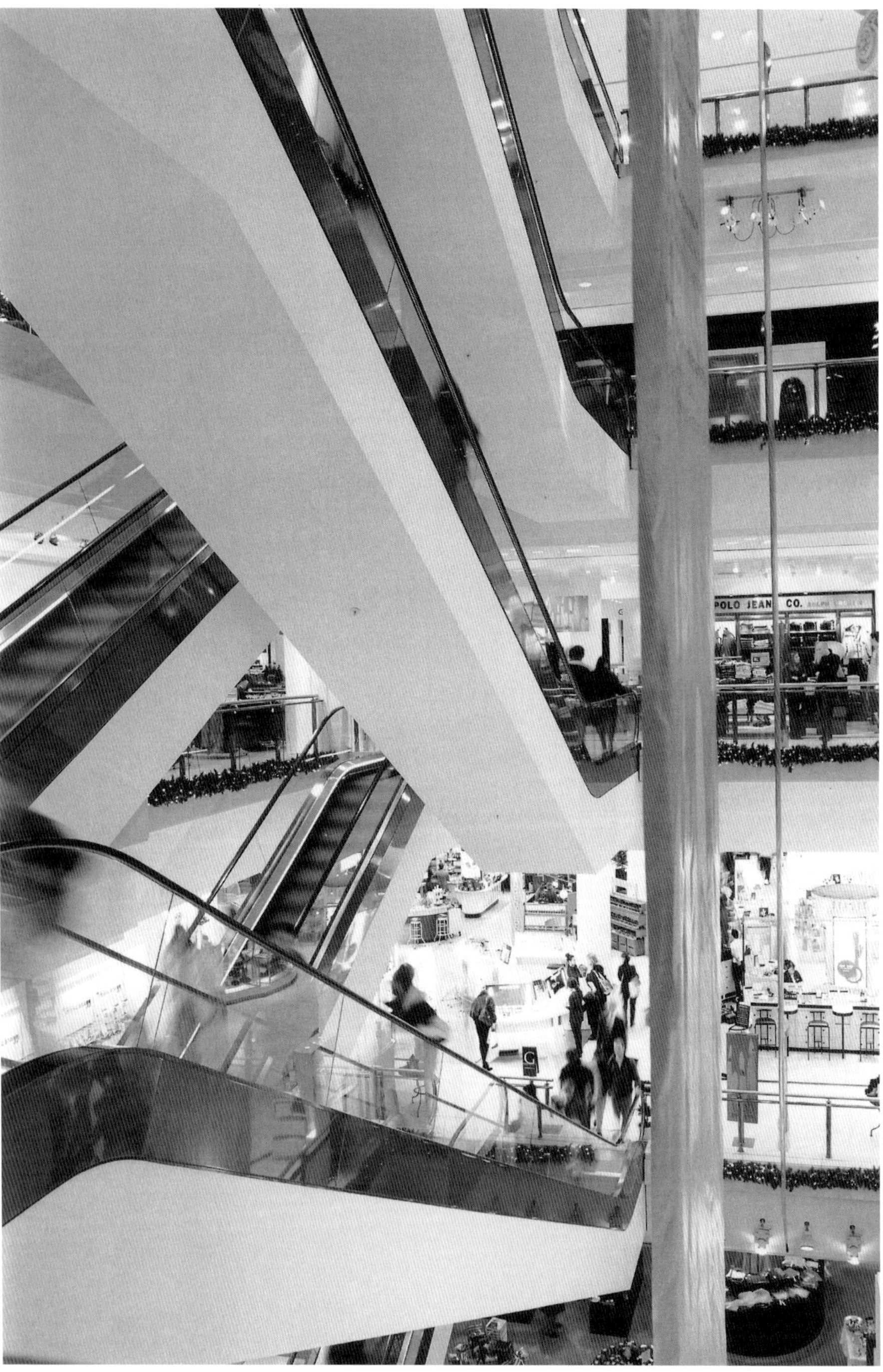

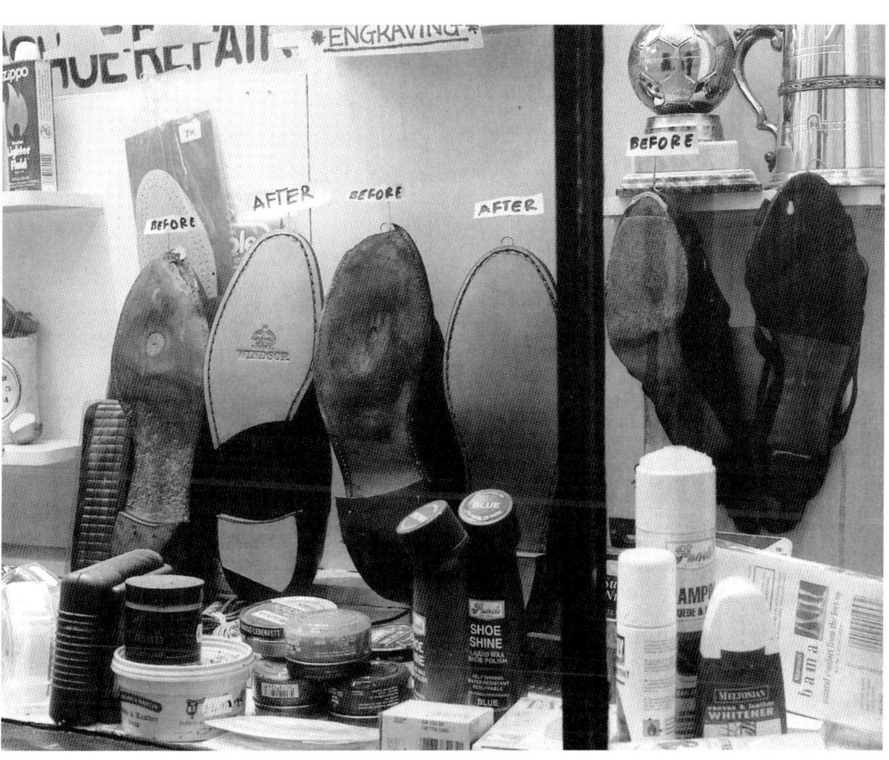

ENGRAVING
BEFORE
AFTER
BEFORE
AFTER
BEFORE
WINDSOR
BLUE
SHOE SHINE
BLUE
MELTONIAN
WHITENER

The Ruin and the House of Porosity

Alex Coles

Walter Benjamin's multi-faceted concept of the ruin felicitously brings into focus much current discussion in art and architectural practice and criticism. Think of Mark Dion's dioromas staging the ruins of the Natural History Museum, Douglas Crimp's work on the museum as ruin, Daniel Libeskind's construction of the monument as ruin, and Jennifer Bloomer's work on the ruin and the writing of a feminist architectural criticism – to name just a few. Elsewhere this optic is also evident in curatorial, historiographical, and ethnographic practice – most recently in the exhibition *Irresistible Decay: Ruins Reclaimed* at the Getty Institute, and James Clifford's reflections on the outmoded and collecting. However, while each of these practices, that represent only a small slice of the ongoing Benjamin reception, puts his theory of the ruin to work – and so transforms its operational procedure – the task of providing a fuller discussion of it has been neglected. Once this has been adumbrated in the first half of the essay, the ruin is telescoped through the glass lens of a contemporary art/architectural work by Dan Graham in the second half. The very act of telescoping the ruin through Graham's *Alteration of a Suburban House* (1978) causes the dynamic concept of porosity that springs from the ruin to be activated, so complicating the theory of the ruin and provoking a reading of many of Benjamin's most widely disseminated texts through a fresh optic.

Reflective Judgement

> ... it is a foregone conclusion for me that there is no such thing as art history.[1]

Benjamin's theory of the ruin unfolds from his sustained exercise of reflective judgement. Developed from a critique of the way Heinrich Wölfflin and Alois Riegl exercise Kant's theory of judgement, it is configured in terms of a series of sustained reflections on the laws that organise works of art.[2] In "First Introduction" Section V to *The Critique of Judgement* (1790) Kant asserts that reflective judgement is "the faculty of finding the universal law when the particular is given." Alternatively "if the universal (the rule, the principle, the law) is given, then judgement which subsumes the particular under it is determinate." Put in another way,

> Judgement can be regarded either as merely an ability to *reflect*, in terms of a certain principle, on a given presentation so as to [make] a concept possible, or as an ability to *determine* an underlying concept by means of a given empirical presentation. In the first case it is the reflective, in the second the determinate, power of judgement .... The reflective power of judgement [*Urteil*] is the one we call the power of judging [*Beurteilung*].[3]

Reflective judgement makes new concepts possible. For "when we reflect ... the underlying concept of the object prescribes the rule to judgement and so takes the place of the principle."[4] In this sense, reflective judgement is productive. The temporal dimension of reflective judgement is premised upon the delay that occurs – upon confrontation with the object – in arriving at the patterning of time in the object. Kant refers to such patterning as the object's *technic*.

The date of Benjamin's reading of Kant's *Critique of Judgement* corresponds with his first – and favourable – experience of Wölfflin in 1912. "There is quite a to-do here [in Berlin] about Wölfflin's *Klassische Kunst* (*Classic Art*). For me, Wölfflin's book is one of the most useful books I have ever read on concrete art."[5] But in 1915 – while attending a series of Wölfflin's seminars at the University of Munich during his doctoral research – Benjamin makes the following punishing judgement regarding the art historian's method:

> I did not recognise right away what Wölfflin was up to. Now it is clear to me that what we have here is the most disastrous activity I have encountered in a German university .... [His] theory might even lead somewhere were it not for the fact that, because of the inability of Wölfflin's capacities to do justice to their object, the only means of access to the artwork remains exaltation .... He does not see the artwork, he feels obliged to see it ....[6]

Benjamin's criticism registers the way he perceives Wölfflin's method as proceeding through a series of determinate judgements. Transposed into the words from his letter, Wölfflin's theories fail "to do justice to their object," directing him to "not see the art work" and thus not derive the law by which the work is judged and interpreted from the mind's intuition of its organisation. Instead it comes from a given system of already determined laws of perception and historical organisation. Congruent with Benjamin's criticism, and published in the same year as his attending the seminars, in *The Principles of Art History*, Wölfflin states: "to expose the individual differences which lead from the style of the sixteenth century to that of the seventeenth must be left to a detailed historical survey which will ... only do justice to its task when it has the *determining concepts* at its disposal."[7]

While Benjamin's rejection of Wölfflin is premised upon a very selective reading of his output, the lens of Alois Riegl is far more conducive to bringing into focus the methodology organising Benjamin's own study of art. For reflective judgement unreservedly forms the entire premise of the most important of his books for Benjamin: *Late Roman Art Industry* (1901). This is on account of three organising methodologies: an unqualititive view of history, the production of the laws by which an individual work is to be judged from reflection on the work, and an interdisciplinary programme across the fine and industrial arts. In this way, Riegl's exercise of reflective judgement arrives at the *technic* of the object no matter from which period or discipline the work originates.

Riegl avoids judging late Roman art by past classical standards – an exercise of determinate judgement which subordinates late Roman art to the classical period, viewing it as a "decay" of standards. Indeed, "to destroy this prejudice [was] the principle object" of Riegl's study. However, in a moment of correspondence with Wölfflin, Riegl holds a point of contention with those art historians that view the progression of artistic style through the qualitative "symbolic analogy" of "bud, bloom, decay." But where Wölfflin suggested that such a qualitative analogy should be renounced, Riegl sustains it, only to warp it, thus relating the full subversive force of his doctrine of judgement.[8] For Riegl maintains that only "a scholar whose interests in the fine arts do not stop at the border of classics" is a scholar who is able to "recognise the seeds and bud of new life even in works of the very late antiquity among signs of death and decay."[9] Under the legislation of reflective judgement, the premise of his task is to "demonstrate the existence of the laws peculiar to late Roman art."[10]

The methodology informing Riegl's interpretation of artefacts from both the industrial and the fine arts is embedded in his conviction that to understand fully the laws governing an age one must look beyond the fine arts, for these "basic laws" are "in effect in all media during the late Roman period. Therefore, observations in each single field are valid for all others and thus support and enhance one another."[11] Whereas for Wölfflin, following his doctoral dissertation *Prologomena to a Psychology of Architecture* (1886), an exclusive survey of only the fine arts was deemed necessary, thus determining the scope of his study prior to its commencement.

Riegl's perpetual exercising of reflective judgement through the three organising methodologies had immense influence upon Benjamin. This suggests that Benjamin absorbed Kant's exegesis of reflective judgement indirectly through Riegl.[12] Benjamin's first reading of Riegl can be dated to as early as 1914, suggesting a further reason for his rejecting Wölfflin the following year. The city portrait "Berlin Chronicle" (1931) finds Benjamin recalling a visit to an antique dealer who held examples of Roman craft work. "I remember distinctly the engrossment with which, under the impression of Alois Riegl's *Late Roman Art Industry*, which I had recently studied, I contemplated the breastplates made from sheet gold and garnet adorned bracelets."[13] Benjamin is especially drawn to Riegl's chapter devoted to the art industry in which he unfolds his theory of perception. This is developed in correspondence with the "last and richest step of development, which belongs exclusively to late Roman times ... represented through works with inlaid garnets, which brought a deep full red colour in contrast to a glistening gold."[14] In fact, Riegl's influence does not find its way into Benjamin's writing until 1916, namely, in the fragment "The Role of Language in *Trauerspiel* and Tragedy". This is announced when Benjamin delivers his judgement of the achievement of the Baroque, and with this, his methodological approach towards history: "The world of the *Trauerspiel* is a particular one that asserts its great and equal stature even against the tragedy."[15] Such a privileging of a marginal domain or epoch of 'decline' was typical of Riegl's practice. This fragment, along with a series of others, forms the beginnings of a whole book devoted to the overlooked and underprivileged genre of the Baroque mourning play, *The Origin of German Tragic Drama* (1928). The book announces Benjamin's fascination with the playwrights and poets of the German Baroque, accounted for through the particularity of their focus on history, nature and time. "Nature was not seen by them in bud and bloom, but in the over-ripeness and decay of her creations."[16] This is also where Benjamin first develops his theory of the ruin – through emphasising how time strips works of art of their former beauty.

In "Books that Remain Alive" (1929) Benjamin clarifies his perception of Riegl's view of history when he refers to "the master, who penetrates so far into the historical conditions that he is able to trace the curve of their heartbeat as the line of their forms. The only such master has been Riegl ... in whom the deep insight into the material will [*Wollen*] of an era expresses itself conceptually as the analysis of its formal canon." Two years later, in his "Rigorous Study of Art" (1933) – a review of a new Riegl-inspired art journal of the second Viennese School – Benjamin makes a number of acute observations regarding how Riegl

> ... differentiates the methodology of the older practice [of art history] based on universal history from a new approach to the study of art to which he himself paved the way. The latter consists of a penetrating interpretation of the individual work which ... uncovers laws and problems of art as a whole.[17]

Benjamin's absorption of Riegl's practice of reflective judgement – namely, his method of undertaking "a penetrating interpretation of the individual work" to uncover "laws ... of art as a whole" – is nowhere more apparent than in his work on art and technology. This also announces the influence of Riegl's sensitivity towards the way technology is patterned in the work of fine or industrial art through artistic technique.

There is a passage from Riegl's "The Modern Cult of Monuments: Its Character and Its Origin" (1903) that Benjamin includes in an earlier version of "The Work of Art in the Age of Mechanical Reproduction" (1935–1939). A discussion of this completely recasts received perceptions about the essay – especially in terms of its underplayed reliance on Riegl. In Section II of the first version of the essay, the appropriated passage from Riegl assists Benjamin in making his most radical move. Benjamin suggests that 'aura' was invented by the Greeks to compensate for the inadequacy of their means of reproduction, which only allowed them to produce replicas of bronzes, terracottas and coins. "All other works of art were unique and technically not reproducible. Therefore they must have been made for eternity. The Greeks were directed by the state of their technology to produce eternal values in their art."[18] Thus reproduction is introduced as a form of compensation. In "The Modern Cult of Monuments: Its Character and Its Origin", Riegl suggests that "the development of modern techniques of reproduction promises that in the near future (especially since the invention of colour photography and facsimile reproduction), new and perfect means of compensating for the loss of originals will be found."[19]

Nevertheless, in the "The Work of Art in the Age of Mechanical Reproduction" Benjamin launches a sustained critique of Riegl. Premised in terms of a criticism of the art historian's inability to correspond the laws by which technology is patterned in the organisation of the object with the organisation of the social bodily collective, Benjamin asserts the critique by reconfiguring Riegl's theory of perception. While this is practised throughout the essay, it is only explicitly mentioned in Section III:

> The scholars of the Viennese school, Riegl and Wickhoff ... were the first to draw conclusions ... concerning the organisation of perception at the time. However far reaching their insight these art historians limited themselves to showing the... formal hallmark which characterised perception in late Roman times. They did not attempt – and, perhaps saw no way – to show the social transformations expressed by these changes in perception.[20]

Benjamin's reliance on Riegl is thus simultaneous with both a critique of him and with the refining of a theory of reflective judgement of his own. This is fulfilled in Section XI with a discussion of avant-garde assemblage, evocatively played out as a comparison between the painter and the cameraman. Articulated in terms of an analogy between the magician and the surgeon, the comparison yields the lucid image of the way the painter (the magician) "maintains in his work a natural distance from reality," while the cameraman (the surgeon) "penetrates deeply into its web." Thus, while the painter works under optical perception, the cameraman makes incisions into reality and so invokes tactile perception. Completing the statement "there is a tremendous difference between the pictures they obtain," Benjamin delivers the often overlooked crux of his argument:

> That of the painter is a total one, and that of the cameraman consists of multiple fragments which are assembled under a new law.

The new artistic media which assemble fragments "under a new law" legislate under reflective judgement. While they produce new artistic media, these new laws also destroy old ones – a point around which the entire essay converges. But Benjamin's theory of reflective judgement developed in "The Work of Art in the Age of Mechanical Reproduction" is more complex than this passage initially suggests. For Benjamin works out these new laws via a close-up shot of a piece of mechanical equipment – obeying Kant's theory of reflective judgement, whereby "the underlying concept of the object [its *technic*] prescribes the rule to judgement."[21]

Benjamin's close-up shot in "The Work of Art in the Age of Mechanical Reproduction", Section VIII, is of a film camera. "Guided by the camerman, the camera continually changes its position .... The sequence of positional views which the editor composes from the material supplied to him constitutes the completed film." This "comprises certain factors of movement which are in reality those of the camera, not to mention special camera angles, close-ups, etc." Benjamin's observance of the way the film camera provides heretofore unknown glimpses of reality through the use of close-ups leads to his perception of the way this assemblage is legislated under reflective judgement. Benjamin's method of reflective judgement *is* that of the cameraman (the surgeon): as close-up shots of details are "assembled under a new law" (*One Way Street* and the *Arcades* project are the apotheosis of this). Zooming-in on such details, whether of mechanical equipment or art works, lends Benjamin's exercise of reflective judgement a striking dynamic range. As before, the *technic* is worked out through a reflection on the way time is patterned in the object, except that now time is cut up and reorganised through the very medium (film). The assemblage of the work of art under new laws enabled by technology strips the work of art of its aura. It re-emerges as a fragmentary, allegorical, ruined work of art. Developed parallel to "The Work of Art in the Age of Mechanical Reproduction", "Paris, Capital of the Nineteenth Century" (the 1935 exposé to the *Arcades* project) consists of a series of sustained reflections on the effects of technology on late nineteenth-century Paris.

> The development of the forces of production reduced the wish symbols of the previous century to rubble even before the monuments representing them had crumbled.[22]

Benjamin is drawn to the way time has demanded the ruination of the iron and glass arcades, and the way this ruination is patterned in their detail. Through this process of reflection Benjamin arrives at the *technic* of the structure. In this way, the section of the exposé entitled "Fourier, or the Arcades" expands the theory of the ruin developed in *The Origin of German Tragic Drama* (as Benjamin's comments attest). With this, Benjamin elaborates Riegl's theory of reflective judgement by not privileging fine art and by giving a penetrating analysis of the particular. Within "Fourier, or the Arcades" a close-up scrutiny of a series of transpositions causes Benjamin to announce, "the ruin of the Paris arcades, the process of decay of an architectural style." Just two of these transpositions are: the revival of old architectural styles through newly developed materials (glass and iron), and the introduction of new forms of lighting – to replace the old gas lighting – into structures for which they were not designed. From these two examples, the way through which the arcades were ruined both by the past (the revival of Pompeian columns), the present ("the development of the forms of production," such as electric lighting), and the future (bearing increased technological development, and its counter tendency of revivalism) comes to the fore.

Splicing Scattered Fragments

Ruination is patterned in Dan Graham's project *Alteration of a Suburban House* (1978) by splicing together two fragments from opposing archetypes of the modern Western home: Mies van der Rohe's glass house, and an American suburban tract house. This is made more complex, however, by the way Graham asserts his methodology in producing an immanent critique of an earlier moment of interrogation of the American suburban house. This earlier moment was undertaken by Gordon Matta-Clark in 1974 in New Jersey.

In *Splitting*, Matta-Clark performs an architectural operation on a suburban tract house. He first "sliced through all the structural surfaces," thereby "dividing the building in half," and then bevelled down the foundation so that the rear half could be slightly lowered, and the 'split' could be introduced by tilting the two halves outwards. Matta-Clark's practice, in Graham's words, of cutting away "sections of the floor or walls to create a view from one space into another," is a gesture that is a direct critique of the configuration of the urban fabric in terms of private and public space.[23]

Setting the *Alteration* project next to *Splitting* highlights the fact that while Matta-Clark's work is *completed* through material ruination, Graham's *begins* with a ruin. "In the spirit of allegory [the work] ... is conceived from the outset as a ruin, a fragment."[24] In this sense, Graham patterns ruination in the *Alteration* project "under new laws". Graham selects the first ruined fragment by sifting through the debris and rubble of Mies van der Rohe's architecture. This material

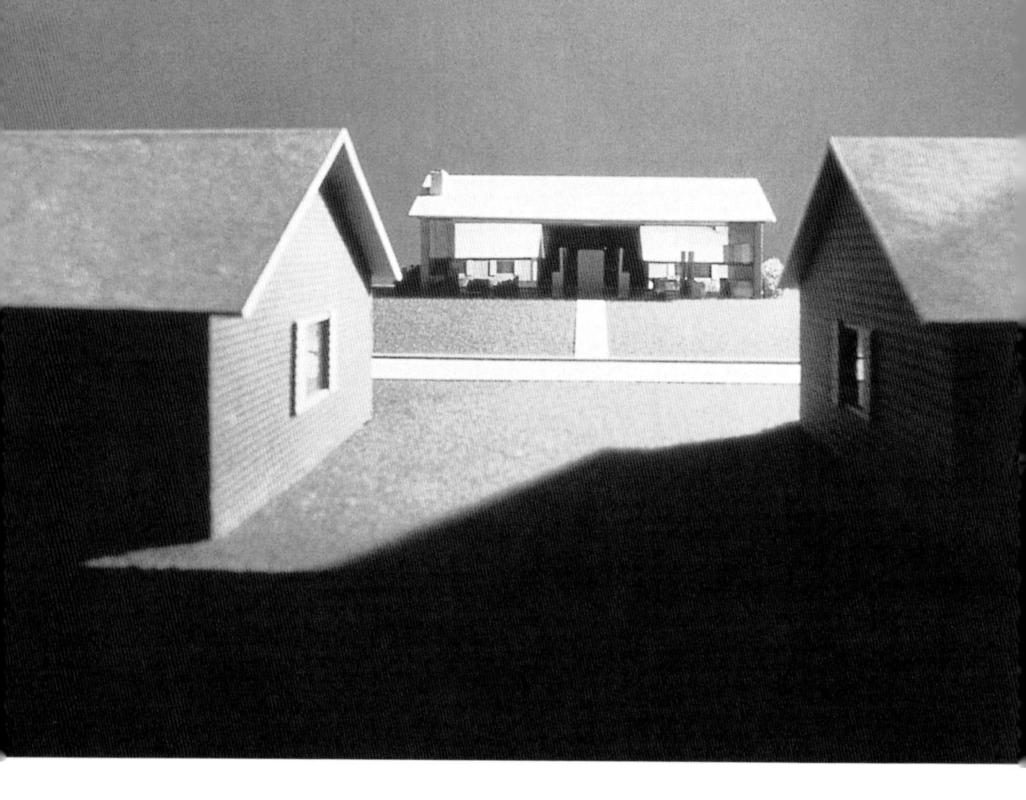

Dan Graham, *Alteration of a Suburban House*, 1978. Courtesy the artist.

is glass. It enables Graham to assert a critique of Mies's rhetoric of 'transparency', heightened in the buildings of the 1940s and 50s, where Mies penetrated dwelling places with light.

Dwelling places made completely from glass were initially a dream of Paul Scheebart's in 1914. While the glass arcades and exhibition halls of the nineteenth century were a reality, the notion of making houses from glass was still revolutionary. In *Glass Architecture* Scheebart states: "Our culture is to a certain extent a product of our architecture .... [Our culture can only be changed] if we take away the closed character from the rooms in which we live. We can only do that by introducing glass architecture."[25] While the notion of transparency is repeated throughout *Glass Architecture* and also in Sigfried Giedion's *Building in France* (1928), it is not put into practice until the 1930s by Mies van der Rohe.

Sigfried Giedion's theory of the glass house is expounded in both *Building in France* and *Space, Time and Architecture* (1941). Although he departed from the type of art Wölfflin discussed, Giedion developed many of his (and Riegl's) theories of perception – Giedion was also a student of Wölfflin's in Munich at the same time as Benjamin. While often critical of Wölfflin, Giedion never betrayed Benjamin's disconcertion towards the art historian.[26] Of glass houses, in 1928 Giedion writes: "[these houses] define themselves neither by space nor by forms: the air passes right through them! .... The separations between interior and exterior fall." Similarly, in *Space, Time and Architecture* (1941), he states "transparency is achieved by penetration through long window strips." It is this long window strip that Graham slices out of Mies van der Rohe's Farnsworth House. There the true deployment of transparency is revealed, as a further boundary between private and public was to be established by Mies at the parameter of the rural park within which the glass house was to be withdrawn. Graham's gesture in the altered house also refers to Mies's urban projects, such as Crown Hall at the Illinois Institute of Technology (1956). Herewith the unavailability of the ideal premises required to control the level of transparency caused Mies to deploy a further strategy, namely the use of tinted glass, so as to reduce the level of the reciprocity between the private and the public. For instead of encouraging a more fluid relationship between the private and public domains of the city suggested by clear glass – so the passer-by can see into the corporate office – tinted glass denies it. This is all the more enhanced by the appearance of the passer-by's reflection in the glass.

Built at the same time as the glass house, but for an entirely different clientèle, was the tract house. Mass-produced, prefabricated and erected on-site, tract houses were a cheap and effective short term answer to the post-war housing crisis. Graham uses a typical 'picture window' house from this period. Instead of being secluded within a vast park or employing expensive materials, such as tinted glass, many tracts were bundled together within small cul-de-sacs and organised in such a way as to enhance the intermingling of the community. However, many owners were to attempt to establish their privacy by furnishing picture windows with blinds and building picket fencing to mark boundaries. Because each house contained a whole family, the attempt to ensure privacy from the exterior through fences and blinds was transposed into the organisation of the interior, which was further divided up into small separated rooms.

Graham's altered suburban house is thus predicated on making imminent the procedure of critique undertaken by Matta-Clark on the suburban house in New Jersey, and is configured in terms of the splicing together of ruined fragments from Mies's Farnsworth House and a New Jersey suburban tract house. Patterned within the *Alteration* project is a multiplicity of time sequences. Like film for Benjamin, fragments are cut up and assembled together. The *technic* that results from this asynchronous configuration becomes even more complex, however, when the viewer's hypothetical relation to the altered house is considered.

Alteration of a Suburban House

In mobilising this critique of the organisation of the urban fabric in terms of private and public space, the *Alteration* project presents the following architectural scenario:

> The entire façade of a typical suburban house has been removed and replaced by a full sheet of transparent glass. Midway back and parallel to the front glass façade, a mirror divides the house into two areas. The front section is revealed to the public, while the rear, private section is not disclosed. As the mirror faces the glass façade and the street, it reflects not only the house's interior but also the street and the environment outside the house. The reflected image of the façades of the two houses opposite the cut-away 'fill in' the missing façade. The glass façade reveals the interior living area and displays it like a show window.[27]

The project consists of a scale model of the proposition, splicing together the frame of the suburban house and the glass façade of the Farnsworth House. In a gesture that subtly remodifies Robert Venturi's tactic of ensuring a reciprocal dialogue between his houses and the details of surrounding vernacular architecture, Graham's commitment to a critique of glass architecture is premised upon two moments in Benjamin's writing: the theory of the ruin developed in the *The Origin of German Tragic Drama*, and the discussion of the organisation of private and public space developed in "Paris, Capital of the Nineteenth Century". In the former, Benjamin states:

> "just as the dramatic structure is emptied, so too is the scenic structure, which looks elsewhere for its justification, now that allegory ... has become a hollow facade."[28]

"Conceived from its very outset as a ruin, a fragment" Graham's *Alteration* project empties the Farnsworth House of its "scenic structure," retroactively turning the private park and the villa into "a picturesque field of ruins."[29] This conception is most pertinent when considering a preparatory montage by Mies of a glass house to be built in Canada in 1937. In the Resor House, the steel frame all but disappears as it is filled in by the scenic structure of the Rockies. In the *Alteration* project, the "hollow façade" is all that remains of the Farnsworth and Resor Houses.

In "Paris, Capital of the Nineteenth Century" Benjamin states: "For the private person, living space becomes, for the first time, antithetical to the place of work. The former is constituted by the interior; the office is its complement. The private person who squares his accounts with reality in his office demands that the interior be maintained in his illusions."[30] Graham is far more assertive regarding his critique of this separation of the private and public in architecture, making a clear incision with relation to the glass buildings of Mies: "the sheer glass-and-steel openwork, like the modern bureaucratic thinking it reflects, is often a measure taken by modern architecture to cover over ... contradictions (particularly contradictions in the definition of public versus private property)."[31] The mirror fragment of the *Alteration* project slices the house in two; the reflections it creates produces a reciprocity between the street and the house as the two interpenetrate. Graham is a surgeon: directing his scalpel amongst the organs of modernist and suburban vernacular architecture.

Graham's assemblage of the *Alteration* project from fragments, sliced scalpel-like from their original context and spliced together, suggests a shift from the contemplative optical perception invoked by the glass house, to tactile perception. This is reinforced by the use of the mirror behind the glass. For the reflection of the passer-by and the inhabitant in the mirror is projected on to the glass: resulting in a situation analogous to Benjamin's discussion of the movie screen in *One Way Street* and "The Work of Art in the Age of Mechanical Reproduction", Section XIV. In the former, Benjamin almost describes the condition of the *Alteration* project when he states: "just as the film does not present furniture and façades in completed form for critical inspection, their insistent, jerky nearness alone being sensational, the genuine advertisement hurls things at us with the tempo of a good film."[32] "The Work of Art in the Age of Mechanical Reproduction", Section XIV, describes the possible effect of this "jerky nearness" of the "furniture and façades." For the images on the optical screen are "interrupted by their constant, sudden change" as both the spectator (the passer-by), and the inhabitant, shift position, culminating in "the shock experience [of] the passer-by."[33] The façade becomes a large advertisement for the interior of the house and the street. But the image it projects changes at the pace of each frame in film. In this sense the advertisement (of the interior) on the glass façade offers a critique of the separation of the private and the public, corresponding with Benjamin's comments, in *One Way Street*, on how the advertisement is superior to criticism. Thus Graham's critique of Mies's invoking of optical perception is announced through the inclusion of the viewer in the work of art (resulting in tactile perception). This also suggests a staging of Benjamin's critique of Riegl's theory of perception: Graham invokes tactile perception so as to disturb the tranquillity of the bourgeoisie's glass house.

The Law of Porosity

> Porosity is the inexhaustible law of the life of this city.[34]

In the same way that Benjamin's critique of historiography is premised upon a sustained reflection on laws of organisation, so it is with the city portraits. Written by Benjamin with Asja Lacis in 1924, "Naples" is the most euphoric of these. It insists that the correspondence between Benjamin's writing and Graham's *Alteration* project is brought to a climax.

While Benjamin toured the ruins of Pompeii during his stay in Italy in 1924, the essay he wrote about the visit focuses on the contemporary process of ruination underway in Naples. Forwarded in terms of panoramic reflections on the "law of the life" of Naples, the essay

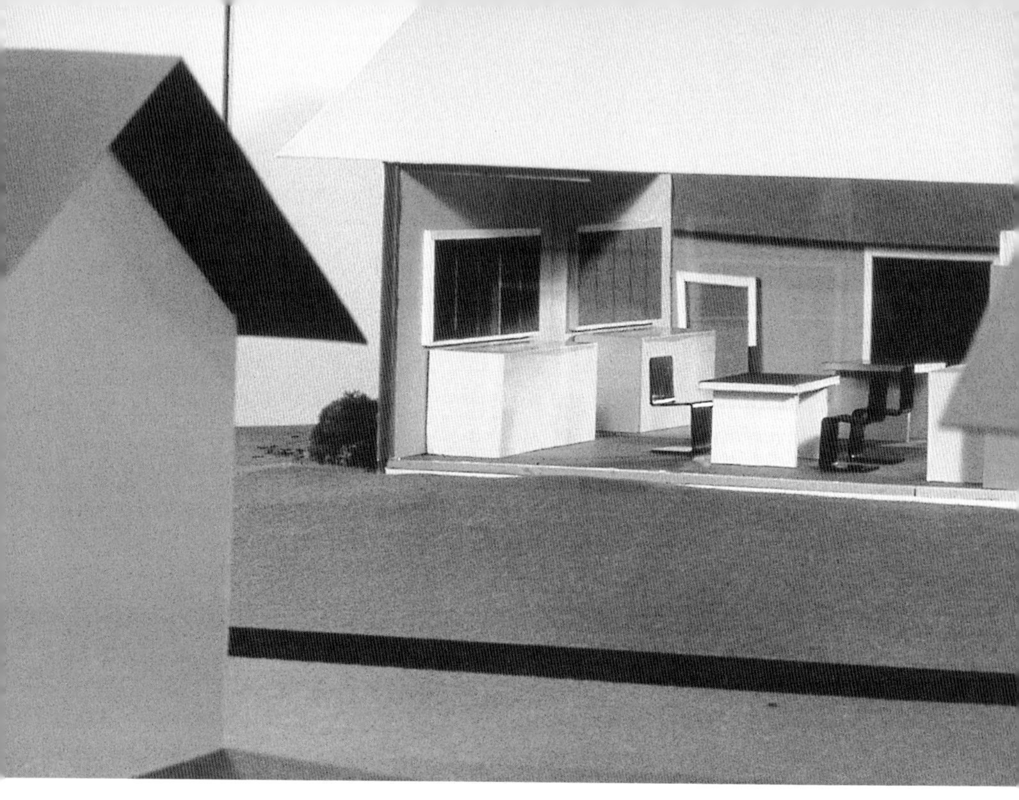

Dan Graham, *Alteration of a Suburban House*, 1978. Courtesy the artist.

works up the raw material of the city into the spatio-temporal organising concept of 'porosity'. As a form of organisation, porosity is the *technic* of the city. Yet, unlike before, this *technic* is configured in terms of a dynamic co-ordination of the spatial and the temporal. Porosity is glimpsed at through a series of close-up shots of "the most binding part of the communal rhythm," namely, Neopolitan architecture – for "as porous as this stone is the architecture." Similarly, it is also produced by the ambivalent condition of the architecture: "one can scarcely discern where building is still in progress and where dilapidation has already set in." Benjamin further divides these close-ups into four categories of reflection. The first focuses on the porous spatial organisation of city life, "each private attitude or act is permeated by communal life;" the second on the temporal organisation of the community, as "the [weekend] festival penetrates each and every working day." The third converges around the possibilities porosity induces for illegal forms of organisation, as the *camorra* are "dispersed over the city and the suburbs." The fourth, and the most nuanced, is found in a number of scattered comments on how porosity can provide the poor with the initiative for joyous innovation: "poverty has brought about a stretching of frontiers that mirrors the most radiant freedom of thought." Benjamin provides examples of familial and criminal organisation. In both cases, and not unproblematically, for Benjamin the poor use the anonymity their dispersal brings to empower themselves.

The first category of close-up in "Naples", the spatial organisation of the city, is the most important for considering Graham's *Alteration* project. Porosity offers an account of the process of dissolving the distinction between the private and the public in the *Alteration* project which is far more complex than the one found in the Parisian city portrait:

> Similarly dispersed, porous, and commingled is private life. What distinguishes Naples from other large cities is something it has in common with the African kraal; each private attitude or act is permeated by streams of communal life.

> To exist, for the Northern European the most private of affairs, is here, as in the kraal, a collective matter .... Here ... there is interpenetration of day and night, noise and peace, outer light and inner darkness, *street and home*.[35]

The correspondence with the *Alteration* project is alarming. But just when it seems as though Benjamin and Lacis could not get any closer to describing the condition of Graham's model of an altered suburban house, they do!

> ... as the living room reappears on the street ... so the street migrates to the living room.[36]

In the *Alteration* project (Graham's house of porosity) "the street migrates into the living room" as the opposite houses "fill-in the missing façade" of the altered house. "The external observer" is situated both in and out of the house. Thus, while the initial activity of splicing results in a montage (of the elements of glass and the suburban house), the relationship engendered by the mirror and the glass façade between the street and the home suggests a more dynamic form of montage. Depending on the hypothetical viewpoint of the passer-by, the street and the interior of the home appear to sit next to each other through their reflection in the mirror – and with a slight move to the side, they retain their former configuration. The permeable glass surface is a membrane shot through with a spatio-temporal dynamic. For as the flickering image of the intermingling of the passer-by and the inhabitant are projected on to the membrane, it dissolves, only reappearing in the image of their activity. Amid the ebb and flow of movement, the flickering image appears as a mirage of suburban porosity to both the inhabitant and the passer-by.

Benjamin's experience in Naples is the reverse to that of Paris, where the law of the life of the city is produced by the strict organisation of the urban fabric in terms of private and public space. Both "Naples" and the *Alteration* project immerse their respective participants in a situation analogous to a theatrical stage: with the law of Neopolitan porosity, in Benjamin's words, inducing "building and action [to] interpenetrate in the courtyards, arcades, and stairways" (and so become "a theatre of new, unforeseen constellations"), and the law of the *Alteration*'s porosity inducing the passer-by in the suburb to, in Graham's words, observe "actual space in the house, as well as the actual space he or she occupies." When considered through the dynamic of porosity, a spatio-temporal dimension – one that is fluid and changing – is added to the theory of the ruin. In this sense, the specificity of the *technic* of the *Alteration* project is in parallax: as the passer-by and inhabitant are always shifting so is "the stamp of the definitive ... avoided." For "porosity results ... from the passion for improvisation, which demands that space and opportunity be at any price preserved."

The co-ordination of the spatial and temporal in "Naples" retro-actively enriches the theory of the ruin developed both in *The Origin of German Tragic Drama* and "Paris, Capital of the Nineteenth Century".[37] For with its emphasis on transience, only the temporal dimension of the concept was emphasised in *The Origin of German Tragic Drama*. And while the spatial and the temporal are developed in parallel in the Parisian portrait, they are not co-ordinated in as an exciting way as they are through the concept of porosity in "Naples".[38] The *Alteration* project thus complicates the adumbration of the theory of the ruin by refocusing the moment of its unfolding in Benjamin's work. However, it is not so much a telescope doing the refocusing – implying a shift from one point of focus to another – but a kaleidoscope. Smashed, the telescope becomes a kaleidoscope. The refractal nature of the kaleidoscope reveals traces of Benjamin's discussion of the ruin scattered throughout his work; not only in his historiography and art criticism, but in the city portraits too, with "Naples" figuring as the apotheosis of this. Given this theoretical correspondence, it is interesting to note that Benjamin wrote "Naples" prior to the "Allegory and *Trauerspiel*" chapter of *The Origin of German Tragic Drama*, while much of the rest of the book was assembled together during the Naples visit. How could Benjamin's experience of a contemporary "field of ruins" not have affected his theory of the ruin developed in the "Allegory and *Trauerspiel*" chapter of the book (written upon his return to Berlin in late 1924)? The experience of walking around Naples and absorbing the law of the life of the city penetrated deeply into his work.

Furthermore, these kaleidoscopic refractions also suggest a different historiographical alignment: "Naples" brings into contemporary focus the ethnographic work undertaken by Aby Warburg.[39] For while the purpose of Wölfflin and Riegl's travels at the turn of the century was to experience what they had seen in reproduction, Warburg visited the Pueblo Indians of New Mexico so as to conduct new fieldwork.[40] "Naples" is an ethnographic portrait of its own, converging around how Neopolitan architecture affects the rhythms of the life of the community.[41] Somewhere in between these works lies the origin of Graham's *Alteration* project in his *Homes for America* (1966), an ethnographic portrait of suburban tract housing and its inhabitants in New Jersey.[42] All three take close-up snapshots of the housing and inhabitants of their respective areas; moreover, like "Naples", by working up the law of the community from the particular, Warburg and Graham's portraits proceed by reflective judgement.

Benjamin's theory of the ruin thus focuses the past and the present *simultaneously*: as the emphasis on fieldwork in "Naples" from 1924 positions Benjamin both as an important precedent for the contemporary (the ethnographic turn in art practice begun by artists such as Graham and Smithson in the 1960s, continued by Martha Rosler in the 1970s and extended by Renée Green, Mark Dion and Fred Wilson) and the past (repositioning Warburg's work from the turn of the century). The recent debate regarding 'the artist as ethnographer' – a debate fuelled by Benjamin – is thus complicated by a consideration of 'the critic as ethnographer' and 'the art historian as ethnographer'.[43]

Aby Warburg in New Mexico, 1896.
Courtesy the Warburg Institute.

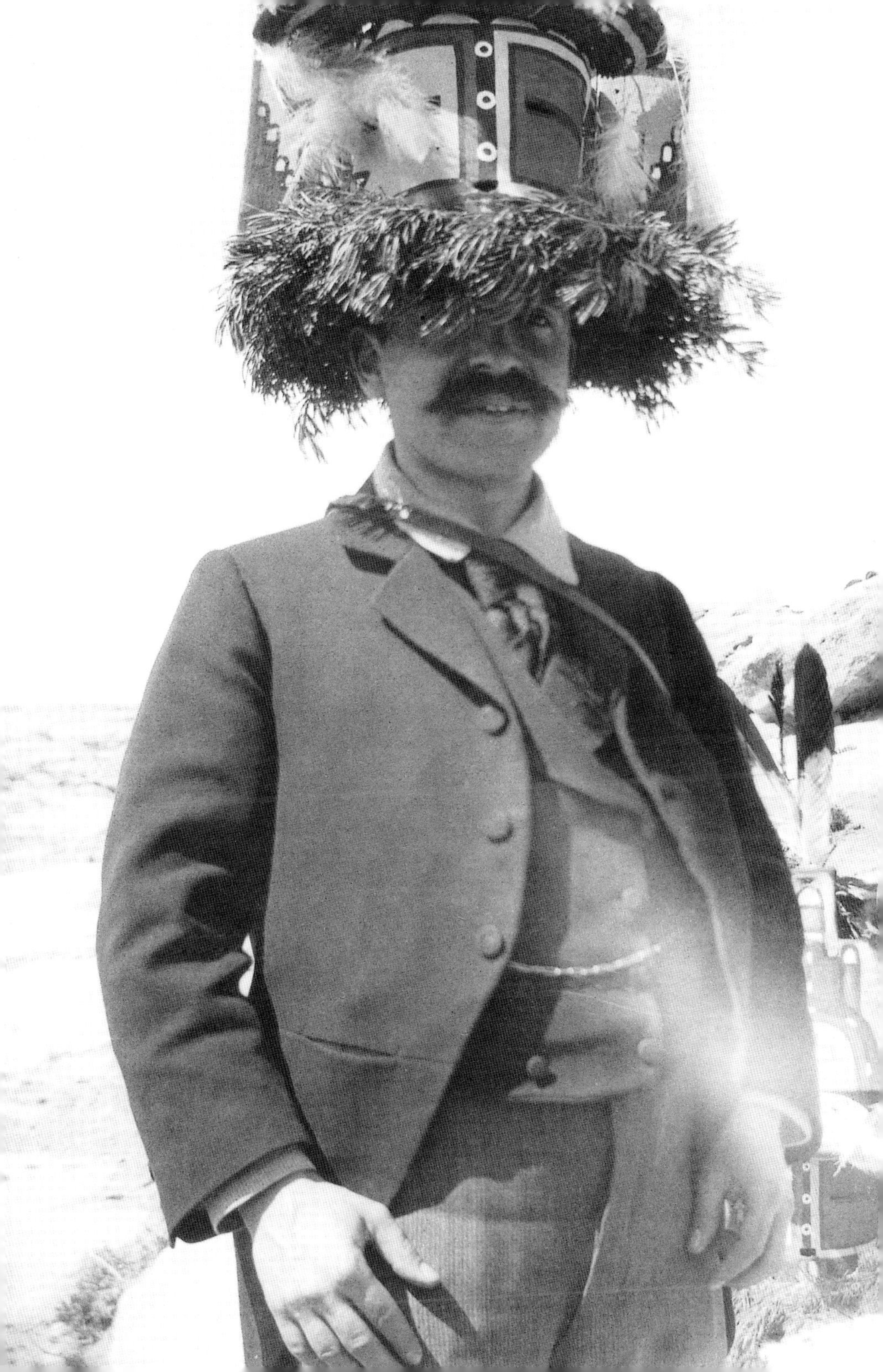

This correspondence between historiography and ethnography also brings the trajectory full circle – back to the lecture hall in the University of Munich in 1915. For after attending Wölfflin's lectures, Benjamin attended those of the American anthropologist and ethnographer Walter Lehmann, on the language and culture of ancient Mexico. This suggests the possibility that Benjamin perceived a correspondence between historiography and ethnography as early as 1915. In this way, Benjamin provides a fresh optic from which a new trajectory can begin.

Footnotes

1 Walter Benjamin, "Letter to Florens Christian Rang, 9 December, 1923", *The Correspondence of Walter Benjamin*, trans., Manfred Jacobson and Evelyn Jacobson, eds., Theodor W. Adorno and Gershom Scholem, Chicago University Press, 1994, p. 223.

2 While Kant's *Critique of Judgement* (trans., Werner Pluar, Hackett, 1987) has had a surprisingly shallow reception in art and aesthetics, with most critics avoiding the very issue of judgement – or the book altogether – the theory of reflective judgement has produced some very important work in feminism (Kimberly Hutchings, *Kant, Critique and Politics*, Routledge, 1996), political judgement (Hannah Arendt, *Lectures on Kant's Political Philosophy*, Chicago University Press, 1989), and socio-ethical judgement (Jean-François Lyotard, *The Differend: Phrases in Dispute*, Manchester University Press, 1988). It is thus time that a theory of judgement was woven into contemporary practice.

3 Kant, *Critique*, p. 399.

4 Kant, *Critique*, p. 400.

5 Walter Benjamin, "Letter to Herbert Belmore, Stolpmunde, 12 August 1912", *Correspondence*, p. 16.

6 Walter Benjamin, "Letter to Fritz Radt, Munich, 21 November 1915", cited in Thomas Y. Levin "Walter Benjamin and the Theory of Art History", *October* 47, 1988, p. 79.

7 Heinrich Wölfflin, *The Principles of Art History*, trans., M.D. Hottinger, Dover Publications, 1950, p. 14. (Emphasis added.)

8 Wölfflin, *Principles*, p. 13.

9 Alois Riegl, *Late Roman Art Industry*, trans., Rolf Winkes, Giorgio Bretschneider Editore, 1985, p. 7.

10 Riegl, *Industry*, p. 16.

11 Riegl, *Industry*, p. 6

12 At the time of commencing his reading of Riegl, Benjamin was still reading the *Critique of Judgment*, which he had begun as early as 1913 in Jonas Cohn's seminars at the Albert Ludwig University. Of these seminars, Benjamin commented: "Cohn's seminars on the *Critique of Judgment* ... have been chemically purified of ideas. The only thing you get out of them is that you read the text." Also, while at the University of Munich in 1915–1916, Benjamin took part in a working group who discussed the *Critique of Judgment*.

13 Walter Benjamin, "A Berlin Chronicle", *Reflections*, trans., Edmund Jephcott, Schoken Books, 1978, p. 32.

14 Riegl, *Industry*, p. 148.

15 Walter Benjamin, "The Role of Language in *Trauerspiel* and Tragedy", in *Selected Writings*, vol. 1, eds., Marcus Bullock and Michael W. Jennings, Harvard University Press, 1996, p. 60.

16 Walter Benjamin, *The Origin of German Tragic Drama*, trans., John Osborne, Verso/NLB, 1977, p. 170.

17 Walter Benjamin, "Rigorous Study of Art", *October* 47, footnote no. 18, p. 88

18 Walter Benjamin, "The Work of Art in the Age of Mechanical Reproduction", first version, *Gesammelte Schriften*, 1.2, p. 446.

19 Alois Riegl, "The Modern Cult of Monuments: Its Character and Its Origin", *Oppositions*, no. 25, pp. 37–38.

20 Walter Benjamin, "The Work of Art in the Age of Mechanical Reproduction", *Illuminations*, trans., Harry Zohn, Fontana, 1973, p. 216.

21 Kant, *Critique*, p. 400.

22 Benjamin, "Capital", *Reflections*, p. 161.

23 Dan Graham, "Gordon Matta-Clark", *Rock My Religion*, MIT Press, 1993, p. 194.

24 Benjamin, "Allegory", *Tragic*, p. 235.

25 Paul Scheebart, *Glass Architecture*, November Books, 1972, p. 41.

26 Wölfflin even wrote to Giedion in 1928 after receiving *Building in France* (a book Giedion had also sent to Benjamin): "Don't you think that secret lines lead from Renaissance and Baroque to Building in France?". See the new edition of Sigfried Giedion's *Building in France: Building in Iron, Building in Ferro-Concrete*, The Getty Centre, 1995.

27 Dan Graham, "Alteration of a Suburban House", *Rock My Religion*, MIT Press, 1993, p. 206.

28 Benjamin, "Allegory", *Tragic*, p. 213

29 In his highly influential essay on Graham's *Alteration* project, Jeff Wall discusses the project in relation to the ruin of "the blitz-krieged remains of a village" and also as "the first ruin in the building of a new conceptual art." See the second version of Jeff Wall's *Dan Graham's Kammerspiel* (1982), Art Metropole, 1991.

30 Benjamin, "Capital", *Reflections*, p. 154

31 Graham, "Gordon", *Rock*, p. 198.

32 Benjamin, "One Way Street", *Selected Writings*, vol. 1, p. 476.

33 Benjamin, "On Some Motifs in Baudelaire", *Illuminations*, p. 173

34 Benjamin, "Naples", *Reflections*, trans., Edmund Jephcott, Schoken Books, 1978, p. 168.

35 Benjamin, "Naples", p. 172. (Emphasis added.)

36 Benjamin, "Naples", p. 171.

37 This runs against the grain of interpretations of Benjamin's theory of the ruin. Usually "Naples" is mentioned only in passing (never in relation to the author's theory of the ruin) and is often referred to as a travelogue akin to those found in Sunday colour supplements; see especially, Susan Buck-Morss, *The Dialectics of Seeing*, MIT Press, 1989, and Peter Szondi, "Walter Benjamin's City Portraits", in *On Walter Benjamin*, ed., Gary Smith, MIT Press, 1988. Of the three most interesting recent books on Benjamin, (namely, John McCole's *Walter Benjamin and the Antinomies of Tradition*, Cornell University Press, 1993; Graeme Gilloch's *Myth*

and Metropolis, Polity Press, 1996; and Howard Caygill's *The Colour of Experience*, Routledge, 1997) only Caygill's really perceives the power of the concept of porosity, and so lets it readjust the very premises of Benjamin's theoretical doctrine. For recent shorter essays, see Victor Burgin, "The City in Pieces", *In/Different Spaces*, University of California Press, 1996, Iain Borden, "Naples: The Emergent Archaic", *Strangely Familar*, eds., Jane Rendell, et al., Routledge, 1995, and Howard Caygill, "See Naples and Die" in *The Anxiety of Interdisiplinarity de-, dis-, ex-.*, vol. 2, Black Dog Publishing, 1998.

38 This correspondence between the concept of porosity developed in 1924 in "Naples" with Graham's *Alteration* project also suggests a retroactive immanent critique of Benjamin's later adumbration of a theory of glass architecture. For in sharp contrast to the subtlety of the theory of porosity developed in the Neopolitan city portrait, in "Experience and Poverty" (1933) Benjamin naively develops the rhetoric of transparency into a theory of porosity: "Things made of glass have no aura. In general glass is the enemy of secrecy. It is also the enemy of possession." In a fragment from the *Arcades* project Benjamin states: "the twentieth century, with its porosity, transparency, light and free air made an end to living in the old sense." Benjamin registers his first experience of the glass arcade in "Naples".

39 Benjamin's most elaborate comments on Warburg are in *The Origin of German Tragic Drama*. Benjamin sent a copy of this book to Panofsky, a member of Warburg's circle, with the hope of a positive reply, especially given their shared interest in the Baroque. It came to no avail. However, Fritz Saxl did give Warburg a copy of the book for his library in Berlin. Now annotated by Warburg, this copy is still in the Warburg Library.

40 Aby M. Warburg, *Images from the Region of the Pueblo Indians of North America*, trans., Michael P. Steinberg, Cornell University Press, 1995.

41 Even in his dreams Benjamin projects himself into the role of ethnographic field worker: "I dreamed I was a member of an exploring party in Mexico. After crossing a high, primeval jungle, we came upon a system of above-ground caves in the mountains .... ," "One Way Street", *Selected Writings*, vol. 1, p. 448.

42 For fieldwork in Naples see Victoria Goddard, "A Brief History of Urban Space in Naples", *Gender, Family and Work in Naples*, Berg, 1996, and I. Pardo, "'Living' the House, 'Feeling' the House: Neopolitan Issues in Thought, Organisation and Structure", *European Journal of Sociology*, 33, 1992. On American tract housing see Gwendolyn Wright, *Building the Dream: A Social History of Housing in America*, MIT Press, 1981, and Peter Rowe, "Tracts", *Modernity and Housing*, MIT Press, 1993.

43 See Hal Foster's "The Artist as Ethnographer", *Global Visions*, ed., Jean Fisher, Kala Press, 1994. Also see Johm Kraniauskas's excellent "Beware Mexican Ruins! *One Way Street* and the Colonial Unconscious", *Walter Benjamin's Philosophy*, eds. Andrew Benjamin and Peter Osborne, Routledge, 1994.

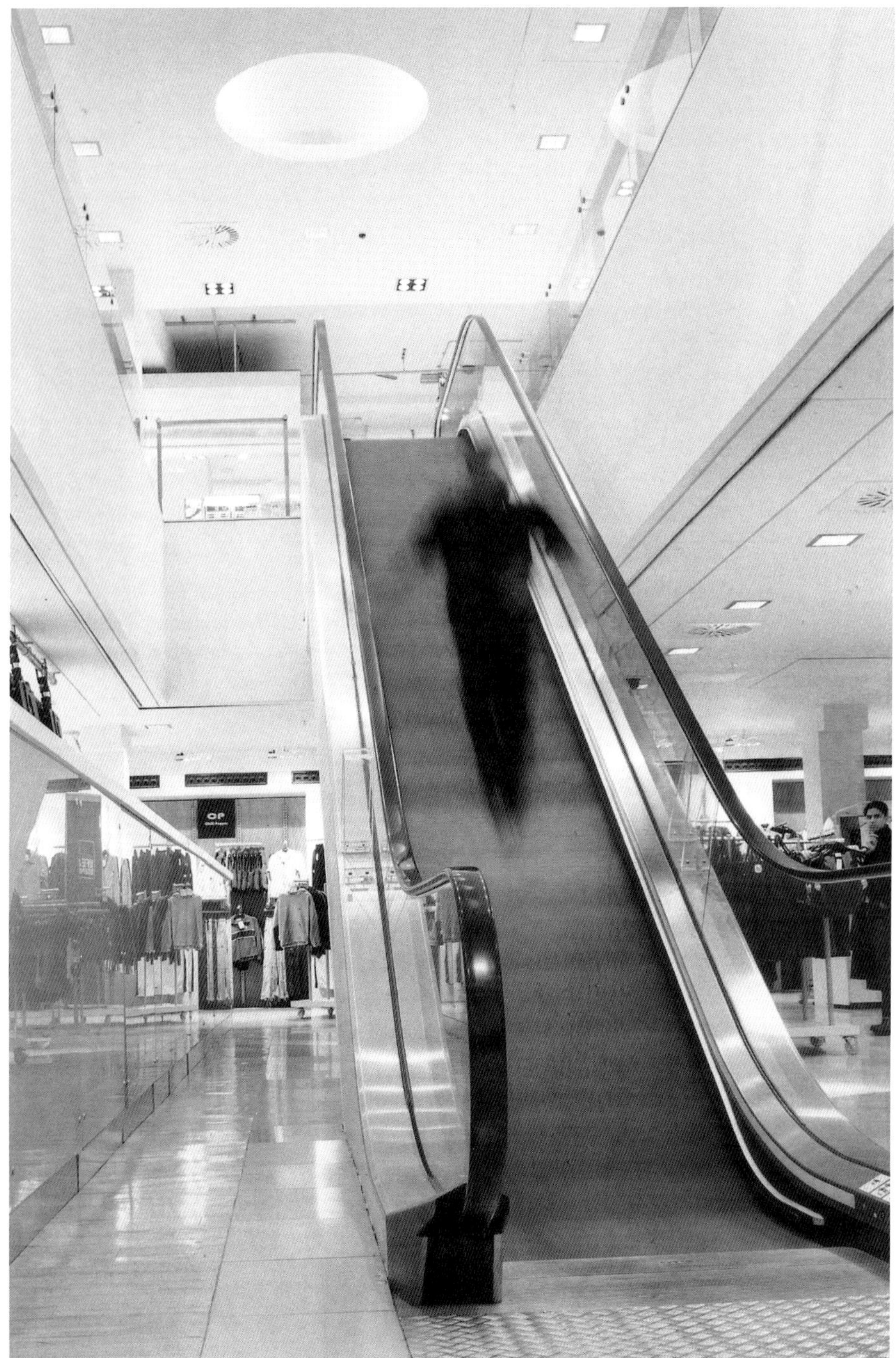

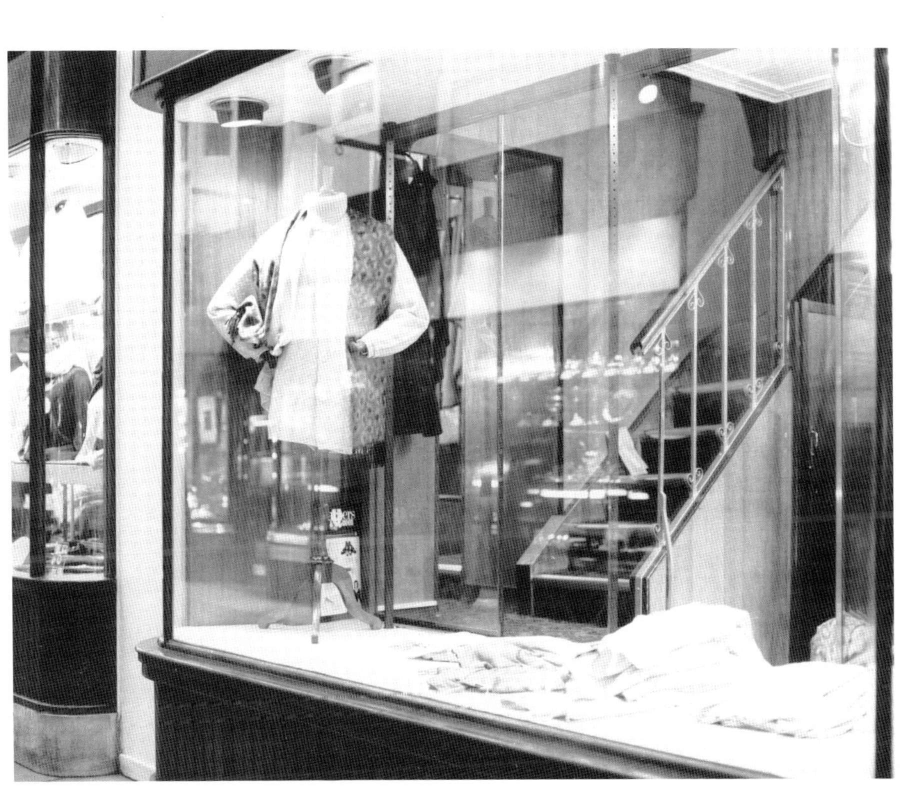

Thresholds, Passages and Surfaces: Touching, Passing and Seeing in the Burlington Arcade

Jane Rendell

> As soon as he set foot in the arcade, he felt a strong tingle of anticipation. The woman who sold costume jewellery was sitting right opposite the door to the side passage. He had to wait until she was busy, selling a brass ring or some earrings to a young working woman. Then he slipped into the passage and climbed the dark, narrow staircase, pressing against the damp, sticky walls. Every time he stumbled on one of the stone steps, the noise gave him a burning sensation in the chest. A door opened, and there on the threshold, dazzling in the white glow of the lamp, he saw Thérèse in her camisole and petticoat, her hair tied up tight in a bun. She shut the door and flung her arms round his neck; she had a warm scent of white linen and newly washed flesh.[1]

Sexual topographies described through the physical morphology of architectural space inscribe a series of territories, boundaries and thresholds, but the precise contours of this sexual geography vary culturally, historically and according to specific locations. In fiction and non-fiction alike, arcades feature as sites of dangerous sexualities in the city – of prostitution and adultery, of desire and fantasy. In

Emile Zola's *Thérèse Raquin*, it is a room above a haberdasher's shop in the Passage du Pont Neuf in 1850s Paris which allows the narrative of a dangerous love affair to unfold. In early nineteenth-century London, arcades with their predominantly female work force and customers were frequently depicted as places of transgressive sexual activity, intrigue, seduction and prostitution. The Burlington Arcade, with its proximate relations of differently owned territories (the external city, the internal walking passage and the individual shop unit) created an erotic choreography of passing, touching and seeing – a series of gendered spaces – which served to articulate male concerns regarding women's presence in the public spaces of the city.[2]

What follows explores the patterning of these gendered thresholds, passages, boundaries and surfaces in the arcades, both in relation to the specific ways in which activities of commodity consumption, display and exchange were historically configured in the Burlington Arcade and its immediate context of early nineteenth-century London; and also in more general relation to the ways in which arcades, and their conflation with the figure of the prostitute, feature in current debates in visual, spatial and gender studies. This is discussed here with reference to the work of two particular critical theorists and philosophers – Walter Benjamin and Luce Irigaray.

Arcades: Pleasure Houses of Commodity Consumption

> These arcades, a new contrivance of industrial luxury, are glass covered, marble-floored passages through entire blocks of houses, whose proprietors have joined forces in the venture. On both sides of these passages, which obtain light from above, there are arrayed the most elegant shops, so that such an arcade is a city, indeed a world, in miniature.[3]

> The commodity clearly provides such an image: as fetish. The arcades, which are both house and stars, provide such an image. And such an image is provided by the whore, who is seller and commodity in one.[4]

The economy – in both the narrow and the broad sense – that is in place in our societies thus requires women to lend themselves to alienation in consumption, and to exchanges in which they do not participate, that men be exempt from being used and circulated like commodities .... In our social order, women are 'products' used and exchanged by men. Their status is that of merchandise, 'commodities'.[5]

Arcades arguably originated in London as the sites of financial exchange and trade located in the city. By siting trade internally and rationalising the layout of booths, these commodity exchanges sanitised and regulated the market place, making it acceptable to a new bourgeois class, providing fancy goods – perfumes and clothes, rather than the food products of traditional markets. The bazaar, a multi-storey building, containing shopping stalls or counters, as well as picture galleries, indoor gardens and menageries, by using a name which evoked the exotic qualities of the merchandise, took the process of commodification one stage further. Under the management of one proprietor, counters were rented out to retailers of different trades, attracting customers to a wider variety of commodities – dresses, accessories, millinery.

Precedents for English arcades also came from France, from the Jardins du Palais Royal (1781–1786), a quadrangle with an arcaded ground floor and shops along one side. This has been described as the prototype of the pre-revolutionary Parisian arcade, a meeting place for wealthy society both pre- and post-Revolution, converted into shops. The first arcades, places of transition as well as exchange, such as the Galeries du Bois, the Passage Feydeau (1791) and the Passage du Caire (1797–1789), followed shortly afterwards. The first two arcades constructed during the early decades of the nineteenth-century in London were the Royal Opera Arcade (1815–1817) designed by John Nash and G. S. Repton, and the Burlington Arcade (1818–1819) designed by Samuel Ware.[6] A third London arcade, the Lowther Arcade, was also part of an urban improvement scheme around Trafalgar Square.

The London arcades were part of plans to promote the fashionable and wealthy residential areas of the West End around Piccadilly, Bond Street, Oxford Street and Regent Street as a zone of luxury commodity consumption.[7]

For Benjamin, describing nineteenth-century Paris, the new arcades were the ultimate image of commodity capitalism.[8] Benjamin's specific interest in the arcades, the first example of the international style of architecture, concerned their role as dialectical image, as a mythologised image of the effects of capitalism and individualistic consumption on communal society. The covered shopping arcades were the external material traces of internal consciousness, "the unconscious of the dreaming collective."[9]

His major work, the unfinished *Arcades* project, was to have been the culmination of all his previous thoughts through a study of Paris, focusing on the arcades as a miniature labyrinth within the larger labyrinth of the city: a "primeval landscape of consumption" through which the "dreaming collectivity" would pass.[10] In Benjamin's methodology, the arcades occupied a threshold position in space, time and consciousness: internal and external, past and present, dream and awakening. The arcade is at once a public and private place, a momentary constellation of past, present and future, as well as a dream landscape composed of everyday matter.

Various configurations of the female figure also resonate as part of what has been described as Benjamin's "micrological and fragmentary method."[11] The arcade is populated by a series of "figures," both real–life and thematic. As Benjamin links some of his most potent dialectic images in the *Arcades* project to prominent male Parisians: for example, Haussmann builds the "new phantasmagoria;" Grandville represents it critically; Fourier's fantasies are "wish–images, anticipations of the future expressed as dream symbols;" and Baudelaire's images are "ruins, failed material expressed as allegorical images." Likewise, all the other more thematic characters, the collector, rag picker, detective, *flâneur* and gambler are men, with the exception of the prostitute.[12] The prostitute occupies a pivotal position in Benjamin's thinking: she is an allegory of modernity, both old – as part of the 'oldest profession' – and new – as a commodity. In Benjamin's work many different temporalities appear in feminine form. Most importantly, an Ariadne figure, a "figure of the beloved woman," who guards the threshold between past and present, she opens the approach to the past, allows the recurrence of what has been – "the present that has been shall eternally be again."[13]

Luce Irigaray's work also allows us to explore the gendered spaces of the arcade, but from a feminist perspective. Irigaray has reworked the Marxist analysis of commodities as the elementary form of capitalist wealth to show the ways in which women are the commodities of patriarchal exchange – the objects of physical and metaphorical exchange among men. Like the commodity in Marxist analysis, the female body as a commodity is divided into two irreconcilable categories – women are utilitarian objects and bearers of value, they have use-value and exchange-value, natural value and social value. In "Women on the Market" Irigaray outlines women's three positions in patriarchal symbolic order: the mother who represents pure use-value, the virgin who represents pure exchange-value, and the prostitute who represents both use- and exchange-value.[14] Irigaray's understanding of how patriarchal culture locates the female figure in terms of her exchangeable qualities allows us to make sense of the representation of all public women as prostitutes. For Irigaray, the market is representative of the spaces of patriarchy as a whole, but it is also the case that "markets" as "real" places of commodity exchange, such as arcades, are the places most associated with prostitution in the city, where women are most likely to be conflated with the commodities on sale and represented as public commodities, as prostitutes, as typically exchangeable women.[15]

As well as providing a feminist critique of women's existing position in patriarchy, Irigaray's writing also offers women a utopian position. For Irigaray, the female subject position radically differs from the male and offers possibilities for a new way of living. The spaces of the female body metaphorically describe these new forms of culture and social exchange between men and women as equal but different subjects. Most importantly, Irigaray proposes an alternative female symbolism based metaphorically on "two lips", one which is not unitary but diffuse, diversified, multiple, decentred, fluid, with a double role as inside and threshold. Female subjectivity is, for Irigaray, a spatial condition, one of topology, space/time, dwelling, reflection, mediated through configurations such as thresholds, passages, boundaries and surfaces. All of which suggest alternative ways of interpreting and imagining the arcade as an architectural space of openness, interiority, mobility, fluidity, porosity, veiling and artifice.

Threshold: The Point of Entry

> ... the man in the gold-laced hat, who guards the entrance to prevent the admission of boys and improper persons.[16]

> There is no doubt, at any rate, that a feeling of crossing the threshold of one's class for the first time has a part in the almost unequalled fascination of publicly accosting a whore in the street. At the beginning, however, this was a crossing of frontiers not only social but topographical, in the sense that whole networks of streets were opened up under the auspices of prostitution. But is it really a crossing, is it not, rather, an obstinate and voluptuous hovering on the brink, a hesitation that has its most cogent motive in the circumstance that beyond this frontier lies nothingness. But the places are countless in the great cities where one stands on the edge of a void, and the whores in the doorways of tenement blocks and on the less sonorous asphalt of railway platforms are like the household goddesses of this cult of nothingness.[17]

> Woman is neither open nor closed. She is indefinite, in-finite, form is never complete in her.[18]

The Burlington Arcade was built for Lord Cavendish, the owner of Burlington House, to create a private realm, protected from the street, for an élite class of shopper. Arcades were represented as safe environments, usually under the management of one proprietor, physically secure with safety features, such as guards and lockable gates. Designed along strict and rational grids, with no hidden spaces or secret activities, these buildings promoted order and control. From the outset, entry to the Arcade was moderated, ex-members of Lord Cavendish's regiment being employed as beadles to guard its entrance and to enforce certain regulations. There were regulations governing opening and closing times – the Arcade closed at eight o'clock in the evening and was locked at night; the kind of movement which could take place – this excluded running, pushing a pram, carrying bulky packages or opening umbrellas; and noise level – there was to be no whistling, singing or playing of musical instruments. In contrast to the surrounding unruly city, associated with danger and threat, emphasis was placed on order and control – everything was in its place. The status of the Arcade was clearly indicated to passers-by at the threshold with the public street, the point of entry, where the presence of the beadles and the colonnaded screens indicated a transition from the unruly and public to the ordered and private.

For Benjamin, there was a resemblance between the threshold of the arcade and the position of the prostitute, both in theory and in everyday life. In the city, prostitutes were to be found on thresholds, framed in windows and on the doorsteps of buildings. As a dialectical image, the prostitute, like the arcade itself, was "wish-image" and commodity storehouse, she lingered on the threshold of desire and fulfilment, hovering between dream-world and awakening.

In nineteenth-century London, the thresholds of the Burlington Arcade represented specific concerns about the sex and sexual status of those who entered. The district immediately surrounding the Arcade at the beginning of the nineteenth-century was described as a "morning lounge" for wealthy young men.[19] The streets in the vicinity housed a large number of male venues, such as the clubs of St. James's Street and Pall Mall, and provided lodgings for single men of the nobility, gentry and professional classes. As such the location provided a concentration of wealthy male custom and played an important part in the commerce of female prostitution. A number of high-class brothels were located in King's Place nearby, and at night the streets of St. James's, Pall Mall, Piccadilly and the Haymarket formed a circuit notorious for street walkers.[20]

As a consequence of this location, the Burlington Arcade was specifically mentioned in contemporary men's magazines as a pleasure resort, and a place to pick up pretty women.[21] It was at the threshold between street and arcade, where decisions were enacted by beadles concerning who could and could not enter the Arcade. Men and women could be excluded on grounds of class, but prostitutes presented a particular threat for they might 'dress up' as respectable women and pass by the beadles or alternatively bribe them. The presence of prostitutes and possible confusion with them, meant that at certain times of day, specifically between three and five o'clock in the afternoon, respectable women would not enter the Burlington Arcade. As such the thresholds to the Arcade represented different emotions for men and women. For women they were signs of moral danger and for men they were sites of desire and the consummation of sexual fantasy. But they also represent something else.

One characteristic of women's sexual bodies is that they are precisely not closed, they can be entered in the act of love and when one is born one leaves them and passes across the threshold. In capitalism, where space as commodity is confined and controlled, thresholds are feared. Likewise, in patriarchy, woman as commodity is confined and controlled as and in space, the threshold that she is and the threshold which contains her are feared. Irigaray proposes the alternative female symbolism based metaphorically on the female genitals, a different syntax of meaning based on two lips – both oral and vaginal – which auto-erotically challenges the unity of the phallus. From the phallic point of view the vagina may be a hole, a flaw, but when viewed as a founding symbol, a new configuration of meaning can occur. The "one" of the male subject becomes "two" constantly in touch with each other, not separated by negation but interacting and merging, not unitary but diffuse, diversified, multiple, decentred, a threat to masculine discourse because of their fluidity and their double role as inside and threshold. Two lips allow openness. To celebrate rather than fear a threshold or opening, a point of entry, is to suggest a different social and spatial order.

Passage: Transition from One State to Another

> ... can't find as fair and fresh a maid, by blundering straight through Burlington Arcade.[22]

> This street is named Asja Lacis Street after her who as an engineer cut it through the author.[23]

> My lips are not opposed to generation. They keep the passage open ....[24]

As symmetrical streets and skylit spaces, arcades give access to the interior of blocks, provide semi-public routes through private property and allow ways of organising retail trade. The spatial layout of the arcades exploited possibilities opened up by divorcing the point of sale from the place of production. Shops could be smaller, allowing narrow strips of unusable urban land to be economically developed. The building of the Burlington Arcade allowed a narrow strip of land alongside Burlington House to be made commercially viable. Samuel Ware's early designs, based on the Exeter Change, described two entrances, four double rows of shops and three open, intervening spaces.[25] But as built, retail opportunities were increased by including unbroken rows of enclosed shops down each side, providing not only a space of static consumption, but also as a space of transition, a place for a promenade.

To consider the passage as a place of transition, a place where we might pass from one state to another, allows us to return to Benjamin. In 1924, an epistemological shift, one frequently referred to, occurred in his work. This was the year in which he met Asja Lacis. Lacis was a Bolshevik, an actress and director active in post-revolutionary Russia, who saw her own work as integral to revolutionary transformation of society. Benjamin and Lacis met in Naples where they collaborated on the first of Benjamin's city portraits, "Naples".[26] 'Porosity', the central idea of this essay and one which will be returned to later, has been attributed to Lacis. *One Way Street* is dedicated to her: "This street is named Asja Lacis Street after her who as an engineer cut it through the author."[27] Just as the passage of the arcade cuts through the surrounding urban fabric, starting at one point and ending at another, so too can we consider changes in epistemological status in terms of space. Whether the "cutting through" refers to Lacis's effect on Benjamin emotionally – he fell in love with her – or whether it describes the influence of her Marxist ideas of historical materialism on his own mysticism remains ambiguous. But it is clear that Lacis's passage through him, reminiscent of the penetrative act of the penis and of masculine phallic knowledge, radically altered the course of Benjamin's work.[28]

To be in one place and then in another, to be in transition, in motion, is a defining feature of the prostitute. Unlike the mobile *flâneur*, whose journeys though the city have been celebrated as forms of urban exploration and the gathering of knowledge, the passage of the prostitute has been cause for concern. The prostitute's movement is transgressive. As an intimate and private female figure moving through the streets and other public places of the city, she blurs the boundaries of public and private spheres, representing the uncontrollability of women on the one hand, and social decay and moral destruction on the other.

The Burlington Arcade was described as an "agreeable promenade," "walk or piazza," "long and commodious archway" and "covered passage."[29] To associate the place with movement was to suggest the possibility of transgression, but it was also the case that the arcade was the site of enacted transgressions. On the public street, according to the 1822 amendments to the Vagrancy Acts, women could be booked for being "disorderly," a definition which described such women as prostitutes.[30] The 'private' street of the Burlington Arcade provided a place with wealthy clientèle where it was possible for prostitutes to solicit in comfort without fear of being arrested.

The notion of the arcade as a passage, as a space of movement, can be thought of somewhat differently if we turn now to Irigaray's work. Irigaray's position regarding the exchange of women in patriarchy allows us to consider more precisely the kind of female movement which might be thought of as transgressive. In patriarchy, men distinguish themselves from women through their relationship to exchange. Men exchange women as and in space. For Irigaray, as mother, woman is off the market, excluded from exchange. Defined as natural use-value, mother is confined as and in private property. As virgin, woman is on the market, but once violated, she is taken off the market, removed from exchange among men. Defined first as natural exchange-value, then as use-value, woman is confined as and in private property.

The prostitute does not fall into the binary opposition of use- or exchange-value, private property or market. Once used, the prostitute is not defined solely as use-value, confined as and in private property, instead the prostitute remains on the market, both useful and exchangeable. Prostitution amounts therefore to "usage that is exchanged."[31] The prostitute stands for exchange, and further, as seller as well as commodity; the prostitute occupies a subject position and stands for the exchange of herself, for self-determined exchange. For women to be moved between men as exchangeable commodities is acceptable in patriarchal culture, but for women to move to exchange themselves of their own free will is not. As a self-motivated moving female body, the prostitute flouts patriarchal rules concerning the exchange and movement of women as and through space.

As well as providing us with a conceptual understanding of the mechanisms of patriarchal exchange, Irigaray's work also suggests an alternative and celebratory way of viewing female movement, from a position of female subjectivity. Here the moving female figure may be considered in terms of the "angel." The angel circulates as a mediator, as an alternative to the phallus, who rather than cutting through, goes between and bridges.[32] The angel cannot be represented in patriarchal terms since she rethinks the organisation of patriarchal space and time. For Irigaray, it is in order to deny the angel, or women's nomadic status, that men have confined women as and in the spaces of the male symbolic systems of law and language. The image of the "angel" in Benjamin's work also concerns women and movement – in passage and at the threshold. At different stages in his writing, Benjamin explored the figure of the angel in various positions at the threshold of past and present.[33] Like the guardian of the threshold of time, the angel allows the present access to the past, indicating that the threshold is not only spatial but temporal. The angel mediates space and time.

Boundary: Limit-line

> They are well acquainted with its Paphian intricacies, and will, if their signals are responded to, glide into a friendly bonnet shop, the stairs of which leading to the cœnacula or upper chambers are not innocent of their "bien chaussée" feet.[34]

> ... just as the living room appears on the street ... so the street integrates into the living room.[35]

> The wall between them is porous. It allows passage of fluids.[36]

The successful selling and buying of goods requires the right kind of environment, a seductive and convincing atmosphere and a consistency between the type of goods on sale and the design of the shop.

For the Burlington Arcade to succeed as a space for luxury consumption the design of the shops required careful consideration. Shops selling high-class goods were distinguished by having workshops either off-site, or at least located in distinct and separate areas. This separation of production and consumption allowed the shallowness of the shops in the Arcade. Such a spatial configuration set up a close proximity between those inside the shops and those passing outside. As a narrow promenade, the space of the passage of the Arcade itself, encouraged casual encounters and provided opportunities for strangers to touch.

In Benjamin and Lacis's "Naples" the central idea of 'porosity' places Naples against the historical disintegration of the Roman Empire where the boundaries of public and private desired by capitalism are as yet unstructured. In this nascent state, architecture does not consist of a series of isolated and monumental objects in space, but rather outside and inside are interwoven to create a city fabric where internal and external are experienced as complementary aspects of everyday life. Just as the inside/outside dichotomy is dissolved in the "Naples" essay, so is the public/private dichotomy blurred in the arcades. For Benjamin, the Parisian arcades are interpenetrations of public and private space, privately owned realms within the public zone, "the arcade is the classical form of the interior."[37]

Each individual shop was designed as a discrete and self-contained unit, with a ground floor, a basement and upper chambers, all accessed via a staircase. The upper chambers of the shops were considered sites of prostitution, and featured in tales of early nineteenth-century London: "the disgraceful and inhuman 'Doings' at the fashionable dress-makers at the west-end of town."[38] While millinery shops were represented as fronts for brothels and scenes of seduction, the upper chambers of haberdashers, for example in *Thérèse Raquin*, and of bonnet shops in the Burlington Arcade, were described in fiction and by contemporary commentators as the site of sex and of prostitution. The precise relation of the staircase from shop to upper chamber remains unclear from existing accounts. It is likely they were connected internally, certainly, originally, the architect favoured letting out the upper floors to the shop tenants themselves and plans from 1818 do show shops with internal staircases only. However, plans of 1815 also exist which show staircases positioned between the shop units, prioritising the likelihood of external letting opportunities.[39] The terminology used to describe the upper floor accommodation further confuses, the chambers being described variously as: "sleeping apartments," "dormitories" and "suites of rooms." But given the separation of upper chambers from shop, it is certainly possible that these rooms were used for prostitution, whether by the shop-girls themselves or hired out by prostitutes or clients.

The role of the boundary – to divide inside from outside – is already gendered. Interior space is most often connected with the female body and exterior with the male. In the Burlington Arcade we find that its original purpose was "to give employment to industrious females"[40] and that many of the shops in the Arcade were often occupied and owned by women. The implicit reference to home in the architectural layout of the shop unit – living below, sleeping above – along with details such as bow-windows, low doorways and fireplaces, allowed associations to be made with everyday domestic space and with the female figure as wife, mother and virginal daughter. But the intimate scale of the architecture, the scaled-down, miniaturised elevations combined with the lack of utilitarian servicing elements usually found on the exterior face of buildings, also suggested the more common interpretation of the arcade, as an unreal and dream-like space. Arcades were connected with fantasy, desire and seduction. Given the historical placing of this experience of the arcade – in the early nineteenth century – it would have been quite rare for an outside space to be covered and lit through roof lights. The quality of the light in the arcade would have been considered unusual, reinforcing an atmosphere of strangeness, of otherworldliness, of the unknowable, connected in patriarchal culture with the feminine.

Spatial analogies can be drawn between the box-like commodities the women were represented as selling and the female body. The words "piece" or "article," often used to refer to the objects sold by women, and "snuff box" or "reticule," often embellished as a "fine fancy gold worked reticule" or an "embroidered snuff box," are metaphors for the female body, specifically the female genitalia.[41] Likewise, the box-like space of the shop/home occupied, if not owned, by women shopkeepers and shop-girls, can also be read as a metaphor for the female body. Here the narrow boundary dividing the territory of exterior public passage from interior private shop was connected with suspense, danger and intrigue. The shop boundary operated as a membrane or skin, separating male from female territory, the known from the unknown, the decent and moral from the indecent and immoral. The places where the boundary was pierced, the door and the window, operate as metaphors of sexual penetration. The threshold of the door represents a point of entry that one may pass over; the threshold of the window, a point of view, offering visibility rather than passage through.

If we reconsider Irigaray's position regarding the exchange of women in patriarchy, this time in specific relation to property, we can start to unravel concerns about women and prostitution in the arcade a little further. In patriarchy, men own property – space and women, and women are property – as and in space. If women can only be owned as property, and cannot own property, then for women to occupy space in a way which suggests property ownership and to be engaged in space as subjects exchanging property (in terms of the buying and selling of commodities) is deeply troubling to patriarchal culture. Representing women as property, either by conflating women with the commodities they are selling or by confusing shop-girls and shopkeepers with prostitutes in their own homes, is an attempt to negate women's empowering relations with property and instead to describe women only as property – in terms of the commodification of their own bodies.

In examining the nature of boundary between passage and shop, we must also explore the material substance of the boundary itself. As qualities of the surface of matter tend to be thought of in relation to femininity and artifice, the surface of the boundary is a gendered one, but there is another way of considering the substance of the boundary in relation to gender. To do this, we must return to Irigaray and her consideration of mucus. For Irigaray, mucus corresponds to sexuality, to speech, to air, to breathing, to singing and to speaking – in short it is a medium which allows exchange between the sexes as different subjects.[42] Mucus exists at the threshold of the interior in order to allow access though touch. (Irigaray has argued that the interior cannot be accessed through sight, cannot be seen in a flat mirror, but understood only through the speculum, through touch). Unlike the penis which is part object, mucus cannot be separated from the body. Mucus is porous, it is neither simply solid nor fluid, it has no fixed form, it is mobile and immobile, it is permanent and flowing with multiple punctuations. Most importantly, the presence of mucus is essential to the act of love, to facilitating exchange between the sexes, and to engendering an understanding of boundaries which delight in their porosity.

Surface: The Outside of a Thing

> ... images of advertisement in a manner that savours of genteel prostitution; the prettier girls are placed at the window to attract male customers and dalliers. The labour is treated as a frivolity, and the girls are being taught to sell themselves.[43]

> The interior was the place of refuge of Art. The collector was the true inhabitant of the interior. He made the glorification of things his concern .... But he conferred upon them only a fancier's value, rather than use-value.[44]

> ... the duplicity of the veil's function ... used to cover a lesser value and overvalue the fetish.[45]

Through their design and materials, shop fronts advertise business, represent social status and attract custom. Luxury commodities require external display and so the shape of windows, as well as the type and amount of glass deployed, is a prime requirement. The shops in the Burlington Arcade maximised display and enhanced viewing possibilities by having shops with shallow depths, wide frontages, including bow-windows. The use of large sheets of plate glass, a modern and very expensive material, added to the perception of the arcades as luxury zones, and its spatial qualities – reflective, transparent and opaque – allowed a number of tensions to emerge between inside and outside.

As a transparent material, glass allowed an opportunity for presenting and protecting commodities. Close visual inspection of shop windows by passers-by was enhanced by the arcade's narrow width, and the transparent glass created a close, though intangible, proximity between inside and outside – commodities could be seen but not touched. As a reflecting material, as well as allowing a look through to the contents of the shop interior, the glass acted as a mirror for consumers to view themselves and passers-by, allowing views of objects in the interior to be conflated with views of the self on the exterior.

The display window, the glass surface of the arcade, where the shop meets the passage, was for Benjamin characterised by the figure of the collector. By desiring but not acquiring, the collector conferred on the displayed items the status of fetish objects, of exchange value rather than use value. Notions of collection reinforced the position of the arcade as interior space, by creating a resemblance between the collector in the arcade crammed full of commodities on display and the collector in his living-room surrounded by art objects on every surface.

Male fascination with the women in the arcade also focuses on the shop windows. Women working in arcades were located as window displays – their bodies operating as signage representing the commodities on sale. In Cheapside in the early seventeenth century, tradesmen's wives sat in purpose-built seats at the doors of shops to engage customers and entice them in. In the early nineteenth century, women were also carefully positioned in retail spaces, such as millinery shops, to attract custom. The pro-active display of the female body in windows and on streets, associative of the codes of prostitution, also suggested to the male viewer that the bodies of the women on display in the shop windows were themselves for sale. Thought of as prostitute, the female commodity represented the possibility of sexual as well as visual consumption.

The arcade was a magical space of enchantment, a site of intoxication and desire, where the enticing display of luxurious commodities promised the possibility of satiation through purchase. This tension between viewing and having, between desire and consummation, was played out through the surface of the woman just glimpsed in the interior, and through the glass of the shop window, the limit-line of the private territory of the shopowner, often a woman. The surfaces of skin and glass may be associated with the "feminine" enigma which provokes a tension between appearance and concealment and the "feminine" surface which provides a screen for the projection of fantasy.[46] The inability to decipher the "true" sexual identity of a woman from her appearance offers sexual titillation – demure exterior might indicate a suppressed wantonness. Likewise a discreet shop front indicates little of its elusive interior.[47]

Although 'looking' and 'being looked at' are, in certain cases, reciprocal positions which can both be adopted by one sex, psychoanalytic theories of the male gaze and the female spectacle tend to consider women only as looked-at objects on display. Female bodies in the arcade are represented in terms of surface display, as sites of the male gaze and male desire. Hence a concern with the surface is connected with femininity, and a problem with the surface in terms of vanity or artifice, is perceived as a female problem: the vanity of the commodity. Irigaray argues that this "troubled" relationship women have with the surface is a result of their role as mothers. As mother, woman represents "place" for man, so that she herself is nude and has to create her own covering.[48]

The displayed surface of the female body, and by extension the surface of a building, is expected to represent exactly what lies beneath. If it seeks to disguise or to cover, as in a veil, then this is perceived as duplicitous. But the displayed surface of the body is yet more complex. Composed of a close relationship between clothes and the fleshy body, clothing is expected to be neither too revealing nor too obscuring of the body that lies beneath. To cover too little is immodest, to cover too much is dishonest. Both transgressions are connected with excess, extravagance and with prostitution. An excess of flesh represents exposure and wantonness, and an excess of clothing in the form of decoration represented artifice and vanity.

The connection of arcades with the sexual availability of women, ornamentation and deceit was reinforced through their origin as a foreign building type. Their precedent, the Galeries du Palais Royale in Paris, was the gathering place for libertines before and during the Revolution. The presence of prostitutes in the arcades was complemented by the commercial activities of gambling, drinking and jewellery-selling in the shops: "where some traded goods while others traded on their charms." In one house, a jewellery shop was located on the ground floor, selling all "descriptions of female ornament," whilst directly above was a café full of men, presided over by a "lady generally of more than ordinary female attractions, who was very much décolleté."[49]

The use of Parisian precedent, providing flats above shops, in John Nash's designs for the arcaded Quadrant Colonnade section of Regent Street increased the association of arcades and colonnades with "foreign" and therefore suspicious attitudes. Some of these lodgings were rented out to performers at the Italian Opera House, often French, Italians and Germans. The mixture of foreign building types and people at a time when France and England were political rivals was perceived as a sign of immorality. Prostitutes were considered to be French, while, conversely, the French women living in the vicinity were thought to be prostitutes. The connection made between places selling ornamental luxury commodities and prostitution may be explained by the French example of prostitution above jewellery shops.

It is also possible to consider the female subject's concern with surface from a different perspective. Woman may well *be* masquerade – the display or performance of femininity (for some an alienated or false version of femininity), but it is also possible to reclaim the masquerade from a subject position. Irigaray's work utilises the operation of mimicry as a conscious subversive strategy for destabilising and defamiliarising masquerade, for flaunting spectacle and speech. Irigaray suggests that by deliberately assuming the feminine style assigned to them, women can uncover the mechanisms which exploit them. Examining the possibilities for flaunting it, for playing out relations of self-reflection and self-display, allows women a liberating notion of being viewed, and so having a different relationship to reflecting and transparent surfaces.

> All these products are on the point of entering the market as commodities. But they still linger on the threshold. From this epoch spring the arcades and the interiors, the exhibition halls and dioramas. They are residues of a dream-world. The utilisation of dream-elements in waking is the text-book example of dialectical thought. Hence dialectical thought is the organ of historical awakening. Every epoch dreams the next, but while dreaming impels it to wakefulness. It bears its end within itself, and reveals it.[50]

> ... woman must be nude because she is not situated, does not situate herself in her place. Her clothes, her makeup, and her jewels are the things with which she tries to create her container(s), her envelope(s). She cannot make use of the envelope that she is, and must create artificial ones.[51]

In the 1830s, arcades and colonnades were synonymous with prostitution. New plans for colonnades around the Italian Opera House in the urban vicinity of the Burlington Arcade were rejected "on the grounds of its liability of continued nuisance."[52] It was the architectural form itself which was believed to be the sole determinant in establishing the use of colonnades or arcades by prostitutes. John Nash thought that some of the problems could be avoided by including minor adjustments to the overall design, such as making the columns round. By mid-century, opposition to new proposals for arcades and colonnaded spaces was still made on the grounds of discouraging prostitution. A conscious attempt was made to promote arcades as sites of domesticity rather than adult pleasure zones. For example, in the Lowther Arcade the character of the shops changed. By the 1860s, the arcade had become known as a place with a family atmosphere where children's toys could be bought.

From Benjamin, we are lead to believe that prostitutes linger on the thresholds of arcades. While it is certainly true that prostitutes haunt the arcades of critical theory, historically the case is not so clear. Does the architectural form of the arcade with its open threshold resemble the body of the prostitute for all time, or is it the prostitute who as fetish commodity, as exchangeable body, reminds us of the arcade, that storehouse of commodity/consumption of the early nineteenth-century?

As seller and commodity in one, the prostitute stands for the refusal of the patriarchal laws of exchange, as described by Irigaray, where women are exchanged between men – as and in property, as and in space. As a barely speaking subject, the figure of the prostitute situated in the artificial envelope of the arcade begins to articulate the unspoken spaces of female subjectivity – openness, interiority, fluidity, mobility, porosity and artifice, as suggested in the writings of Irigaray.

Footnotes

1 Emile Zola, *Thérèse Raquin*, Oxford University Press, 1998.

2 See Jane Rendell, "Subjective Space: A Feminist Architectural History of the Burlington Arcade", *Desiring Practices: Architecture, Gender and the Interdisciplinary*, eds., Duncan McCorquodale, Katerina Ruedi and Sarah Wigglesworth, Black Dog Publishing, 1996; Jane Rendell, "Industrious Females" and "Professional Beauties," or, Fine Articles for Sale in the Burlington Arcade", *Strangely Familiar: Narratives of Architecture in the City*, eds., Iain Borden, Joe Kerr, Alicia Pivaro and Jane Rendell, Routledge, 1995; Jane Rendell, "Displaying Sexuality: Gendered Identities in the Early Nineteenth Century Street", *Images of the Street: Representation, Experience, and Control in Public Space*, ed., Nick Fyfe, Routledge, 1998. See also "Doing it, (Un)Doing it, (Over)Doing it Yourself: Rhetorics of Architectural Abuse", *Occupied Territories*, ed., Jonathan Hill, Routledge, 1998.

3 Walter Benjamin, "Paris, Capital of the Nineteenth Century", *Charles Baudelaire: A Lyric Poet in the Era of High Capitalism*, trans., Harry Zohn and Quintin Hoare, NLB/Verso, 1997, p. 159.

4 Benjamin, "Capital", p. 171.

5 Luce Irigaray, "Women on the Market", *This Sex which is not One,* Cornell University Press, 1985, pp. 170–191.

6 Samuel Ware, "A Proposal to Build Burlington Arcade", (16 March 1808), and schematic plans for the Burlington Arcade and Burlington House, (1815, 1817 and 1818), Collection of Lord Christian, Royal Academy of Arts Drawing Collection, London.

7 The most useful secondary sources on arcades are Margaret MacKeith, *Shopping Arcades: a Gazetteer of British Arcades 1817–1939,* Mansell, 1985 and Johann Friedrich Geist, *Arcades: the History of a Building Type,* MIT Press, 1983.

8 Benjamin, "Capital", pp. 157–160.

9 Susan Buck–Morss, *The Dialectics of Seeing*, MIT Press, 1991, pp. 97–112, p. 39.

10 David Frisby, *Fragments of Modernity,* Polity Press, 1985, p. 192.

11 Frisby, *Fragments*, p. 215.

12 Benjamin, "Capital", pp. 157–176.

13 Sigrid Weigel, *Body- and Image-Space: Re-reading Walter Benjamin*, Routledge, 1996, pp. 89–91.

14 Irigaray, *Sex*, pp. 172, 176, 185–187.

15 It is interesting to note that in the eighteenth and early nineteenth centuries, the word "commodity" was used to describe a woman's sex, and the term a "public commodity" described a prostitute.

16 Amateur, *Real Life in London*, Jones, 1821–1822, vol. 2, p. 365.

17 Walter Benjamin, "A Berlin Chronicle", *One Way Street*, trans., Edmund Jephcott and Kingsley Shorter, NLB/Verso, 1992, p. 301.

18 Luce Irigaray, *The Speculum of the Other Woman*, Cornell University Press, 1985, p. 229.

19 Pierce Egan, *Life in London*, Neely and Jones, p. 213.

20 A. R. Henderson, *Female Prostitution in London 1730–1830,* University of London, 1992, p. 130.

21 *Ramblers Magazine or Fashionable Companion*, vol. 1, no. 1, 1 April 1824, p. 16 and *Ramblers Magazine or Annals of Gallantry, Glee, Pleasure and Bon Ton*, vol. 2, 1820, pp. 28 and 207.

22 Egan, *Life*, p. 16.

23 Benjamin, *One Way Street*, p. 45.

24 Luce Irigaray, *Elemental Passions*, The Athlone Press, 1992, pp. 65–66.

25 Ware, "Proposal", n. p.

26 Benjamin, "Naples", *Street*, pp. 167–176.

27 Benjamin, *Street*, p. 45.

28 Buck–Morss, *Dialectics*, p. 21. For a more detailed account of the relationship between Benjamin and Lacis from Benjamin's perspective see Walter Benjamin, *Moscow Diary*, Harvard University Press, 1986.

29 "The Opening of the Burlington Arcade", *Gentleman's Magazine*, vol. 87, part II, September 1817, p. 272; Ware, "Proposal", n. p; John Tallis, *Tallis's Illustrated London: in Commemoration of the Great Exhibition*, London: J. Tallis, 1851, p. 153; "Covered Passage, Burlington House", *The Times,* 3 April 1815.

30 See for example, *Charge Book of the Parish of St. James's D2113*, (26.05.1818–09.11.1818) and *Charge Book of the Parish of St. James's D2116*, (30.01.1821–26.08.1821).

31 Irigaray, *Sex*, p. 186.

32 Luce Irigaray, *An Ethics of Sexual Difference*, The Athlone Press, 1993, p. 15.

33 For a fascinating discussion of Benjamin and angels, see Weigel, *Body*, pp. 54–60.

34 Bracebridge Hemyng, "The Prostitution Class Generally", *London Labour and the London Poor, London Morning Chronicle 1861–-1862*, eds., Henry Mayhew and Bracebridge Hemyng, vol. 4, Frank Cass, 1967, p. 217. "Paphian": pertaining to Paphos in Cyprus, and sacred to Aphrodite, also means whore or prostitute. See *Oxford English Dictionary*, CD ROM, 2nd edition, 1989.

35 Benjamin, "Naples", *Street*, p. 174.

36 Irigaray, *Passions*, p. 66.

37 Benjamin, "Capital", p. 150.

38 George Smeeton, *Doings in London; or Day and Night Scenes of the frauds, frolics, manners and depravities of the Metropolis*, Smeeton, 1828, p. 83.

39 See Geist, pp. 319–20 and "The Parish of St. James's Westminster, Part 2, North of Piccadilly", *The Survey of London,* ed., F. H. W Shepperd, The Athlone Press, University of London, 1963, vol. 32, p. 433, fig. 77.

40 "The Opening of the Burlington Arcade", p. 272.

41 *Ramblers Magazine*, 1828, v. 1, p. 251 and v. 2, pp. 27–28.

42 Margaret Whitford, *Luce Irigaray: Philosophy in the Feminine,* London, 1991, p. 162.

43 Fanny Burney, *The Wanderer*, 1816, Oxford University Press, 1991, p. 452.

44 Benjamin, "Capital", p. 168.

45 Irigaray, *Speculum*, p. 116.

46 Laura Mulvey, "Cinematic Space: Desiring and Deciphering", *Desiring Practices: Architecture, Gender and the Interdisciplinary*, eds., Katerina Ruedi, Sarah Wigglesworth and Duncan McCorquodale, Black Dog Publishing, 1996, pp. 206–215.

47 Marguerite Gardiner, *The Magic Lantern or Sketches of Scenes in the Metropolis*, Longman, Hurst, Rees, Orme and Brown, 1823, p. 28.

48 Luce Irigaray, *Difference*, p. 10

49 Captain Gronow, *Reminiscences of Captain Gronow*, Smith Elder and Co., 1862, p. 119.

50 Benjamin, "Capital", p. 176.

51 Irigaray, *Difference*, p. 11.

52 Shepperd ed., *Survey*, vol. 29, footnote no. 183, p. 241.

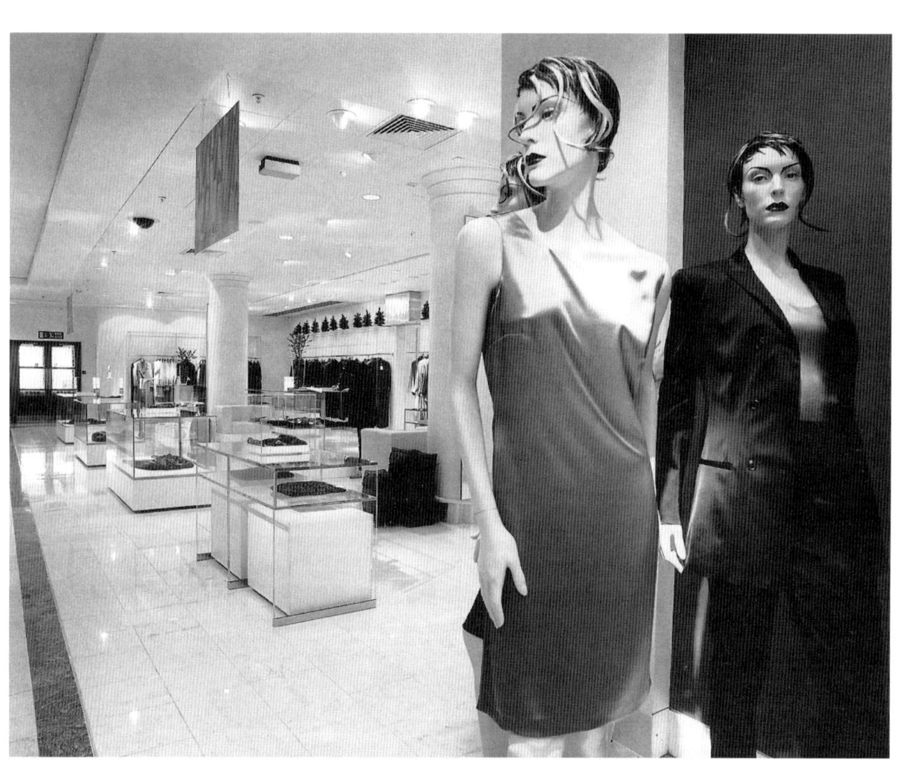

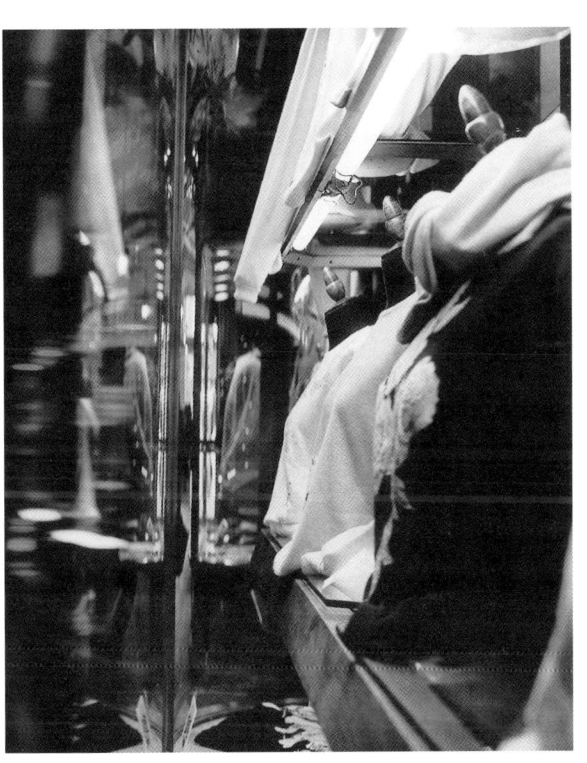

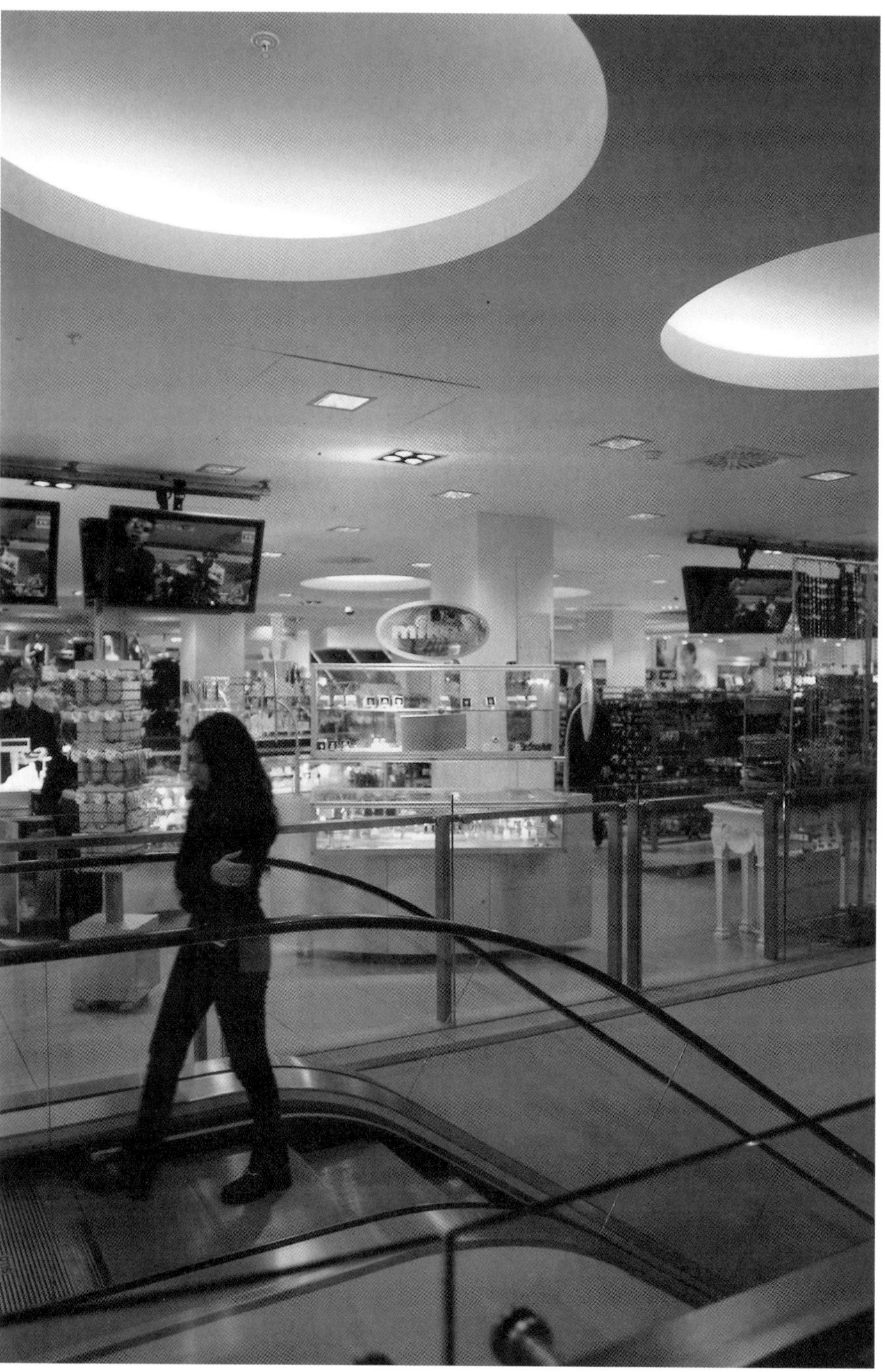

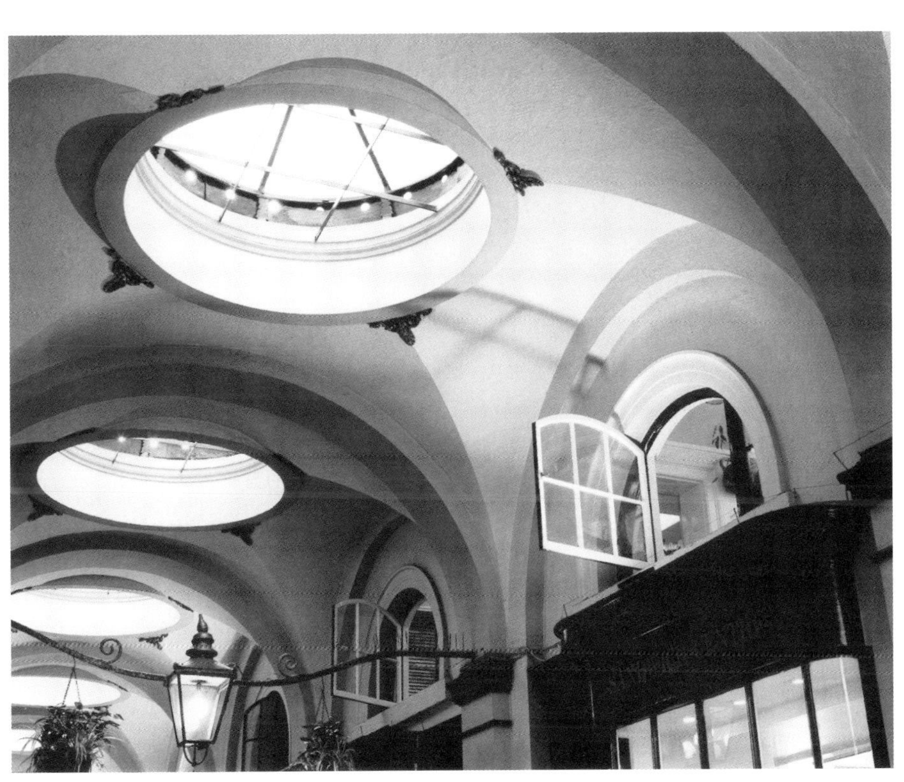

Walter Benjamin and the Tectonic Unconscious: Using Architecture as an Optical Instrument

Detlef Mertins

The writings of Walter Benjamin include appropriations and transformations of modernist architectural history and theory that offer an opportunity to broaden the interpretation of how the relationship between the 'unconscious' and technologically aided 'optics' is figured in his commentaries on cultural modernity. This essay focuses on three moments in his writings, each of which touches on this topic in a different way: first, on Benjamin's reading of Carl Bötticher's theory of architectural tectonics as a theory of history in which the unconscious serves as a generative and productive source that challenges the existing matrix of representation; secondly, on Benjamin's transformation of Sigfried Giedion's presentation of iron structures into optical instruments for glimpsing a space interwoven with unconsciousness, a new world of space the image of which had seemingly been captured by photography; and thirdly, on Benjamin's suggestion that the mimetic faculty continues to play within representation, history and technology to produce similarities between the human and the non-human. In each instance, Benjamin reworked the dynamic dualism of nineteenth-century architectural tectonics – (self)representation seeking reconciliation with alterity – into a dialectic. In so doing, he set the cause of revolution (of a modernity yet to come) against metaphysical and utopian claims, progressive and regressive alike.

Technical Forms

In the opening segment of his well-known exposé for the *Arcades* project of 1935 – "Paris, Capital of the Nineteenth Century" – Benjamin referred to the architect and historian Carl Bötticher, and he was not flattering.[1] He associated Bötticher with what he elsewhere referred to as the nineteenth-century's deficient reception of industrial technology, that is, the problematic production of images in which the old persists and intermingles with the new. He called these "wish-images" in which "the collective seeks both to preserve and to transfigure the inchoateness of the social product and the deficiencies in the social system of production." Benjamin explained that, Janus-like, such wish-fulfilling images (which is how Freud had characterised dreams) tended to direct the visual imagination "back to the primeval past," thus linking their power of prophecy (for that which is to follow appears first in the images of dreams) to "elements from prehistory, that is, of a classless society." Intimations of a classless society, archived in the collective unconscious, mingle with the new "to produce the utopia that has left its traces in thousands of configurations of life, from permanent buildings to fleeting fashions." Benjamin offered Charles Fourier's utopian vision of a community housed in a phalanstery as such an image that combines promise and problematics. He considered its architecture a "reactionary transformation" of the arcades into "the colourful idyll of Biedermeier" inserted into the austere, formal world of the Empire.

For Benjamin, it was the destiny of the working masses to realise the non-instrumental potentiality of industry and yet the latent physiognomy of technical forms remained constrained under the rule of the bourgeoisie, just as the workers were themselves. Concurring with Max Weber's analysis of how Enlightenment rationality had "disenchanted" the world, he nevertheless recognised that modernity was not yet free of myth. Things produced as commodities under the conditions of alienated labour were enveloped by false mythologies, as evident in advertisements, fashion and architecture. "Capitalism," he noted in the *Arcades* project, "is a natural phenomenon with which a new dream-sleep came over Europe, and in it, a reactivation of mythic powers." [K 1a, 8] These myths, to which Georg Lukács had drawn attention to as being characteristic of the class consciousness of the bourgeoisie, gave the world of reified commodities the appearance and status of "nature" – a second nature that occluded the original as it exploited it.[2] To awaken from the nightmare of capitalist phantasmagoria, to dissolve mythology into the space of history was Benjamin's principal aim for the *Arcades* project, which he thought of – in terms similar to the work of dreams and dream analysis – as his *Passagenarbeit*, or work of passage. In Jeffrey Mehlman's apt formulation, "Benjamin's work on the phantasmagoric glass and iron arcades of Paris constituted a devastating enactment of the messianic dream of plunging into evil, albeit to defeat it from within."[3] Benjamin's reading of modern architecture and photography during the late 1920s in Germany (*neues Bauen* and *neue Optik*), like his reading of their histories, was informed by these problematics of dream-consciousness – the resistance posed by the old for passage across the threshold of modernity into an undistorted and fully revolutionary state of redemption.

Having noted in the exposé that the emergence of construction in iron was critical for the appearance of the skylit and gaslit Parisian arcades during the fashion boom around 1820, Benjamin referred to Bötticher's conviction that the art forms of the new system of iron construction must follow the formal principle of the Hellenic mode. As Mitchell Schwarzer has shown, Bötticher's tectonic theory centred on the hermeneutic problem of architectural ornamentation or (self)representation seeking to interpret the raw ontological moment in which artifice is created out of unformed matter, drawing new and unassimilated appearance into the already given system of architectural representation.[4] Benjamin went on to describe the Empire style, which conformed to Bötticher's prescription, as being the equivalent in architecture to "revolutionary terrorism" in politics, for which "the State was an end in itself." Invoking a kind of functionalism against the politics of historicism, which served to legitimate the present by reiterating the forms of the past, he wrote,

> Just as Napoleon little realised the functional nature of the State as an instrument of the rule of the bourgeois class, so the master-builders of his time equally little realised the functional nature of iron, with which the constructional principle entered upon its rule in architecture. These master-builders fashioned supports in the style of the Pompeian column, factories in the style of dwelling-houses, just as later the first railway stations were modelled on chalets.[5]

That Benjamin sided with the engineer against the architect is clear from the first part of the exposé, in which he suggested that engineering had a revolutionary role to play, not only for architecture but for society. Having already introduced this theme in his essay "Surrealism" of 1929 and again, more radically, in "Erfahrung und Armut", ("Experience and Poverty") of 1933,[6] Benjamin returned to it at the end of the exposé. There he took up what he called the surrealists' gaze across "the ruination of the bourgeoisie" and observed that,

> The development of the forces of production had turned the wish-symbols of the previous century into rubble, even before the monuments which represented them had crumbled. This development during the nineteenth century liberated the forms of creation from art, just as in the sixteenth century the sciences freed themselves from philosophy. A start is made by architecture as engineering.[7]

By linking "artistic" architecture to the phantasmagoria of bourgeois capitalism, while at the same time linking "engineering" architecture to social revolution, Benjamin radicalised and politicised the conflict between engineering and architecture that had marked the nineteenth-century. He drew it into the overarching dialectical struggle between the classes and the new and old.

In this context, Benjamin's reading of Bötticher's tribute of 1846 to Karl Friedrich Schinkel takes on a rather strategic significance for the dialectical theory of architecture that may be glimpsed between the lines of his writings. It was, of course, in this text – "The Principles of the Hellenic and Germanic Ways of Building with Regard to Their Application to Our Present Way of Building"[8] – that Bötticher had extended his theory of tectonics to the matter of iron. Having previously analysed the two great historical styles – the trabeated Hellenic system and the vaulted Germanic-Gothic – he turned to speculate on the architecture of the future, the new architecture that so many in the nineteenth century longed for so intensely. In the notes of the *Arcades* project, Benjamin assembled the following excerpts:

> Another art will emerge from the womb of time and will take on a life of its own: an art in which a different structural principle will sound a more ringing keynote than the other two .... A new and so far unknown system of covering (which will of course bring in its train a new world of art-forms) can appear only with the adoption of an unknown material, or rather a material that so far has not been used as a guiding principle .... Such a material is iron, whose use for these purposes began in our century. Further testing and greater knowledge of its structural properties will ensure that iron will become the basis for the covering system of the future and that structurally it will in times to come be as superior to the Hellenic and medieval systems as the arcuated medieval system was to the mono lithic trabeated system of antiquity .... The structural principle is thus to be adopted from the arcuated system and transformed into a new and hitherto unknown system; for the art-forms of the new system, on the other hand, the formative principle of the Hellenic style must be adopted .... [F 1, 1][9]

For Bötticher, the new iron architecture had a double origin – structure pursuing a "new and hitherto unknown system," while art assimilated the new with the old principles of antique form. In his earlier writings, Bötticher had introduced the twin notions of *Kernform* and *Kunstform* (technical form and art form) precisely to account for what he took to be the necessary relationship between material origins and idealised re-presentations of material properties and structuring forces in Hellenic and Gothic architecture. This relationship was central to his understanding of architectural style *per se*, as an integrated system of production and symbolisation. He conceived of unmediated material and structural self-expression on the one hand, and interpretative self-representation through ornament on the other, as mutually mediating and hence indivisible. In transposing this historical schema into the future, into his speculations about the physiognomy of a new iron architecture, he clearly hoped to promote the emergence of an equally integrative architectonic system for the new epoch.

Yet in positing the split between nature and culture as a condition of modernity, Bötticher inscribed into his tectonic theory an unending struggle to maintain their mutuality over the process of historical development. If in linking "technical form" and "art form" to the opposition between Germanic and Hellenic styles Bötticher had hoped

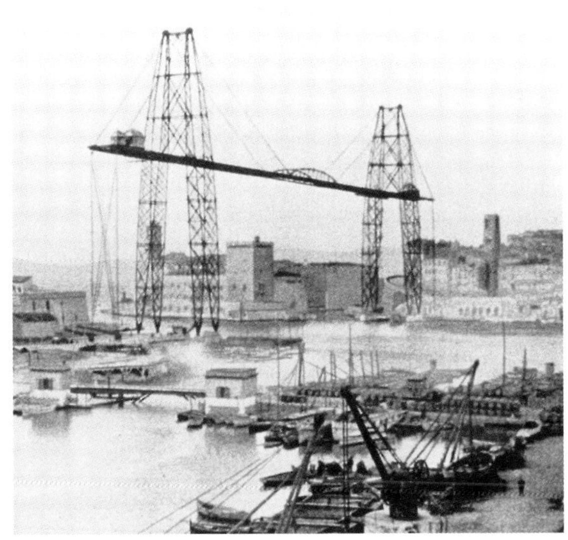

Sigfried Giedion, Pont Transbordeur spanning the industrial harbour of Marseilles, built by the engineer Ferdinand Arnodin in 1905.
From Sigfried Giedion, *Bauen in Frankreich: Bauen in Eisen – Bauen in Eisenbeton*, 1928.

to draw on the integrative strength of his dualism to forge a new and higher architecture through *stylistic* synthesis, his strategy may have had the opposite effect. It merely confirmed the split that was becoming increasingly apparent and freed the impulse for a new structural principle from the obligation to represent itself through the mediation of old tectonic systems.

Benjamin's brief commentary on these passages reveals that he took Bötticher's notion of a double origin as a sign of conflict rather than the complementary relationship that Bötticher had intended. Subtly reworking Bötticher's dualism, Benjamin noted that his history demonstrated the "*dialectical* derivation of iron construction" (emphasis added). In so doing, Benjamin was informed by Alfred Gotthold Meyer's prior reworking of tectonic theory in his posthumously published *Eisenbauten (Iron Constructions)* of 1907.[10] Benjamin held Meyer's book in the highest esteem calling it a "prototype of materialist historiography." He singled it out in 1929 as one of four books that had "remained alive," the others being Alois Riegl's *Late Roman Art Industry* (1901), Franz Rosenzweig's *The Star of Redemption* (1921), and Georg Lukács's *History of Class Consciousness* (1923). In his book, Meyer had been critical of the Berlin tectonic school inaugurated by Schinkel, for its insistence that traditional forms and principles of architectonic expression, developed for stone and wood, be used to assimilate iron construction into the art of architecture. Instead, Meyer adopted engineering as the vital and dynamic basis of a new architecture that would grant to technical forms the potential of a new self-generated beauty. Where Bötticher found, in 1846, that the various efforts to "shake off the shackles of the past" had not yet achieved persuasively original art forms *or* structural systems, Meyer spoke of the Eiffel Tower of 1889 in terms of a "new beauty, the beauty of steely sharpness" and the expression of a new tempo of tectonic vitality. While Bötticher argued that "the acceptance and continuation of tradition, not its negation, is historically the only correct course for art ... leading it toward the destined emergence from tradition to a newborn, original, and unique style," Meyer's later more *sachlich* and anti-representational approach to the relation between art and iron technology was distinguished by his refusal of any wilful symbolisation. Instead he favoured the supposed immediacy of material properties, calculations, purposes and modes of production. He conceived of beauty as the immanent expression not only of the material but of the society that produced it. Where Bötticher feared what remained outside the system of order, Meyer embraced the rush and terror of the technological sublime.[11]

While rejecting Bötticher's prescription for contemporary architecture, Meyer and Benjamin both reiterated aspects of the theory of history that underpins his tectonics, in which material and structural innovations are seen to emerge from a mysterious source – "the womb of time" – to play a leading role in the formation of a new system. For Bötticher, a new structural system specific to a new material was to be born out of the old in the same way that a distinctive and integral Roman vaulted architecture had emerged out of the Hellenic through a process of hybridisation, mutation and rationalisation. Meyer, too, was interested in the unknowable source of new architectures, but instead of Bötticher's metaphors of birth and metamorphosis, Meyer suggested that a new style is always precipitated by an "unconscious urge" and that "any generation destined to create a new style ... [will] need to start the process of formal creation from the beginning." In the case of iron construction, the drawing board of rational engineering calculations and structural diagrams constituted such a new beginning, with the path to formal self-realisation moving from elementary to complex and from part to whole. In "Experience and Poverty", Benjamin likewise mobilised the blank rationality of the engineer's drawing board as a groundless ground for a new (proletarian) society, for starting again at the beginning, albeit within the phantasmagoria. In the exposé, he referred to construction as the "subconscious of the nineteenth-century," taking the phrase not from Meyer but from the young architectural historian Sigfried Giedion, whose book of 1928,

Building in France – Building in Iron – Building in Ferro-Concrete,[12] Benjamin admired almost as much as Meyer's.[13]

Conflating metaphors of organic growth and subconscious impulses, Giedion held that the new forms of iron construction, and the new forms of life (mass society) that emerged with them, began as kernels struggling within the old to gradually assume their own identity. His story of the historical passage of iron construction follows a morphological evolution – from the simple iron roof frame of the Théatre Français of 1786 to the full realisation of iron's potential in the vast spans and gracefully engineered arcs of the Palais des Machines of 1889. This natural progression was, in his portrayal, hindered by the persistence of tradition among architects, until the twentieth-century, when they finally took up the task of bringing what had emerged in the dark subconscious of industrial labour into the clarity of a self-conscious architectural system, distinguished by a new kind of spatial experience.

Benjamin's quotation of Giedion's thesis about construction as the subconscious of the epoch may be considered in relation to a pair of images that Giedion used graphically to present what he took to be the line of development from the glass façade of an exhibition hall of 1848 to the curtain wall of Walter Gropius's Bauhaus at Dessau of 1925–1926 – the technical form "finally" purified, refined and

Sigfried Giedion, View of the water, boats and ferry platform in the harbour of Marseilles, taken from the top of the Pont Transbordeur. From Sigfried Giedion, *Bauen*.

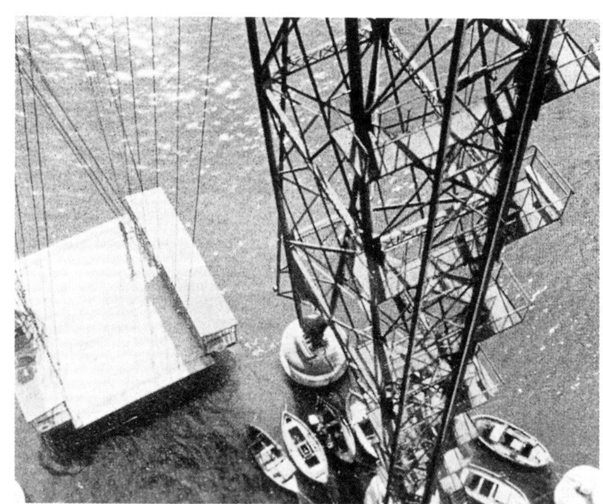

self-reflexive. But it should also be read in conjunction with Benjamin's commentary on it: "Shouldn't one rather," he suggested, "substitute [for the subconscious]: 'the role of the bodily processes', on which 'artistic' architecture would then lie like dreams supported by the scaffolding of physiological processes?" [V 1027] In reworking Giedion's dualism into a dialectic between physiological processes and phantasmagoric dreams, Benjamin pointed to the immanence of truth within the expression of bodily labours and the physiognomy of historical events. This immanence, however, remained impeded by bourgeois controls, albeit less in the technical realm (unworthy of bourgeois attention) than in the artistic.

The architecture of emerging mass society could, then, be seen as beginning not only in the corrupt form of the bourgeois arcades but also in the less deficient forms of utilitarian structures – engineered bridges, train stations, grain silos, exhibition halls and, of course, the factory, the nascent home of workers and engineers. "It is," Benjamin wrote, invoking Bötticher's terms, "the peculiar property of technical forms (as opposed to artistic forms) that their progress and their success are proportionate to the transparency of their social content. (Whence glass architecture.)" [N 4, 6] Even in the technical realm, Benjamin treated this transparency as mediated – historically, materially and perceptually. With respect to the artistic realm, he suggested, "One can formulate the problem of form for the new art in this way: When and how will the form-worlds of the mechanical, in film, in the building of machines, in the new physics, etc. rise up without our help and overwhelm us, make us aware of that which is natural about it?" [K 3a, 2] When and how, in other words, would construction – pursuing its own inherent logic of purification, working within but against the system of production, working within but against the object riddled with error – bring about the ruination of bourgeois culture and society, and do so without overt politics, but rather through a collective physiological labour that had the character of a constantly renewed originary upsurge?

Optical Instruments

By considering tectonics within the problematics of representation, Benjamin was able to both clarify and radicalise the terms of the tectonic discourse, while functionalist architects and historians of his generation merely eschewed representation, confident of their capacity to step beyond it and materialise the elemental primitiveness of utopia in the here and now of white prismatic volumes, curtain walls and cantilevered slabs. For Benjamin, the process of physiognomic immanence freeing itself from distorting mediations was not only incomplete but could not, in fact, be fulfilled by humanity alone. In seeking to cojoin radical messianic Judaism and revolutionary historical materialism, he considered such redemption contingent on suprahuman intervention. The hope and even excitement that Benjamin revealed in describing the arcades, exhibitions and panoramas of the nineteenth-century as "residues of a dream world" at the beginning of the bourgeois epoch came from a conviction that in them it was possible to glimpse the true face of prehistory, which remained opaque in the artefacts of his own time, that is at the beginning of the next epoch ushered in by the proletariat. "For us," he noted, "the enticing and threatening face of prehistory becomes clear in the beginnings of technology ... in that which lies closer to our time, it has not yet revealed itself." [K 2a, 1]

Benjamin's historicised theory of technological productivity in the field of architecture underscores the significance of metaphors of passage for his theory of history. At the same time, it sets up another constellation of metaphors concerning a new optics – the expansion of vision made possible by modern technologies including iron structures that provided unprecedented views of the city, glimpses perhaps of the "enticing and threatening face of prehistory" yet to come. As is well-known, Benjamin's "Artwork" essay of 1935–1939 introduced the idea that an equivalent analytical practice had emerged in the realm of the visual to psychoanalysis in the realm of the psyche. Sigmund Freud's *Psychopathology of Everyday Life*, Benjamin observed, had "isolated and made analysable things which had heretofore floated along unnoticed in the broad stream of perception. For the entire spectrum of optical, and now also acoustical, perception the film has brought about a similar deepening of apperception."[14] The technique that Benjamin singled out to exemplify how "the camera introduces us to unconscious optics as psychoanalysis does to unconscious impulses" was the close-up – the blow-up, the enlargement, the cropped image, the fragment. "With the close-up," he observed, "space expands." Moreover, "the enlargement of a snap-shot does not simply render more precise what was in any case already visible, though unclear: it reveals entirely new structural formations of the subject matter .... It thereby becomes tangible that a different nature speaks to the camera than to the eye. For in place of a space interwoven with human consciousness one interwoven with unconsciousness steps in."[15]

Such a space interwoven with unconsciousness was palpable for Benjamin, who consistently located the unconscious in the material world itself, not outside, behind, above or below it, but within – as he did the "truth content" of the work of art and "traces" of prehistory. In his first essay on surrealism, "Traumkitsch" (Dreamkitsch) of 1925, he distinguished the analytics of the surrealists from those of Freud precisely for tracking down "the traces not so much of the soul as of things."[16] For Benjamin, truth was hidden from casual observation, but resided in traces within the welter of base material. He considered it the task of criticism, like the task of history, to make fragments of truth visible and dominant. Regardless of medium, he considered criticism an activity of stripping its objects bare, mortifying them, dragging the truth content of what is depicted in the image out before it, not as "an unveiling that destroys the mystery but a revelation that does it justice."[17] Thus the negativity and destructiveness of criticism opens up a moment of revelation, which in turn opens the future potentiality of the object. This notion of potentiality was related to Benjamin's proposition that phenomena have a natural history, that their nature lies in the full and concentrated scope of that history – in their pre-history as well as their present state. The idea that this natural history could be fulfilled may be understood within Benjamin's thought as approaching his hope for redemption from yet another perspective.

In the "Artwork" essay, Benjamin was concerned with the problem of the work of art in the modern industrial epoch, distinguished not only by mechanical reproducibility but by phantasmagoria and commodity fetishism. In this context, Benjamin's concern for the intermingling of old and new focused on the perpetuation, into the era of capitalism, of the old phenomenon of aura, which he defined as a uniqueness that, in earlier times dominated by ritual, had enveloped the work of art as "the unique phenomenon of a distance however close the object may be." During the nineteenth-century, the phenomenon of aura had become an agent of bourgeois mythology working to maintain dominance over the masses. Without such constraint, he suggested, the class consciousness of the masses would tend to destroy aura as a function of a desire to "bring things closer spatially and humanly." The photographic image enabled them to get hold of an object at close range, prying it (in its objectivity) from its auratic encasement. Elsewhere, he wrote of other tactics for achieving similar ends: proceeding eccentrically and by leaps to rip things out of context in order to highlight the seemingly inconsequential details of larger structures ignored by the dominant class; and inventing a *historiographic telescope* capable of seeing through the phantasmagoric fog – a haptic-optic instrument for bringing the tangible, tactile concreteness of things closer to view.[18]

Just as psychoanalysis treats dream images as rebuses or picture puzzles whose manifest content must be deciphered, so Benjamin discovered in the photographic close-up a technique for reading latent content *within* the manifest, for seeing hidden significance *within* the surface. But what was it that he hoped to see? Perhaps justice with respect to the past; repressions and oppressions worked through; the object or event released to fulfil its mysterious potentiality; the enticing and threatening face of prehistory.[19] And how might this have appeared? In his "Surrealism" essay of 1929, he suggested that "We penetrate mystery only to the degree that we recognise it in the everyday realm, by virtue of a dialectical optic that perceives the everyday as impenetrable, the impenetrable as everyday." Perhaps these were the affects of the close-up that he had in mind when, in a well-known passage of the "Artwork" essay, he wrote that the moment of the close-up bursts open the prison-world of the everyday metropolis, the milieu of the proletariat – the taverns and metropolitan streets, offices and furnished rooms, railroad stations and factories "that appeared to have us locked up hopelessly ... so that now, in the midst of its far-flung ruins and debris, we calmly and adventurously go travelling."[20]

Benjamin left several concrete clues to the kind of (impenetrable) images that he associated with such adventurous travelling. Twice in the notes of the *Arcades* project, he recorded his interest in Giedion's photographs of the Pont Transbordeur in *Building in France*. His letter to Giedion, a few weeks following the publication of the 'Surrealism' essay, reveals the strong affinity that he felt for Giedion's historiography – his admiration for what he called Giedion's "radical knowledge." In the *Arcades* project, he wrote that "just as Giedion teaches us we can read the basic features of today's architecture out of buildings of the 1850s, so would we read today's life, today's forms out of the life and the apparently secondary, forgotten forms of that era." [N 1, 11] Familiar with the discourse of the new optics (led in the late 1920s by Giedion's friend Lázsló Moholy-Nagy), Benjamin took this ability to read the future in the past as contingent on a new

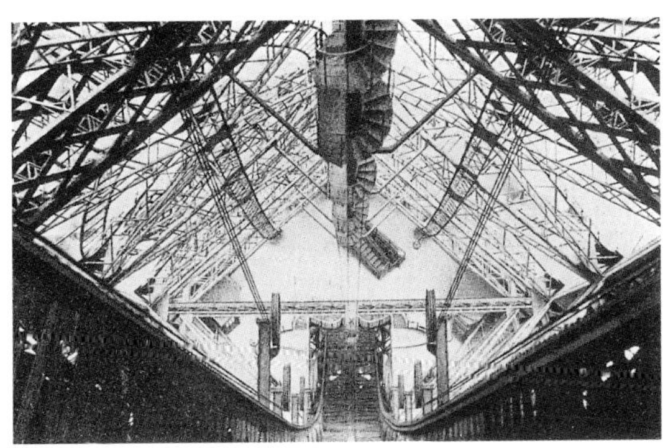

Sigfried Giedion, View inside the Eiffel Tower. From Sigfried Giedion, *Bauen*.

technologically mediated vision. Implicitly, he affiliated this with the tactics developed by the surrealists to produce profane illuminations, glimpses of a sur-reality within the banal experiences of everyday life – within, for instance, the extraordinary iron and glass structures of nineteenth-century Paris. One of Benjamin's notes begins by citing Giedion's "encounter" with the "fundamental aesthetic experience of today's building" in the "windswept stairwells of the Eiffel Tower, and even more in the steel supports of the Pont Transbordeur ... [where] things flow through the thin net of iron spanning the air – ships, sea, houses, masts, landscape, harbour. Lose their definition: swirl into one another as we climb downward, simultaneously commingling." He then went on to note that the "glorious views of the cities [which] the new iron structures afforded were initially the exclusive privilege of the workers and engineers." [N 1a, 1] Elsewhere he continued, "For who else but the engineers and proletariat climbed these steps, which alone at that time provided an opportunity to recognise the decisive, new spatial feeling of these iron constructions." [F 3, 5][21]

While similar structures had been built in Rouen, Nantes and Bordeaux, it was the swaying, hovering and dizzying Pont Transbordeur, built by the engineer Ferdinand Arnodin in 1905 across the industrial harbour of Marseilles, that assumed special significance among the avant-garde. Giedion observed how this "balcony springing into space" – photographed by Moholy-Nagy, Germaine Krull, Herbert Bayer, Man Ray and others – had entered the unconscious of modern architecture in Germany.[22] In his words, "The 'new architecture' has unconsciously used these projecting 'balconies' again and again. Why? Because there exists the need to live in buildings that strive to overcome the old sense of equilibrium that was based only on fortress-like incarceration."[23] Giedion had even featured the astonishingly delicate yet bold "transporter," built to carry a small ferry across the harbour without interfering with the boats, on the cover of *Building in France*. His photographs, as well as his words, treat its spatial and optical affects (like those of the earlier Eiffel Tower) as paradigmatic of the emerging epoch. Of course, Meyer had already taken exciting images of technology, such as the bridge over the Firth of Forth as demonstrating that "the power of [iron] speaks to us and in us in every great train station and exhibition hall, in front of every great iron bridge and in the fast-paced modern metropolis." Giedion, too, mobilised a rhetoric that echoed the aesthetics of the sublime, but not as aesthetics. Invoking dematerialisation, spatial extension, shadowless light, and air as a constitutive material, he revelled in the fluid and gravity-free interweaving of subject and object and in the unsettling movement, formlessness and metamorphosis engendered by the pulse of life in iron structures. Both Meyer and Giedion eschewed bourgeois aesthetic categories, and instead treated these new spatial experiences as the structural conditions of the emerging era. For them, technology's transformation of buildings into fleshless open bodies of skeletal transparency, like its transformation of the nature of vision with microscopes, telescopes, aerial photography and X-rays, marked the emergence of new modes of perception, cognition and experience specific to the emerging era.

Hovering weightlessly and breathlessly above the harbour of Marseilles, Giedion's "iron balcony" served to reframe and shatter the familiar, harsh world of the industrial metropolis, providing Benjamin with a graphic image of the "threshold" of awakening from the false dream-consciousness of the bourgeoisie. It is telling that Benjamin focused on photographs by Giedion that were quite distinct from his dizzying and destabilising images of the Eiffel Tower, which Giedion had described as the first instance of the montage principle and exemplary of the tendency of the new structures to "open themselves to all kinds of possibilities," to blur the boundaries of their autonomy in favour of relationships and interpenetrations in which the subject is united with the object in the creative process of space-forming.[24] Instead, by selecting abstracted, fragmented close-up views of the harbour's edge taken from the top of the structure and through its open framework, Benjamin effectively distinguished between two moments in Giedion's thinking: one Benjamin identified as "radical knowledge" serving historical self-consciousness and justice; the other, enthusiastically proclaiming that a new immediacy had already arrived under the sign of a vitalist, technologically mediated transparency in which "there is only one great, indivisible space in which relationships and interweaving rule instead of fixed borders." Benjamin focused, not on images of the great iron structures themselves, but on the unprecedented views of the city that they afforded. Among Giedion's photographs, only the ones singled out by Benjamin treated the view as mediated, and only in them was the unacknowledged misery of working-class life both revealed and simultaneously transformed into the site of revelation, just as they had been in Moholy-Nagy's constructivist film *Marseille, Vieux Port* of 1929.

While Benjamin admired the rationalised technical forms of these montage structures (he too referred to the Eiffel Tower as the first instance of montage), he focused on their role as viewing instruments. Their web-like structures provided opportunities to crop, cut, reframe and abstract the familiar. Like the lens of a camera, they could reveal hidden secrets and provide glimpses of the estranged within the city of representation, "the tiny spark of contingency, of the here and now with which this reality has so to speak seared its subjects." Benjamin called these views glorious, for they released something of a magnificent potentiality locked within the reality of alienation and exploitation. With Giedion's camera and the power of the close-up to expand space and reveal secrets, Benjamin collapsed Bötticher's tectonic dualism, transforming the hermeneutics of origins into an immanence within representation whose visibility in the present was, however, contingent on technology's most powerful instruments of optical analysis. To open the object riddled with error, Benjamin mobilised a dialectical optics that "extends our comprehension of the inevitabilities which rule our Being and at the same time manages to secure for us an immense and unexpected space of play."[25]

Magical Similarities

The effects attributed by Benjamin to the Pont Transbordeur bear a striking resemblance to his treatment of photographs by David Octavius Hill, Karl Dauthendey and Karl Blossfeldt in his essay "A Small History of Photography" of 1931.[26] The fact that a portion of this is repeated verbatim in the section of the "Artwork" essay that deals with the power of close-ups to explode the experience of the metropolis invites a reading of Giedion's photographs in terms parallel to Benjamin's reading of these other images. In this way, a third reformulation of the tectonic problematic may be inferred from his writings.

In his essay on photography, Benjamin suggested that, in contrast to painting, with photography "we encounter something new and strange." His interest was captured, to begin with, by one of the numerous calotypes that Hill had made of fishwives, fishermen and children in Newhaven, Scotland between 1843 and 1847. Unlike the precision and fidelity of the more expensive daguerreotypes, the soft orange-brown and sepia calotypes, with their diffuseness and transparency, were considered by some the most engaging and truly artistic medium, and came to be admired for their power to evoke personality, to find the presence below the surface, to probe behind appearances. Referring to Hill's portrait of Mrs. Elizabeth Hall, Benjamin observed,

> In Hill's Newhaven fishwife, her eyes cast down in such indolent, seductive modesty, there remains something that goes beyond testimony to the photographer's art, something that cannot be silenced, that fills you with an unruly desire to know what her name was, the woman who was alive there, who even now is still real and will never consent to be wholly absorbed into art.
> "And I ask: how did the beauty of that hair, those eyes, beguile our forebears: how did that mouth kiss, to which desire curls up senseless as smoke without fire."[27]

To underscore his concern for the immediacy of lived experience, as captured by the photographer in a tense relationship with his own artful idealisations, Benjamin turned briefly to a picture by Karl Dauthendey, a German post-mortem photographer of the late nineteenth-century living in Moscow at the time the photograph was taken. Benjamin's description invokes an image of Dauthendey himself, together with the woman he was engaged to, lying in the bedroom of his home, shortly after the birth of her sixth child. Her arteries were severed and her gaze absorbed in "an ominous distance." The silent violence of this image is both shocking in relation to Hill's and revealing of the unconscious realm that Benjamin saw opened up by the new optics. With these photographs already in mind, Benjamin then continued,

> Immerse yourself in such a picture long enough and you will recognise how alive the contradictions are, here too: the most precise technology can give its products a magical value, such as a painted picture can never again have for us. No matter how artful the photographer, no matter how carefully posed his subject, the beholder feels an irresistible urge to search such a picture for the tiny spark of contingency, of the Here and Now, with which reality has so to speak seared the subject, to find the inconspicuous spot where in the immediacy of that long-forgotten moment the future subsists so eloquently that we, looking back, may rediscover it. *For it is another nature that speaks to the camera than to the eye: other in the sense that a space interwoven with human consciousness gives way to a space interwoven with the unconscious .... It is through photography that we first discover the existence of this optical unconscious, just as we discover the instinctual unconscious through psychoanalysis.* Details of structure, cellular tissue, with which technology and medicine are normally concerned – all this is in its origins more native to the camera than the atmospheric landscape or the soulful portrait. Yet at the same time photography reveals in this material the physiognomic aspects of visual worlds which dwell in the smallest things, meaningful yet covert enough to find a hiding place in waking dreams, but which, enlarged and capable of formulation, make the difference between technology and magic visible as a thoroughly historical value.[28]

Adding yet a third image to this constellation, Benjamin turned to the "astonishing" plant photographs of Professor Karl Blossfeldt, designer and teacher at the United States Schools of Free and Applied Art in Berlin. The images appeared in Blossfeldt's book of 1928, *Art Forms of Nature*,[29] together with an introduction by the gallerist Karl Nierendorf, whose thoughts share certain affinities with Benjamin's own – thoughts on the "unity of the creative will in nature and art;" their respective embodiment of a profound sublime secret; "joining the two poles of the Past and the Future;" how the modern techniques of photography and film as well as microscopes and astronomical observatories "bring us into closer touch with Nature than was ever possible before, and with the aid of scientific appliances we obtain glimpses into worlds which hitherto had been hidden from our senses."[30]

Paraphrasing Nierendorf, Benjamin wrote that Blossfeldt's uncanny photographs,

> ... reveal the forms of ancient columns in horse willow, a bishop's crosier in the ostrich fern, totem poles in tenfold enlargements of chestnut and maple shoots, and gothic tracery in the fuller's thistle. Hill's subjects, too, were probably not far from the truth when they described 'the phenomenon of photography' as still being 'a great and mysterious experience'; even if for them this was no more than the consciousness of 'standing before a device which in the briefest time could produce a picture of the visible environment that seemed as real and alive as nature itself'.[31]

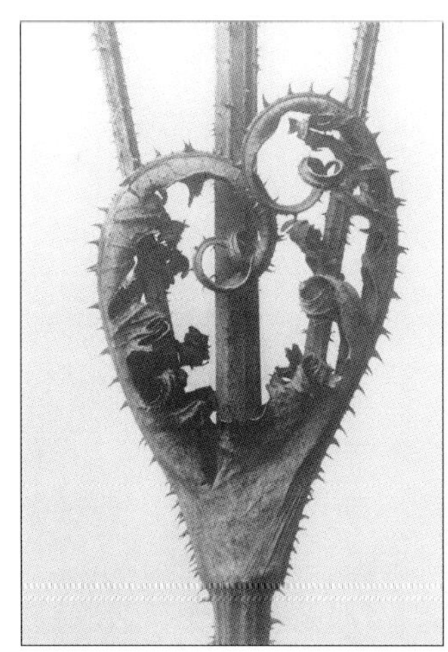

Karl Blossfeldt, *Fuller's Thistle*. From Karl Blossfeldt, *Kunstformen der Natur*, 1928.

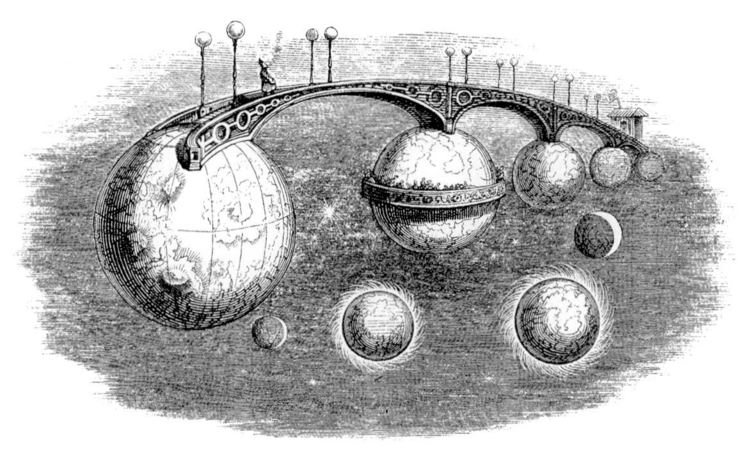

J.J. Grandville, *An Interplanetary Bridge: Saturn's Ring is a Balcony*. From J.J. Grandville, Un Autre Monde, 1844.

At the risk of reduction, condensing Benjamin's eloquently woven thoughts may help to register more emphatically the link between these various ideas: that the most precise technology can give its products a magical value; that the photographic enlargement can reveal a secret within the physiognomic surface of things; that that secret is visible in a tiny spark of contingency with which reality has seared the subject, in inconspicuous spots where in the immediacy of that long-forgotten moment the future subsists so eloquently that we, looking back, may recognise it; and recognise it as another nature, one interwoven with unconsciousness. All of this makes possible a great and mysterious experience, an experience of the natural within the human and the human within the natural; an experience whereby the difference between technology and magic is seen to be strictly historical, implying not only their commonality, but also a future potentiality.

That magic – the correspondence between the natural and human – has a history and that this was subsumed into the history of technology was most explicitly treated by Benjamin through the concept of similarity in his essays "Doctrine of the Similar" and "On the Mimetic Faculty", both of 1933.[32] There he described how humanity's special gift for seeing and producing similarities between the human and non-human has a history that is both phylogenetic and ontogenetic – that is, a history within the species that parallels its history within the life of each of its members. In other words, this faculty changes over the course of historical development as it does over the life of each person. Just as "children's play is everywhere permeated by mimetic modes of behaviour ... the child plays at being not only a shopkeeper or teacher but also a windmill and a train," so in other essays Benjamin characterised the proletariat as the new-born children of the emerging industrial age, whose games always try to begin again at the beginning.[33] While it appears that the mimetic faculty has decayed over time, that "the observable world of modern man contains only minimal residues of the magical correspondences and analogies that were familiar to ancient peoples," Benjamin suggested that this faculty has, rather, been transformed into a *non*-sensuous similarity, now borne exclusively by language. "The coherence of words and sentences (the semiotic aspect of language) is the bearer through which, like a flash, similarity appears."[34]

But Benjamin's apparent exclusion of the sensuous here needs to be qualified by the dependence of language on the sensuous media of speech and script, just as flames rely on substances that burn. Notwithstanding his emphasis on modern semiotic language, Benjamin also treated modern technologies of mechanical production and reproduction – photography and film, glass and iron – as bearers of correspondences between the human and the non-human. Benjamin's concept of similarity concerned the effects of things as much as their attributes. As technical forms that had been reduced to the limit of their objectification, these media (like the sober technical language that Benjamin admired in Bertolt Brecht and Paul Scheerbart) held the special potential of not only materialising similarity in their elemental form, but bringing the similarity hidden in other things into momentary visibility. They were instruments capable of producing glimpses, which the snap of the shutter, the dynamite of the tenth-of-a-second, was able to rip from the flesh of history and preserve.[35]

Believing that every epoch dreams its successor, Benjamin was especially attentive to utopian schemes. One of his earliest versions of the Arcades project was even named after an image by the French humorist J.J. Grandville, from his 1843 satire of modernist utopias, *Another World*.[36] In his précis of 1928–1929 "The Ring of Saturn or Something about Iron Construction", Benjamin suggested that a small cosmic vignette by Grandville might demonstrate, in the form of a grotesque, the infinite opportunities that the nineteenth-century saw opened up with construction in iron. Focusing on the adventures of a small goblin trying to find his way around in space, Grandville's story was accompanied by an etching that depicts an iron bridge with gas lanterns springing from planet to planet in an indefinite perspective, an unending passage into the infinite depths of space. The 333,000th pillar, we are told, rests on Saturn, where the goblin sees that the ring of this planet is nothing but an iron balcony on which the inhabitants of the planet take the evening air. Preceding Bötticher's text on iron by two years, and the Crystal Palace by nine, the bridge and balcony are remarkably modern and free of historical stylisation. Later, in the exposé of 1935, Benjamin still included this image in the section on "Grandville, or the World Exhibitions", calling it a "graphic utopia."

To be able to commune with the cosmos, to link the past and future, to produce similarities between representation and alterity without restriction – such could be the opportunities of technology and industrialisation pursued rationally to their ultimate potential beyond the exploitation of nature under capitalism. But let us remember that this image of absolute unity and openness was a satire of utopians like Fourier and the Saint Simonians, that Benjamin admired the caricatures of Karl Kraus for "creeping into those he impersonates in order to annihilate them" and that he concluded his tribute to the utopian fantasist Paul Scheerbart, written in the final months of his life, by recalling that "art is not the forum of utopia .... Of that greater (some)thing – the fulfilment of Utopia – one cannot speak, only bear witness."

An earlier version of this essay was published under the title "Walter Benjamin's 'Tectonic' Unconscious", in ANY, *14.*

Footnotes

1 Walter Benjamin, "Paris, Capital of the Nineteenth Century", *Reflections*, Harcourt Brace Jovanovich, 1978, pp. 146–162/"Paris, die Hauptsadt des XIX Jahrhunderts", *Gesammelte Schriften*, Suhrkamp, Frankfurt, 1974–1982, V, 1, pp. 45–59. Notes given in the text in square brackets refer not to page numbers but to the classification of items, which are the research notes for the unwritten book *Passagenwerk*, Walter Benjamin, *Gesammelte Schriften*, vol. V, Suhrkamp, 1982.

2 Georg Lukács, *History and Class Consciousness*, trans., Rodney Livingstone, MIT Press, 1971.

3 Jeffrey Mehlman, *Walter Benjamin for Children: An Essay on the Radio Years*, University of Chicago Press, 1993, p. 80.

4 Mitchell Schwarzer, "Ontology and Representation in Karl Botticher's Theory of Tectonics", *Journal of the Society of Architectural Historians*, Vol. 53, September 1993, pp. 267–280.

5 Benjamin, "Capital", p. 147.

6 Walter Benjamin, "Erfahrung und Armut", *GS*, II, 1, pp. 213–219.

7 Benjamin, "Capital ", p. 161–162.

8 Karl Botticher, "Das Prinzip der hellenischen und germanischen Bauweise hinsichtlich der Übertragung in die Bauweise unserer Tage", *Allgemeine Bauzeitung*, vol., 11, 1846, pp. 111–125; Carl Gottlieb Wilhelm Botticher, "The Principles of the Hellenic and German Ways of Building", *In What Style Should We Build? The German Debate on Architectural Style*, trans., Wolfgang Herrmann, The Getty Centre for the History of Art and Humanities, 1992, pp. 147–167.

9 Translation taken from Botticher, "Principles".

10 Alfred Gothold Meyer, *Eisenbauten*, Paul Neff, 1907.

11 In his introduction to the English translation of Sigfried Giedion's *Bauen in Frankreicht*, Sokratis Georgiadis observed that "What Meyer experienced as non-aesthetic, he actually described in terms of an aesthetic of the sublime." See note 12.

12 Sigfried Giedion, *Bauen in Frankreicht: Bauen in Eisen – Bauen in Eisenbeton*, Klinkhardt and Biermann, 1928/*Building in France: Building in Iron – Building in Ferro-Concrete*, trans., J. Duncan Berry, The Getty Centre for the Study of Art and the Humanities, 1995.

13 For a more detailed treatment of Benjamin's reading of Giedion and Meyer, see Detelf Mertins, "The Threatening and Enticing Face of Prehistory: Walter Benjamin and the Utopia of Glass", *Assemblage* 29, pp. 7–23.

14 Sigmund Freud, *The Psychopathology of Everyday Life*, trans., Alan Tyson, W.W. Norton, 1960.

15 I have altered Harry Zohn's well known translation of this passage to render Benjamin's use of "durchwirken" as "interweaving" rather than "exploring" and "penetrating".

16 Walter Benjamin, "Traumkitsch", *GS* II, pp. 620–622

17 Walter Benjamin, "Ursprung der deutschen Trauerspiel", *GS* I, 1, p. 211/ *The Origin of German Tragic Drama,* trans., John Osborne, Verso, 1977, p. 31.

18 Walter Benjamin, "Benjamin an Kraft. Paris, 28.10.1935", *Das Passagenwerk, GS* V, 2, p. 1151.

19 Eduardo Cadava has given a more precise reading of this in "Words of Light: Theses on the Photography of History", *Diacritics* 22, 3–4, Fall–Winter 1992, pp. 84–114.

20 Walter Benjamin, "Das Kunstwerk im Zeitalter seiner technischen Reproduzierbarkeit", *GS* I, 2, pp. 471–508/"The Work of Art in the Age of Mechanical Reproduction", *Illuminations,* trans., Harry Zohn, Schoken Books, 1968, pp. 217–251.

21 The significance of these notes was first recognised by Susan Buck-Morss in *The Dialectics of Seeing: Walter Benjamin and the Arcades Project,* MIT Press, 1989.

22 See exhibition catalogue, *Le pont Transbordeur et la Vision Moderniste,* Musées de Marseille, 1991.

23 Giedion, *Building*, p. 147.

24 See Walter Benjamin, *Das Passagenwerk, GS* V, 1, p. 223.

25 Benjamin, "Reproduction", p. 236.

26 Walter Benjamin, "A Small History of Photography", *One Way Street,* trans., Edmund Jephcott and Kingsley Shorter, NLB/Verso, 1979, pp. 240–257/"Kleine Geschichte der Photographie", *GS* II, 1, pp. 368–385.

27 Benjamin, "Photography", p. 246.

28 I have altered the translation by Edmund Jephcott and Kingsley Shorter by using the more palpable phrase "interwoven with consciousness" instead of their "informed by."

29 Karl Blossfeldt, *Kunstformen der Natur,* Ernst Wasmuth, 1928/*Art Forms in Nature,* E. Weyhe, 1929.

30 Karl Nierendorf in Blossfeldt, *Nature.*

31 Benjamin, "Photography", p. 224.

32 Walter Benjamin, "Doctrine of the Similar", trans., Knut Tarnowski, *New German Critique* 17, Spring 1979, pp. 65–96/"Lehre vom Anlichen", *GS* II, 1, pp. 204–210.

33 See Detlef Mertins, "Playing at Modernity", *Toys and the Modernist Tradition,* Canadian Centre for Architecture, 1993, pp. 7–16.

34 Walter Benjamin, "The Mimetic Faculty", *One Way Street,* p. 335.

35 See Benjamin, "Doctrine", p. 68.

36 J.J. Grandville, "Une Autre Monde", *Bizarreries and Fantasies of Grandville,* Dover Press, 1978.

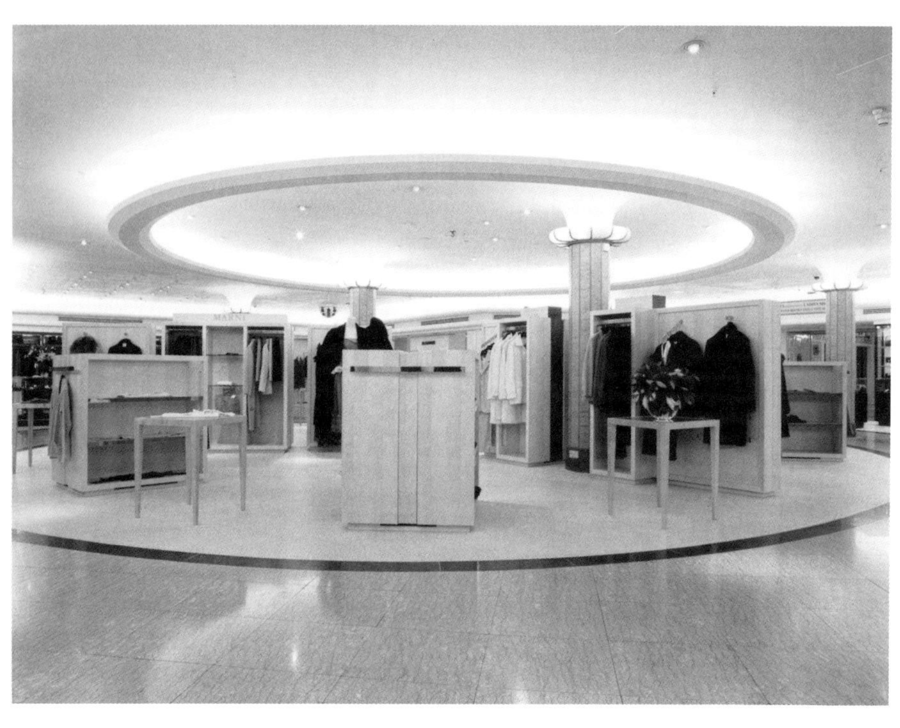

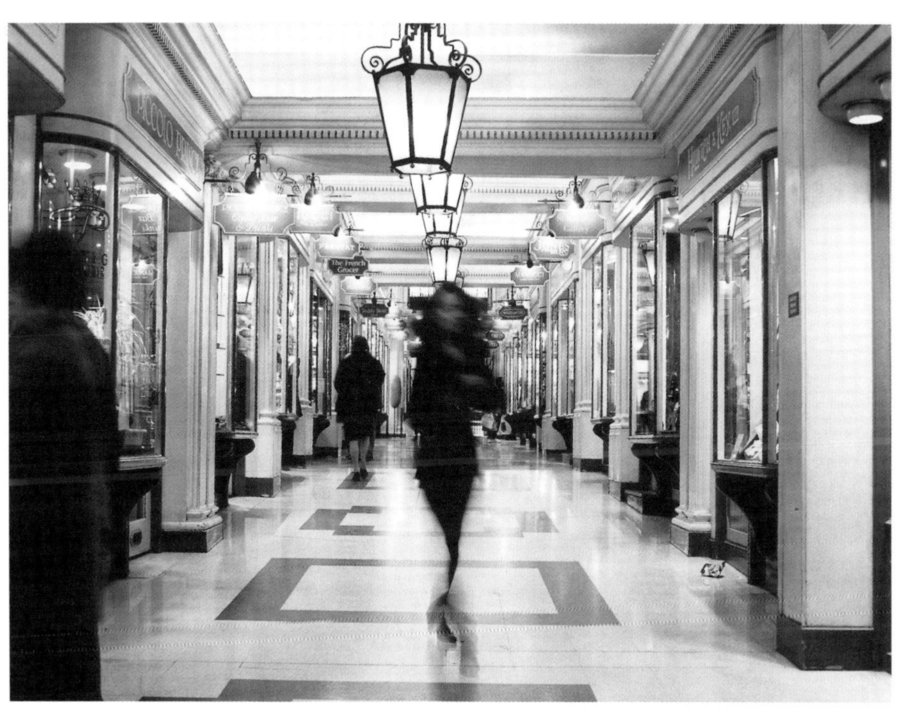
The French
Grocer

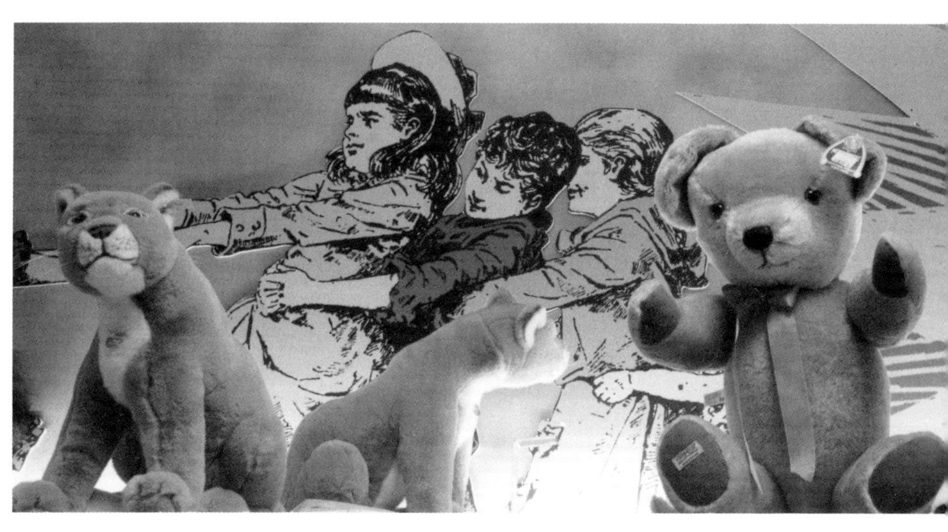

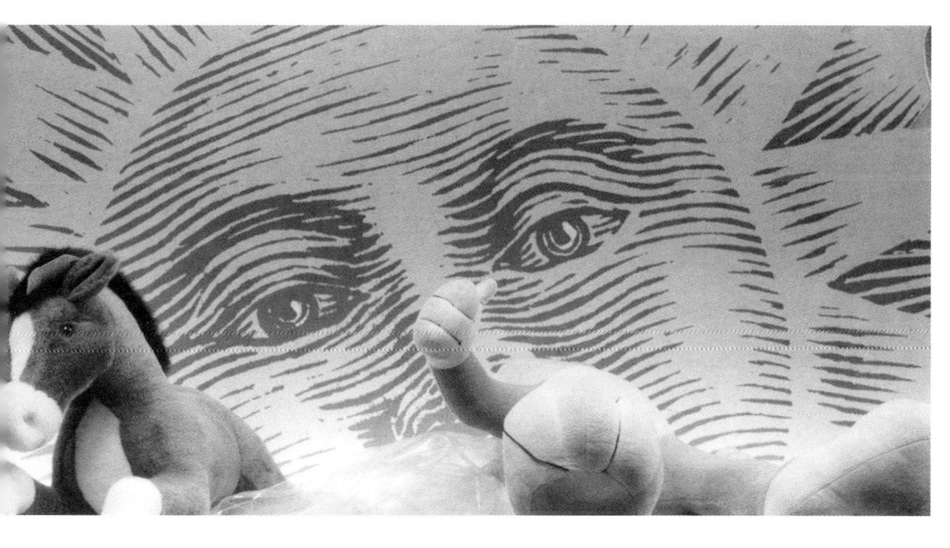

List of Contributors

Benjamin H.D. Buchloh is Professor of Art History at Barnard College, Columbia University. His collection of essays, *Open Book*, will be published by MIT Press in 1999.

Mark Dion is an artist and naturalist. He exhibits internationally.

Esther Leslie is a lecturer in the Cultural Studies Department at the University of East London. She is currently writing a book on animation and the avant-garde and is an editor of the journal *Historical Materialism*.

Mathew Rampley is a Principal Lecturer in Art Theory and the Co-ordinator of Graduate Studies at the Surrey Institute of Art & Design. He has published articles on historiography and post-war painting. His book, *Nietzsche. Aesthetics and Modernity* (Cambridge University Press) is due for publication in 1999.

Donald Preziosi is Professor of Art History at the University of California, Los Angeles. He is author of *Rethinking Art History* (California University Press, 1989) and *Brain of the Earth's Body* (forthcoming), and editor of *The Art of Art History* (Oxford University Press, 1998).

Clifton Steinberg is an artist who lives and works in London and exhibits internationally. He photographs display mannequins, architectural interiors and exteriors, stuffed animals and members of the public.

Alex Coles is founding editor of *de-, dis-, ex-.* and co-author of *Walter Benjamin for Beginners* (Icon Books, 1998). He is currently undertaking Phd research at Goldsmiths College where he is also a visiting lecturer.

Jane Rendell is lecturer at the University of Nottingham. An architect and architectural historian, she is co-editor of *Strangely Familiar* (Routledge, 1995), *Gender Space Architecture* (Routledge, 1999), and *The Unknown City* (MIT Press, 1999).

Detelf Mertins is an architect, historian, and critic teaching at the University of Toronto. He is editor of *The Presence of Mies* (Princeton Architectural Press, 1994), and has a collection of essays forthcoming from MIT Press.

Acknowledgments

Thanks to Arcadia Group plc, Andrew Brighton at the Tate Gallery, Alexia Defert, Harrods Ltd, Christian Küsters, Lisa LeFeuvre at The Photographers Gallery, Dan Graham, Rory Logsdale at the Lisson Gallery, Nicholas Mann at the Warburg Institute, Timothy Martin, Duncan McCorquodale, Alessandra Santarelli at London Projects, Sue Rose, Selfridges, Gerald Steinberg and Barbara Steinberg.

Also, thanks to Icon Books for the invitation to work with Howard Caygill and Andrzej Klimowski in thinking through Benjamin in words and images, Susan Kandel and Paul Foss for the invitation to initially engage with the work of Mark Dion in the pages of *Art&Text*.

A very special thanks to Art in Ruins and Howard Caygill – while absent from the volume, their work underpins its methodology.

Colophon

Black Dog Publishing Limited PO Box 3082 London NW1 UK
T 44 (0)171 380 7500 F 44 (0)171 380 7453

All opinions expressed in material contained within this publication are those of the authors and not necessarily those of the publisher.

Produced by Duncan McCorquodale.
Designed by Christian Küsters.

Printed in the European Union.

ISBN 1 901033 41 4

British Library cataloguing-in-publication data. A catalogue record for this book is available from The British Library.

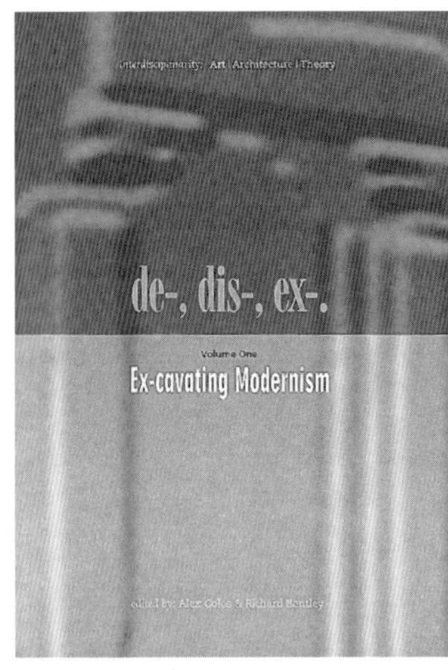

de-, dis-, ex-. Volume 1

EX-CAVATING MODERNISM

Edited by Alex Coles

Contributors include:
Jon Thompson, Juliet Steyn, Peter Halley, Fred Orton and Nikos Papastergiadis.

Soft Cover, 200 pp, 32 b & w reproductions
15 x 21cm / 6 x 8.5 in, 1 901033 05 8
UK £9.95 / US $14.95

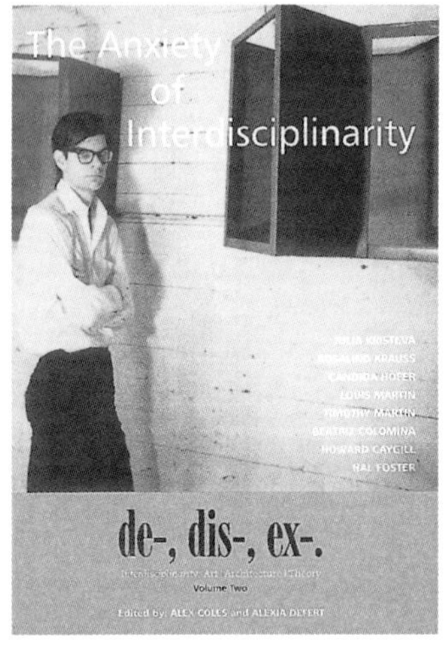

de-, dis-, ex-. Volume 2

THE ANXIETY OF INTERDISCIPLINARITY

Edited by Alex Coles and Alexia Defert

Contributors include:
Julia Kristeva, Rosalind Krauss, Louis Martin, Beatriz Colomina, Howard Caygill and Hal Foster.

Soft Cover, 208 pp, 25 b & w reproductions
15 x 21cm / 6 x 8.5 in, 1 901033 75 9
UK £9.95 / US $14.95